Truancy

Truancy: Short and Long-term Solutions is a practical and accessible guide to dealing with the problem of truancy and non-attendance. It is the first book on the issue to actively focus on solutions to the problem, rather than just the causes.

The book is full of practical examples of the latest ways in which schools, teachers, education welfare officers and LEAs try to overcome their attendance difficulties. The author identifies 120 short-term solutions as well as several long-term strategic approaches. He also considers issues such as parental-condoned absenteeism, alternative curriculum themes and mentoring, while the final chapter presents some strategic issues which policy makers and politicians need to overcome.

The book provides all teachers, heads of year, deputy heads, head teachers, education welfare staff, social workers, learning mentors and other caring professionals with a repository of up-to-date ideas and potential solutions. It is essential reading for anyone involved in addressing the challenge of truancy.

Ken Reid is Deputy Principal at Swansea Institute of Higher Education. He is also the author of *Truancy and Schools* and *Tackling Truancy in Schools*, both published by Routledge.

Truancy

Short and Long-term Solutions

Ken Reid

London and New York

First published 2002 by RoutledgeFalmer
11 New Fetter Lane, London EC4P 4EE

Simultaneously published in the USA and Canada
by RoutledgeFalmer
29 West 35th Street, New York, NY 10001

RoutledgeFalmer is an imprint of the Taylor & Francis Group

Typeset in Gill and Goudy by BC Typesetting, Bristol
Printed and bound in Great Britain by
TJ International Ltd, Padstow, Cornwall

British Library Cataloguing in Publication Data
A catalogue record for this book is available from the British Library

Library of Congress Cataloging in Publication Data
A catalog record for this book has been requested

ISBN 0–415–27575–X

Contents

List of figures   vii
Acknowledgements   viii
Foreword: About this book   ix

1 The challenge of truancy and school absenteeism   1

2 Typical schools   20

3 Short-term solutions I   31

4 Short-term solutions II   57

5 Short-term solutions III   72

6 Short-term solutions IV   95

7 Long-term strategic approaches I   112

8 Long-term strategic approaches II   130

9 Parents and parental-condoned absenteeism   141

10 Alternative curriculum schemes   157

11 Mentoring   173

12 The way forward   184

Bibliography   189
Index   191

Figures

3.1	100 plus short-term strategies currently in use in schools	32/3
3.2	Recommended daily home learning-based activities	54
6.1	Percentage of pupils working during term-time by region	106
6.2	Type of illegal work amongst school-age pupils by region	107
7.1	The five-year cycle using the PSCC scheme	114
7.2	Adapting the PSCC scheme in a numerical way	123
7.3	The Davison model of the PSCC scheme (the RAG project)	124
7.4	Using the colour-coded PSCC system for exclusion	128
8.1	Panel-based approaches to combating absenteeism	132
8.2	Key staff who could be involved in the panel processes	133
8.3	Standardising processes between PSCC scheme and panel-based SSTG approach	137
8.4	Longer-term strategic approaches utilising the panel scheme	139
9.1	Categories of parental-condoned absence	148
9.2	Profiles of categories of parental-condoned absence: Category 1	149
9.3	Parental-condoned absence: Category 2	150
9.4	Parental-condoned absence: Category 3	151
9.5	Parental-condoned absence: Category 4	153
9.6	Parental-condoned absence: Category 5	154
10.1	Some existing alternative curriculum strategies	158
10.2	Pupils' preferred out-of-school activities by year	168
10.3	Activities available through the MAP programme	170
10.4	The MAP Project	171
11.1	Popular mentoring schemes	174

Acknowledgements

I would like to thank several people for all their help during the preparation of this book. First and foremost I offer my thanks to Angela Harris for typing the manuscript and for her patience and help during the editorial process. Second, I would like to thank Alison Foyle, Anna Clarkson and all their colleagues at RoutledgeFalmer for their help and advice during the production of this book. Third, I would like to thank a number of colleagues for their assistance in facilitating issues covered in the text. These include: Mike Weston, assistant headteacher at Davison High School, Worthing, and Sheila Wallis, headteacher at the same school; Elaine Reynolds, senior teacher at Mountain Ash Comprehensive School and her headteacher, Mick Guilfoyle, for permission to use evidence from the MAP Project (The Mountain Ash Partnership Out-of-School Learning Project funded by the New Opportunities Fund) for which the author is acting as the objective, external evaluator; Andrew Harvey, Kerica Hunt and Richard Hillary of Chamberlayne Park School, Southampton.

I would also like to thank: Professor Lou Cohen, Emeritus Professor of Education, University of Loughborough, Professor Carl Parsons, Canterbury Christ Church University College, Lesley Thomas and Anne Taylor for their help and assistance, and Merle Davies, Robin Boyden, Barnaby Shaw and Karpana Somasundram, School Attendance Support Team from the DfES.

Foreword: About this book

The focus of this book is on helping schools to find short and long-term solutions for their non-attendance and truancy problems. Thus, Chapters 1 and 2 help to set the current national scene partially by providing relevant case studies. Chapters 3 to 6 concentrate on a whole host of recent short-term initiatives within schools. These ideas emanate from current work taking place within schools, LEAs and education action zones with which the author has been personally involved.

The remainder of the book concentrates upon longer-term solutions and current issues which impinge upon establishing short and long-term solutions. Thus, Chapters 7 and 8 present an outline of two different types of long-term and more strategic ideas for schools to consider. Thereafter, the key issues discussed in the remaining chapters are truants and absentees, parents and parental-condoned absenteeism, alternative curriculum approaches, and mentoring. Re-integration strategies are considered at appropriate points throughout the book. The final chapter concludes with a series of recommendations on the best way forward in the continuing fight against truancy and other forms of non-attendance.

Ideally, this book should be used alongside *Truancy and Schools* (Reid, 1999) and *Tackling Truancy in Schools* (Reid, 2000) both published by Routledge. In fact, this new book represents the third and final volume in a series on truancy previously referred to in the Epilogue on page 333 of *Truancy and Schools*. The provisional title has been changed from *The Challenge of Truancy* to *Truancy: Short and Long-Term Solutions*. This text is intended to be a helpful resource material for all those caring professionals involved in the process of combating non-attendance and truancy. These include headteachers, senior staff, middle managers, form tutors, education welfare officers, education social workers, attendance support staff, educational psychologists, social workers, pupil referral unit staff, LEA administrators, magistrates and their clerks and, finally, and not least, parents whose role in the prevention of truancy is vital.

Most of the case studies, examples and exemplars have been taken directly from schools, LEAs, projects and EAZs with whom the author has been personally involved. In some cases where it is generally about 'good' news the actual title of the institution involved has been named. However, in cases of high truancy schools or in order to protect individuals or their institutions, some fictional names of real people or their institutions have been used. Therefore, Seaside School represents a real school by the sea somewhere in south-west England. By contrast, the MAP Project at Mountain Ash School details are given in full as not only is the author acting as the external evaluator for the scheme, but because the school is rightly proud of its endeavour and achievements, and the Project Co-ordinator, Elaine Reynolds, has agreed to 'field' any subsequent interest from readers of the book.

The chapters on the alternative curriculum and mentoring have been included because these two emergent fields are likely to become increasingly important in the near future. Equally, the chapter on parents and parental-condoned absenteeism is long overdue and utilises data gathered by the author in a variety of projects on truancy and persistent school absenteeism since 1977 and reworked to form the five categories now outlined. Much more work needs to be done to confirm the precise boundaries of these groups. However, Chapter 9 reminds us that parental-condoned absenteeism is far from being a simple and uniform problem. In fact, it is made up of a whole host of parental groups some of whom try very hard not to condone their children's absence but are not very successful in achieving their aim.

Finally, to help readers who are new to the subject of truancy, Chapter 1 describes some of the latest developments in the field. It tries to provide a potted introduction suitable for a reading of the rest of the book on where we are now in the current state of play on truancy and related attendance issues. Conversely, the final chapter summarises ideas for consideration by policy makers and practitioners on some of the best ways of reducing and combating truancy and other forms of absence based on the author's thirty years' experience in the field.

The book is intended to be a good read as well as providing up-to-date and relevant case work and information about truancy. I hope you will enjoy it and find it helpful.

Ken Reid
Swansea Institute of Higher Education

Note: Owing to the recent name change of the old DES and DfEE to DfES in 2001, the latter acronym is used throughout the text.

Chapter I

The challenge of truancy and school absenteeism

The extent of effort

More is happening to combat truancy and absenteeism in schools throughout the United Kingdom than ever before. The real question is: how much difference are all these initiatives making? And the simple truth is that no one really knows or can be certain.

Certainly, no one can be blamed for making a lack of effort. Not the DfES, Scottish Parliament or Welsh or Northern Ireland Assemblies. In fact, after reading this book, you may feel it is a question of initiative-itis. Moreover, no one can be really certain of which preventative initiatives are working better than others. Perhaps there is a feeling amongst high office holders that all new innovations to improve school attendance are helpful even if only from a raising awareness perspective.

Equally, teachers and headteachers in schools are playing their part. Many of them and their staff are spending long hours in the detection, prevention and investigation of their pupils' non-attendance. Most schools now have policy documents on attendance and promote a range of school-based solutions. Re-integration strategies to enable pupils to return and re-settle in schools generally remain weak and are often non-existent. This is generally true irrespective of whether the cause for the absence is a long-term illness, visit abroad or a period of truancy. In fact, many schools do not currently even have appropriate short-term re-integration or return to school strategies in place if evidence from truancy patrols is to be believed. In Swansea, for example, truancy patrols are regularly picking up the same pupils in the afternoon as those they returned to their schools in the morning, even though the process involves the school signing a form to acknowledge their pupils have been returned safely to them. Certainly, therefore, some schools are not retaining their disaffected pupils for very long.

Education welfare officers, too, are working their socks off despite national restructuring issues. Unfortunately, this service is notoriously blighted by having no national and uniform conditions of service. In some parts of the UK the service is seriously under strength. One EWO in north-west England told a conference in Manchester in March 2001 that she was responsible for attendance issues at fourteen comprehensive schools and all their feeder primaries. Imagine trying to do that job! Following an internal review, one authority in South Wales will have only two full-time EWOs after September 2001. The same area once had thirty-five employees. So, on the one hand, whilst more initiatives than ever are taking place, and whilst schools are playing their part, the service with overall responsibility for attendance issues locally is struggling hugely. Moreover, the range and responsibilities given to the education welfare service are ever increasing partly because of new initiatives and partly because of legislative requirements. Thus, as from April 2001, the education welfare service has taken on a key role as part of the Connexions Service in England. The devolution pilot review results of the EWO service will not now be known before mid 2002 at the earliest.

The extent of truancy

Against this background of sheer gritty professional effort, illegal work for under-age schoolchildren continues to thrive. The TUC/MORI (2001) poll reported that nearly half a million school-age children are engaged in illegal work. Of these, approximately 100,000 truant from school on a daily basis in order to be able to do so.

And, herein, lies another serious deterrent to successful professional practice. No one can be really sure precisely how many pupils are missing school daily. The DfES would have us believe that there are only 50,000 truants from schools in England on a regular basis. This is 0.7 per cent of the English school-age population. But, how do they reach this conclusion and are they certain of their data? If the real figure for truancy from schools in England is only 50,000, do we really have such a major problem? In fact, one might ask why is so much time being spent on one new initiative after another if this is the real extent of the phenomenon? Why, indeed, are the DfES and other departments spending millions of pounds annually to combat it?

The issue is, of course, one of definition. Where does the 50,000 truancy figure come from? There are no universally agreed and uniform national statistics and those which have been collected in earlier decades suggest the national truancy rate *per se* is around 2.2 per cent of pupils daily (Reid, 1985). The suspicion is that the current truancy rate being used by the DfES excludes certain categories of pupils such as parental-condoned absentees because these are often marked as authorised absences within schools. Yet, parental-condoned absentees are really parental-condoned truants. And, in a whole array of surveys conducted over the past forty years, parental-condoned absentees tend to make up the single largest category of truants. Equally the returns to the DfES exclude post-registration truants and specific lesson absentees. In some schools these can also make up the largest single category of truants (O'Keefe et al., 1993).

And, there is a much greater and more serious contributory problem – the recording of absence within schools. At present, the system is much too complicated and open to abuse, sometimes for the best of reasons. The major issue revolves around detecting and recording authorised from non-authorised absence. In some schools staff are instructed not to record unauthorised absence unless it is for exceptional circumstances. For example, pupils who turn up to school after a period of absence without good reason are asked to return the following day with a note providing a reason for the absence. The pupil's absence is then recorded as authorised in whichever category is subsequently chosen. By contrast, the same pupil under a different school's internal practices is marked as unauthorised absence. Surprisingly, some schools now go as far as giving returning pupils a list from which they are asked to tick a box selecting the reason for their absence. Thus, some schools are deliberately colluding with their pupils in order to maintain high attendance figures. In these cases, no unauthorised absences are ever recorded. Therefore, practical and policy differences between internal procedures for recording absence is one of the main reasons for the large variations in rates between schools' attendance. These differences are exacerbated by league tables although there are several other reasons for this phenomenon as well.

Take another example. Regulations regarding the taking of family holidays during school time are frequently misunderstood or misinterpreted. Officially, pupils are entitled up to ten days' holiday time during the school year with the prior consent of the head-teacher. The parental application should be made in writing to the school. However, in practice in many schools, pupils who are taken on family holidays during term-time, are marked as authorised absence even though they do not have the prior consent of the headteacher. In other schools, they are marked as unauthorised. At one conference held in the north of England, on a show of hands around half the teacher delegates reported that pupils on family holidays were marked as authorised absence; provided the school had been sent an official note or letter from a parent. In the other half of schools, taking family holidays is marked as unauthorised absence. Hence, it is clear that all the guiding regulations are simply not understood by schools. Given the constant changes of staffing in some schools and LEAs, perhaps this is hardly surprising. In one LEA in north-west England more pupil absences are attributable to family holidays than for all other categories put together. This is by no means unusual. In fact, there are several LEAs which currently report that absences due to family holidays are the single largest category of non-attendance and their greatest cause for concern.

Another grey area is parental-condoned absence. Again, a high proportion of schools mark parental-condoned absence as authorised absence. This practice can occur irrespective of whether parents retrospectively provide a note or whether a pupil is found to be with a parent in say, a shopping centre during a truancy sweep. This is one of the reasons why so many non-attenders currently being picked up by truancy sweeps are carrying 'excuse notes' in their pockets. Some of these notes have been found to be written by a parent, others by the truants themselves or by a friend. This practice shows that even some truants are getting the message. As long as you have a note of some kind, the school is less likely to be as concerned about your absence.

All the variations between schools in practice mean that it is difficult to establish an accurate daily figure either for truancy or for other forms of non-attendance. Surveys suggest that between 600,000 and 1.2 million pupils miss school daily. Of these, a high proportion are young pupils who are away from primary or infants schools for reasons of illness. Official studies undertaken of attendance during a day, a week, a term and a school year continue to confirm findings emanating in the 1970s that the national daily average for attendance is between 85 and 92 per cent of secondary-aged pupils (Reid, 1985, 1999). The one-day national study on attendance of all secondary and middle schools in England and Wales (DES, 1975) reported that 9.9 per cent of all pupils were absent on the day. Of these, 22.7 per cent (2.2 per cent of all pupils) had no legitimate reason for their absence. The NACEWO Survey (1975) of secondary pupils in sixteen LEAs found 24 per cent of pupils to be absent on the day. The Pack Report (Scottish Education Department, 1977) found 15 per cent of pupils to have been unaccountably absent on at least one occasion during a six-week period.

Today, a quarter of a century later, variations in attendance rates continue to abound. There are huge local variations by school, by time of year, by day of the week and by geographical location, with some large urban inner cities amongst the highest for non-attendance rates. Some rural areas are also disproportionately high. South Wales and

Glasgow continue to have some of the highest rates for truancy and non-attendance in the United Kingdom.

But, whereas collecting accurate attendance statistics used to be a fairly routine matter, nowadays, with so many different categories being used to classify authorised absence, it is almost impossible to classify like with like. Not only do internal school policies and practice vary but so do those within LEAs. After all, no headteacher wishes her school to be at the bottom of a league table on attendance. Neither do LEAs wish to appear bottom of their regional league tables on attendance.

Classifying attendance would in some ways be very much simpler if the registration process reverted to the old system of merely recording those 'present' or 'absent'. Or, using today's terms, the absence column could be simply divided into two categories: either authorised (e.g. a visit to the dentist) or unauthorised absence (e.g. truancy, parental-condoned absenteeism). At least we might then have more accurate daily totals for pupils in school as well as for those who were not. Currently, too many headteachers have a vested interest in ensuring that their unauthorised non-attendance returns are kept as low as possible by obfuscating the reasons between authorised and unauthorised absence.

As the author has travelled around the United Kingdom on visits to schools, LEAs and to attend conferences on attendance-related issues, it has become increasingly obvious that the officially published statistics do not add up. You only have to consider the large number of secondary schools recently put into special measures partly because of their low attendance. Or, the number in which attendance is the first issue on Ofsted or Estyn action plans. Or, the large number of secondary schools whose overall attendance rates are below 80 per cent. Or, the large number of schools who have reported a decrease in attendance particularly in years 10 and 11 since the introduction of the National Curriculum. Or, the large number of headteachers, LEA officers and EWOs who will tell you in private with professional dismay about the differences between their official attendance returns and the reality on the ground. In an age when blame culture thrives, headteachers and directors of education can lose their jobs (and have done so) for appearing bottom of performance-related and attendance league tables, is it hardly surprising that the issue is fudged? After all, within this process, everyone benefits and no one is really sure quite who to blame.

So, despite all the good work of government departments, schools, LEAs, caring professionals and EWOs, truancy and other forms of non-attendance continue to flourish in British schools almost unchanged over previous decades and generations (Hoyle, 1998). And, whatever the true daily figure for truancy and other forms of non-attendance, the evidence from schools and professionals is that the problem is at least as great today as it was thirty, fifty, seventy or a hundred years ago. Moreover, we still need to find better ways of detecting and recording specific lesson absence, post-registration truancy and parental-condoned absence/truancy.

Professional issues

There remain several outstanding professional issues which continue to cause concern. One of these is the work of the magistrate's court in attendance cases. Here, also, there is very little consistency in practice. Variations in outcomes by magistrate, locality and region abound. Some magistrates are keen on parenting orders. Others are not. The DfES believes parenting orders are used too infrequently. Some impose high fines. Others do not. Some clerks plan for attendance cases to be heard on the same day one after another. Most do not. In fact, in some areas clerks tend to fit attendance cases in and around other perceived more significant matters, thereby giving attendance cases too low a priority. Unfortunately, too few magistrates or magistrates' clerks have been trained in the subtleties or implications of attendance-related issues.

Similarly, some local authority social service departments have increasingly given attendance-related issues a lower priority than they should, often leaving attendance cases to the social-work skills of education welfare officers. Again, differences in local practices vary enormously. In many parts of the UK, it is becoming accepted as the norm that the social services are only seriously concerned in attendance cases when the child (or a parent) is perceived to be at risk perhaps because it is a child abuse matter or the subject of a care order. This is unfortunate and often seriously hampers joined-up inter-disciplinary good practice.

The reverse is true in the case of the police. The police have become much more interested in attendance cases since the 1998 Criminal Justice Act and the introduction of truancy patrols. Following the publication of the first report on truancy and social exclusion (Cabinet Office, 1998) which highlighted the clear link between the genesis of truancy and day-time crime conducted by truants, as well as the link between juvenile and adult criminality, New Labour has been making a concerted effort to combat the links between truancy and crime. During March 2001, the DfES and Home Office launched a series of major seminars throughout England on the theme of Truancy and Crime: Together We'll Tackle It. Two hundred and fifty invited professionals from across the caring professions attended each of these events. From these people, new regional committees have been established to practise and share joined-up inter-disciplinary and multi-disciplinary good practice on truancy and school attendance issues. Partners in the venture include headteachers, teachers, the police, education welfare officers, magistrates, social workers, youth workers, community team workers, pupil referral unit staff and social inclusion officers as well as civil servants from the DfES. These regional committees provide a unique opportunity to establish agreed ways forward to combat truancy and crime and to further improve the boundaries between the professions. Emergent local information technology web-sites on good practice are to provide a key form of linkage between the groups alongside a national DfES database. This regional initiative is, of course, also supporting some of the DfES's other policy initiatives relating to truancy and attendance.

Truancy and crime

Why is truancy so important in the fight against crime? Apart from the fact that many thousands of pupils are missing school daily, some of whom could be at risk, there are other reasons: 23 per cent of young people sentenced in court have engaged in truancy. A high proportion of young offenders are truants and often commit serious crimes while truanting (Reid, 1986). Moreover, truants are more likely to end up unemployed and have poor life chances – socially, professionally and economically (Reid, 1999).

In England, there have recently been a whole host of central government initiatives aimed at reducing the link between truancy and youth crime. These include:

(a) a co-ordinated nationwide programme of truancy sweeps;
(b) new legislation which ensures that parents of persistent truants have to go to court and face tougher fines;
(c) new funding of £11 million for electronic registration schemes in 500 schools in 2002/3; Sheffield LEA, for example, is one authority at the forefront of these developments;
(d) truancy buster awards;
(e) the formation of a cross-Whitehall Group including DfES, Home Office, CYPU, Department of Health and Social Exclusion Unit which meets regularly to discuss issues affecting the truancy and crime agenda.

Further government-led schemes are included in the next section on new initiatives in England.

We will now consider how police and schools working together can tackle truancy, crime and disorder. First, this is what schools can do. Headteachers can give a public commitment to local initiatives to reduce crime and anti-social behaviour. Schools can help to identify pupils who are at a high risk of being involved in anti-social or criminal behaviour and work with local agencies to help combat this behaviour. They can help to establish a youth action group focusing on crime prevention. They can involve police in classroom activities, where appropriate, to help pupils form positive relationships with the police. They can advise the police of any actual criminal activity or suspicious behaviour. Finally, they can have effective first-day absence schemes: in particular, have in place competent electronic registration schemes which will enable them to contact parent(s) or guardian(s) on the first day of a child's absence.

Second, the police can do the following:

(a) participate in truancy sweeps;
(b) work closely with schools to help challenge young people's attitudes to criminal behaviour;
(c) develop youth participation in community projects;
(d) work with schools to develop joint truancy protocol.

Other local issues for schools and the police to consider together are: protocols with other caring agencies; information sharing; the vexed problem of confidentiality; the relationship between drugs-related activity and truancy; multi-racial dimensions; mobile phone policies and the use or otherwise of restorative justice in schools.

Working in partnership means that schools should be readily involved with other partners to support anti-truancy initiatives. Schools should appoint a dedicated teacher as police liaison officer. Schools need to work with other local key players in the area such as community agencies, child guidance and, at a practical level, bus companies. Schools should also be represented on community safety partnerships. Evidence suggests that the best and most successful results tend to happen when police and schools target their efforts on high-risk individuals and help to identify 'hot spot' locations. Some of these 'hot spot' locations can often be frequented by truants.

New initiatives in England

The DfES is spending large sums of money on a variety of initiatives to combat truancy and, in some cases, related crime. The main schemes implemented by New Labour and organised by the DfES include:

(a) *Social Inclusion: Pupil Support (SIPS) grant*
    The government has set schools a target to reduce truancy and exclusion by a third and provide a full-time education to all pupils who are excluded by 2002. To help schools and LEAs meet these targets, the DfES is providing £174 million to schools and LEAs in 2001/2; 33 per cent more than available in 2000/1 and a ten-fold increase since 1996/7. The majority of the grant is devolved to schools so that they can decide how best to meet the needs of disaffected pupils before the need to exclude. The £174 million includes £127 million for schools and £36 million for authorities under the Social Inclusion: Pupil Support grant. In addition, a further £10 million is available from the Capital and Infrastructure grant to fund new on-site learning support units in schools. Finally, the department provides a further £1 million to flexibly support the national drive against truancy.

(b) *Connexions Service*
    Connexions is the name of the multi-agency support service that is available for all 13–19 year olds and which commenced on 1 April 2001 and is being phased in over the next 2–3 years. Connexions brings together a range of partners currently working with young people, such as schools, colleges, career services, the youth service, EWS, health agencies, and youth offending teams in order to provide a coherent, holistic package of support that enables every young person to remain engaged in learning and make a successful transition to adulthood. Connexions is designed to ensure that every teenager receives individual and appropriate learning and career advice.

(c) *Children's Fund*
    The Children's Fund has been established as a key part of the government's strategy to tackle child poverty and social exclusion. It attempts to ensure that vulnerable children get the best start in life, remain on track in their early years, flourish in secondary school and choose to stay on in education and training at 16.
    The Children's Fund supports two major programmes. £380 million of the Fund is distributed to local partnerships to develop preventive services to identify children and young people aged between 5 and 13 who are showing early signs of difficulty and provide them and their families with the support they need to overcome barriers and disadvantage. £70 million is distributed directly to local community groups through a network of local funds.

(d) *National Strategy for Neighbourhood Renewal (NSNR)*
    The NSNR is about turning round the most deprived neighbourhoods by tackling the underlying causes of urban and rural poverty. It is a key priority for No. 10 and has cross-Whitehall ownership. The document 'A New Commitment to Neighbourhood Renewal: National Strategy Action Plan' was launched by the Prime Minister on 15 January 2001 in East London. It marks a radical change in the way government is tackling social exclusion. The idea is to gradually rid the country of a

sub-culture of dependence, deprivation and violence that is the breeding ground for disaffection, truancy and crime.

(e) *Sure Start*

Sure Start promotes the physical, intellectual, social and emotional development of young children by ensuring that children are ready to flourish when they start school. By 2004, the DfES will be investing almost £500 million each year in Sure Start, reaching a third of children under the age of 4 born to poor families. In addition, New Labour is planning bursaries for all new children at birth which will be invested for their later use in education or to provide them with a start in adult life.

(f) *Learning mentors in Excellence in Cities*

There are some 1,500 learning mentors in post in Excellence in Cities secondary schools and by the end of 2001 there will also be 900 in primary schools in the areas. By 2004, there will be an estimated total of 3,200 learning mentors in primary and secondary schools in Excellence in Cities and the new Excellence Clusters.

As part of the Excellence in Cities programme, learning mentors are school-based employees who, together with teaching and pastoral staff, assess, identify and work with those pupils who need extra help to overcome barriers to learning inside and outside school. In this way, they take some of the burden off teachers, who often feel as though they should be helping pupils to overcome problems inside and outside school. Having a learning mentor to help pupils tackle these problems frees teachers to teach. Some headteachers who are not in Excellence in Cities areas are using their school improvement funding to recruit their own learning mentors.

(g) *Education Action Zones*

Education Action Zones (EAZs) were proposed in the White Paper 'Excellence in Schools' and have their legislative basis in the School Standards and Framework Act, 1998. EAZs are intended to create urgent focus on raising standards through local partnerships between parents, schools, businesses, LEAs, TECs and others. Zone initiatives generally focus on four main themes: improving the quality of teaching and improving the quality of learning; social inclusion including attendance; providing support to families, and providing support to pupils; and working with business and other organisations. EAZ's will shortly be merged with the Excellence in Cities programme.

(h) *On Track*

On Track is a long-term crime reduction programme aimed at preventing children at risk of getting involved in crime. It is a key element of the government's agenda on tackling the causes of crime. The programme was launched at the end of 1999. Twenty-four areas were initially selected to develop On Track projects. Partnerships in each area consisting of the key agencies that work with families and children have put together detailed delivery plans and are implementing them. Each area initially receives funding of around £400,000. The programmes are expected to be funded for seven years. The projects are based in high crime, high deprivation communities.

The On Track programme is currently being led by a team made up of staff from the Family Policy Unit and the Research, Development and Statistics Directorate of the Home Office. It is overseen by a project board involving a range of government departments. Since April 2001, On Track has been incorporated into the new

Children's Fund and the projects are monitored and supported by the government's Children and Young People's Unit.

The National Curriculum

There is considerable anecdotal evidence amongst teachers that the originally prescribed and rigid nature of the National Curriculum was hampering their efforts within schools to combat disaffection and attendance-related issues. Yet, no one can be certain of the real extent of pupils' non-attendance which is related to the National Curriculum. We do know that a lot of pupils are taking subjects in schools, including GCSEs, in which they have little interest or aptitude. As some pupils begin to recognise that they are unlikely to achieve good passes at GCSE-level, and have little interest in some of their subjects, so their attendance starts to become more erratic.

It is for this reason that the DfES empowered schools to introduce more flexibility into the National Curriculum. First, schools were permitted to allow disaffected pupils the chance to spend up to half their allocated time on vocationally-orientated subjects often outside schools in, for example, a further education college. Second, schools are in the process of introducing vocational GCSEs which it is hoped will cater better for disillusioned pupils. Third, the DfES is considering extending vocational partnerships for pupils aged 14 or over. These partnerships might involve longer work placements with local business partners or other special partners which could mean that certain categories of pupils might remain at school after 14 in a part-time capacity.

Headteachers and teachers' professional organisations are welcoming the advent of much greater flexibility in the management and implementation of the National Curriculum within schools. Only time will tell whether these new initiatives will make a real impact upon truancy and other forms of non-attendance.

Familial breakdown

Despite all the considerable efforts being made by a whole host of caring professionals and by government, truancy and other forms of non-attendance from school are constantly being refuelled by another parallel factor. Most persistent school absentees emanate from deprived home backgrounds often suffering from multiple deprivation, low social class and with a whole host of social, psychological and institutional aspects providing the root cause for their non-attendance in school (Reid, 1985, 1999). Yet, just as standards in school are being driven up, so the number of children attending schools from broken or turbulent homes is ever increasing.

Truancy, in one very real sense, mirrors the spiralling decline in society's standards. Far too many children are being caught up as the innocent victims of marital break-up, familial disharmony and familial dysfunction. Given their lack of stability at home, many pupils' self-concepts are being lowered often to the point where the natural parental support they need for their schooling is non-existent. As their personal confusion at home is compounded by a lack of success at school, some pupils decide to play truant or start missing occasional days or lessons. Whereas before the 1950s and early 1960s, divorce or parental separation was unusual, today it is becoming the norm for up to half of all pupils as they go through their school lives. And this figure keeps on rising.

Moreover, there is often a communication gap between the parents of the needy child and the school.

Therefore, the origins of truancy are thriving. The increasing number of pupils who require regular emotional help and support means that however hard teachers and caring professionals work to support their pupils, they are losing out against the sheer weight of numbers. And it is this key factor that is at the heart of the need for vigilance in the continual fight against truancy and other forms of non-attendance. As professional practice improves, so people are having to work harder all the time in order to maintain the status quo by containing the ever growing numbers of potentially serious child-related problems. Just imagine what would happen if all the professional and state help and support currently being given to these children and their families stopped overnight. In what condition would British society be left?

Whilst familial breakdown appears to be on the continual increase, so professionals are having to learn to cope with the consequences of working and living in a multi-cultural society which also brings with it new pressures for schools. Early studies suggest that underachievement, truancy and related criminal activity appear to be higher in inner city and cosmopolitan regions (Social Exclusion Report, 1988). Yet, there remains very little specific information on the reasons for this trend or on whether the causes of truancy amongst minority multi-racial groups are the same as those for the indigenous population.

The pressure of truancy

The pressure upon schools caused by the local consequences of truancy tends to vary dependent upon its nature, extent and the efforts of the local media. There are three major forms of truancy. The first is low-level truancy which can be equated with harmless fun, growing up and natural child rebellion. This is manifest by usually regular attending and able pupils taking the occasional day off school as an alternative to their strict daily routines. Such truancy is regarded as less than serious and almost as a healthy part of growing up.

The second type is of persistent low levels of truancy which is manifest by significant parental-condoned absenteeism, specific lesson absence and post-registration truancy. To the majority of the public, persistent low levels of truancy are not seen as a major symptom of social dysfunction but of the extent to which schools are in or out of control of their pupils and are educating or not educating them properly.

The third type is high-level truancy. This equates with pupils whose schooling is seriously damaged by non-attendance, disruptive behaviour and links with crime. It is normally this latter form of truancy which grabs the national and local headlines and receives most attention.

Yet, at present, there is no way of differentiating between the extent of these forms of truancy. Indeed, most schools probably include pupils from all three categories to a greater or lesser extent. Clearly, high truancy schools will contain a greater proportion of high-level truancy cases than those with lower levels of absenteeism.

Equally, apart from the author's own work (Reid, 1985, 1999), there is no way of distinguishing between the extent of traditional, psychological and institutional absence on a school-by-school basis. There is also no current way of distinguishing between the five different types of parent(s) who are perceived by the authorities to 'condone' absence.

The data presented in Chapter 9 will reveal that there are in reality four different types of parent(s) who condone their children's absence while the fifth category actually endeavours to do everything possible to ensure their children attend school but are unable to do so. Hence, the study of truancy *per se* is by no means quite as simple as some people seem to believe.

Truancy and the UK

One of the questions repeatedly asked is why high truancy and absenteeism rates are such a hallmark of schools in Britain when, for example, in many other countries in Europe equivalent rates are minimal. So far, no one can answer this question with certainty. We know that rates of truancy and absenteeism have been high in the UK since the introduction of compulsory schooling. We know the rates increased significantly in some parts of Britain after the introduction of comprehensives. We also know that absences have always been much higher in years 10 and 11 than in earlier years. Recent evidence however, indicates that the onset of absenteeism is becoming younger and younger. Whereas thirty years ago, truancy from primary schools was almost unknown, today up to 35 per cent of pupils begin their histories of non-attendance whilst at primary school (Reid, 1999)

It is also well known that the causes of non-attendance amongst persistent school absentees are unique and diverse (Reid, 1985). Schools are notoriously poor at detecting the causes of initial absentees and taking early steps to rectify the situation (Reid, 1985). Moreover, the more pupils absent themselves, the more confident and brazen they tend to become over a period of time.

Ofsted have shared the concern of the DfES about attendance rates within some primary and secondary schools. This is why school attendance targets were raised in late 2001 from 90 to 92 per cent for secondary schools and to 95 per cent for primary schools. Ofsted and the DfES are also worried about the increasing numbers of 'missing children' from school rolls, the numbers of pupils who are not on any official school register, and the number of pupils for whom the 'specific trigger' for their absence appears to be the primary secondary transfer stage or the selection of public examinations between years 9 and 10.

Pupils' traits

Evidence from research so far suggests that there are certain psychological traits within some pupils which make them more prone to absenteeism than their peers. These include lower general levels of self-esteem, lower academic self-concepts, a tendency (especially amongst institutional absentees) towards neurotic and anti-social conduct, a susceptibility towards being vulnerable to peer group pressure (especially amongst traditional and psychological absentees) and bullying, reacting badly to poor academic progress and social failure within schools, having vulnerable personalities, being prone to illness or psychosomatic conditions (allergies, asthma, and so on), having unusual appearances (e.g. obesity) or being picked upon by staff within schools (Reid, 1999, Chapters 3 and 6). It is quite probable that further personality aspects will be linked to persistent absentees over time although, to date, research has not proved any other clear-cut traits.

What we do know is that the age of maturation amongst pupils – both boys and girls – is becoming younger all the time. Whereas the age of puberty amongst girls a hundred years ago was around $15\frac{1}{2}$ to 16, today it is between 12 and 13. Many girls now start to menstruate at primary school. Even some boys have broken voices by the age of 12. Therefore, the tendency towards even earlier maturation begs the question as to whether schools have changed sufficiently over time in recognition of their pupils' needs.

The answer is almost certainly no. Average secondary schools only allow 'special' privileges in school for 'sixth formers'. Even the application of these rights varies from school to school. Within most comprehensives, there are few, if any, facilities for younger age pupils. Explicitly, year 9, 10 and 11 pupils tend not to have their own separate common rooms, tuck shops, counsels or quiet rooms. In many schools, they do not even have their own independent access to information technology or their own lockers. Typically, in most schools, space is limited, pupils are cramped and the design and state of repair of some buildings woefully inadequate. Is it any wonder therefore, that some underachieving pupils who already feel inadequate because of their adverse social and home backgrounds and perceived limited aptitude react in the way they do by missing school? These psychological feelings of inadequacy are exacerbated by the fact that today there is much more peer and social pressure exerted upon pupils than in previous generations. The effects of advertising aimed at teenagers means that they are all wanting to grow up as soon as possible. In real terms, the childhood phase is shortening. Secondary schools are catering for young adults who wish their near-adult status to be recognised.

Ask many parents and you will find that one of the chief complaints of their children is that teachers should have more respect for them. The typical daily school regime for most pupils is rule-orientated, monotonous and geared towards the masses rather than focused upon individual needs. In fact, the increased pressures upon teachers since the introduction of the National Curriculum, attainment targets, records of achievement and policies of devolution to schools, had meant that many pupils feel even more vulnerable than before. It is becoming more and more difficult to find individual time for pupils. Against this argument, of course, is the increased emphasis upon literacy and numeracy, on mentoring, or providing classroom assistants as well as more proactive special needs policies. There is little doubt that schools are becoming busier and busier. And, the demands of paperwork are equally ever increasing.

Nevertheless, it is clear that regular non-attenders are found among those pupils whose literacy and numeracy scores are two or more years (often three or four) behind their peers by the ages of 7, 9 and 11. Unless these pupils receive sufficient and appropriate individual and group support to assist them with their numeric and literacy skills, they will remain at risk of long-term school failure and of dropping out of a system in which they receive constant negative reinforcement in the form of low grades, being placed in the bottom sets and being unable to choose subjects for public examination from the same list as their higher achieving peers (for example, second languages).

The challenge to teachers and to teaching as a profession is to find ways of being able to get to know and work with all pupils on a needs-orientated and individual basis which not only protects pupils' levels of self-esteem but also enables them to feel that they are being successful and making progress. Sadly, despite some laudable recent initiatives, the opposite fate continues to be the norm for far too many pupils. And it is precisely these pupils who become truants and persistent non-attenders.

There is good evidence for making this assertion. Reid (2000, Unit 9) has presented evidence on factors which cause pupils to miss school; a checklist of pupil-related factors which cause truants to miss school; a checklist of teacher-related factors which cause pupils to miss school; reasons given by persistent absentees for missing school; how regular attenders in years 9, 10 and 11 think school can be improved; how truants think schools can be improved and the qualities which truants and regular attendees in years 9, 10 and 11 look for in good teachers.

Reid's work has also shown that once pupils have begun to absent themselves from school, and the initial 'cause' lies undetected, it is likely that the pattern of absence will continue and escalate throughout the pupils' subsequent school careers. This reinforces the need for (a) early identification; (b) early preventative strategies operating in schools; and (c) for schools to implement appropriate re-integration strategies for short and long-term absentees once they return to school. Future research may be able to show that absentees will return to school and start to attend regularly when they see it as being relevant to their individual needs.

Through my research, teaching and consultancy activities over more than thirty years with truants and persistent absentees, certain points stand out clearly. First, playing truant imposes significant psychological consequences upon the individuals concerned. Second, the first act of truancy requires a certain amount of courage. Third, the vast majority of truants and persistent absentees are bored when absent from school. Fourth, the majority would never become persistent absentees or truants if they had their time over again. Fifth, the effects of playing truant include further reducing already fragile self-concepts, often to the point that it encourages a dependency culture to develop which, in some cases, continues throughout adult life. It is this very vulnerability which leads some absentees and truants into a shadowy and unhappy life ahead which can be punctuated by crime, failed relationships, poverty and frequent job changes. Very few school-aged truants become successful employees, businessmen or upstanding citizens within society. Many become totally dependent upon the state throughout their adult lives at a major cost to the taxpayer.

Teachers' attitudes

Research also shows that the causes of truancy are unique, multi-dimensional and inter-disciplinary (Reid, 1985). Sometimes teachers and schools are to blame in individual cases. Sometimes it is a pupil's own fault. Sometimes, it is the parent(s) and the pupil colluding together. Sometimes, it is the fault of schools, parent(s) and pupils. Too often however, pupils' own problems are exacerbated by the attitudes and/or culture within some schools. Examples of these unfavourable attitudes towards non-attenders are now presented. These views have been recorded verbatim from statements made by delegates at conferences on attendance and/or truancy over a two-year period starting in February 1999. Whereas most teachers are empathetic towards pupils with attendance problems, this is not universally the case; indeed, some teachers are notoriously unsympathetic towards truants and absentees as well as the whole notion of social inclusion.

My school asked me to attend this course today. To be frank, I'd rather have been sent on anything else. It makes me feel that my head doesn't value my contribution to the school.

(Male teacher, Conference in north of England, June 2000)

When my head asked me to take charge of attendance I nearly flipped. Why me? I had no idea where or how to start.

(Male teacher, Conference in Birmingham, May 2000)

Quite frankly, when I find the class has only got twenty pupils instead of thirty I jump for joy and get on with it.

(Female teacher, Manchester, November 1999)

As a form tutor I can tell you that I have had no problems with any of my truants – apart from not seeing any of them.

(Female teacher, Leeds, October 2000)

I came into teaching to help people. Why should we be interested in helping people who do not want to help themselves?

(Cardiff, October 2000)

Headteachers' attitudes towards truancy

This unsympathetic attitude held amongst some teachers is also shared by some head-teachers as the examples below show:

I object to the Government telling me that I have to spend my time on down-and-out pupils like truants and exclusion cases. I have enough paperwork already for three people without worrying any further about those who have either rejected the system or have caused my school serious problems.

(Male headteacher, London, July 2000)

In our school we have a simple philosophy. If they don't want to attend and learn, we are not going to force them. The school has enough problems without chasing any new ones.

(Male headteacher, Liverpool, June 2000)

I think schools should only have to teach and support those pupils who want to be there.

(Female deputy headteacher, Bristol, October 2000)

I care for all my pupils. However, I have to admit that the most frustrating are those who never attend and whose parents can't be bothered either.

(Male primary head, Weston-Super-Mare, May 2000)

There now follow some interesting statements made by good attenders about persistent school absentees. Finally, some verbatim statements made by pupils in Scotland for missing school (Scottish Office Focus No. 5, 2000) concludes this short section.

Good attenders' attitudes towards persistent school absentees

Many regular school attenders also tend to hold pupils like persistent absentees and truants in contempt as the following verbatim examples illustrate:

> If I had my way, I'd give them the cane, stop their pocket money and make them catch up with all their work on Saturdays and Sundays.
>
> (Year 9 boy, Cardiff, October 2000)

> I couldn't care whether they come to school or not as long as they don't interfere with me. My parents have told me that all truants come from broken homes and are jealous of people like me.
>
> (Year 6 boy, Ormskirk, July 2000)

> I feel sorry for truants. It must be awful being so dull that you can't read or write and are afraid of coming to school in case a teacher sees you.
>
> (Year 7 girl, Rhondda Cynon Taff, February 1999)

> I don't blame Shaun for not coming to school. Most of the class picks on him and so does Mr J. If I was him, I'd stay away as well.
>
> (Year 10 boy, South Midlands, December 2000)

> Kevin used to come to school until he got blamed for something which wasn't his fault. He was made to stay behind and got put in detention when everyone in the class knew it was Harrison who flicked the pellet. I liked Kevin. Now, I never see him and he hates Mr C.
>
> (Year 9 girl, Leeds, November 2000)

Some reasons for not going to school in Scotland

Finally, it is worth noting the range of excuses given by pupils in Scotland for not attending their schools on a regular basis (see Scottish Office, 2000).

> 'I just felt sick every time I thought about turning the corner and seeing that school in front of me.'

> 'I was always in the top class. I just couldn't stand everyone saying I was a swot. After second year I never went back.'

> 'There's nothing I'm good at. What's the point going every day just to learn what you already know – nothing.'

> 'I don't mind school but most of my pals just say let's go down the town, so you go.'

> 'The teachers all look down on you because you're from the scheme. It's like you're contaminating their lovely school.'

> 'Mr X makes me stand in the middle of the floor and say I am a pratt. It is humiliating. I'd rather have the hassle for dogging it than put up with that.'

'You can't go to the toilets or you get beaten up. Half the time you can't go into the playground because someone will do you over, and if they don't get you in school they get you on the way home.'

'I stay off sometimes when I'm at my dad's. My mum is really strict and makes me go in even if I've got a headache.'

'The only time I don't go in is when I have nae done ma homework. That can be quite often mind.'

'The white boys all slag me and my family. Sometimes they wait behind a hedge and throw stones at me.'

'If I'm late I think, well, maybe it's better to stay off sick than get a big row an that.'

'I often get a sore stomach or a sore throat and my mum just lets me stay in my bed.'

'I can be a lot mair use staying in the hoose looking after the weans for my ma.'

'I had a puni and it got doubled and I couldn't do it so I just thought I'd no go in.'

'I start my milk round at four. If I've been up late the night before I'm too knackered to go to school, I should maybe give it up but it's 45 quid a week and that's a lot of dough.'

'The only day I dog it is PE days. I just can't stand it.'

In another detailed study, Reid (1985) in *Truancy and School Absenteeism*, produced a breakdown of the detailed initial and later causes of the reasons given by 128 persistent absentees for missing school for at least 65 per cent of school time based on a three-year project undertaken with pupils in years 9, 10 and 11 from schools in South Wales supported by appropriate case studies. He found that school-based reasons were named most frequently by the persistent absentees for missing school with aspects relating to the curriculum, school transfers (all types), bullying, rules and punishment, boredom and poor teacher–pupil relationships to the forefront.

Why then should Britain top the European league tables on truancy and absenteeism? The answers seem to be in the resolution of the following points. First, by making sure that all pupils have their learning needs met on an individual as well as a group basis. Second, by preventing and overcoming the direct causes of truancy. These include poverty, the anti-educational attitudes of some parents, low literacy and numeracy skills, boredom amongst certain pupils whilst in school, poor undemanding teaching and adverse peer pressure allied to unattractive school buildings and adverse school climates. Is it purely coincidence, for example, that until now Britain has been one of the few parts of Europe not to have a complementary vocational curriculum for appropriate pupils alongside an academic one? And even now, there is a very long way to go before British schools have a proper alternative vocational curriculum which is valued by all parties in the education enterprise.

Pupils' perspectives

It is clear that the government has begun its fight back against these festering negative ills. It will take a great deal of resources, time, effort and capital funding before the United Kingdom will cease to continue to top league tables for absenteeism in Europe. If the government is eventually to be successful, it has to take account of the needs of pupils like Sara, Kelly, Ryan and Jake and to ensure that all pupils are treated with respect; after all, this is everybody's fundamental human right.

Sara

Sara is 14. She truants from school regularly usually condoned by her mother. She says she misses school because the 'teachers pick on me. I have all the dull teachers. Some of my friends have got really good teachers. The school needs more younger teachers like Mr P who really understands kids and knows how to talk to us. Some of the teachers should be put out to graze. They don't like teaching and they don't like kids. If I had good teachers, I'd go to school every day.'

Kelly

Kelly is 12. She started to miss school at the age of nine. She is now a persistent absentee missing on average two to three days a week.

'I started to miss school because I did badly in my tests. Miss R read out my results in front of the whole class and said I could do better. The other kids started to call me names like "stupid". Then, when I came here, they told me I had to go into the bottom set for maths so I thought "Why should I bother?". Since then, things have got worse. I wish they would help me to read and write properly 'cause I know I've got to learn and one day get a job. At the moment, going to school is a waste of time. But, I'd like to go and start again if I could.'

Ryan

Ryan is 14 and misses a lot of school to go surfing about which he is a fanatic. He accepts the problem is entirely of his own making and his truancy will do him no good in the long run.

'One day my parents will find out and they'll kill me. I get up and wait for the school bus. Then I hang around until my parents have gone to work. Every morning I wait for the mail to come in case there's a letter for my parents from the school. So far, I've ripped two up. When they come, I go back to school for a few days before bunking off again. I'd like to go to school part-time but I know no one will let me.'

Jake

Jake is 15. Up until the age of 13, he was achieving well at school. After entering year 10 and starting his GCSE programme things started going badly wrong. 'I used to like all my subjects. Then, I was told what I could and could not take. I thought that I would leave school with a lot of good exam passes. Then, my year tutor told me that I was likely eventually to do GNVQs rather than A levels so I thought "Why bother?" I've decided to join the army and so will probably go to college and take subjects I like after leaving school. I tried to explain my point of view to the teachers at school but they would not listen. They said they knew what was best for me. So, I lost interest and now you're talking to me. It's all a shame because I thought I was doing well. But why should I have to take what I'm told when everyone else could choose their subjects?'

The costs of non-attendance

No one can be sure of, probably not even estimate, the long-term costs of truancy and non-attendance from school. All we know is that there are a multiplicity of reasons why some pupils do not attend school regularly (Reid, 1999) and that subsequently these pupils cost the taxpayer enormous sums of money; not least in terms of the social security, unemployment, housing, crime prevention and adult psychiatric budgets. More-over, a lot of truants become young offenders; some committing their first offences whilst away from school. If we could find ways to successfully prevent and/or stop truancy and other forms of non-attendance, we would save the Exchequer millions and millions of pounds annually. And, we would help these types of youngsters become more useful citizens in adult life and, probably, better parents as well.

There is, however, another cost of non-attendance. This is the cost to the caring professions – especially teachers – of dealing with the consequences of non-attendance, including often the resulting abusive behaviour.

Finally, there is the cost to the professions. In Scotland in 2001, five headteachers and two deputy heads were suspended for falsifying attendance data. The Scottish Parliament launched an investigation into the causes of this phenomenon. In South Wales, a director of education, his deputy and a headteacher were dismissed for claiming too much public funding for 'shadow' pupils. A similar incident has occurred at a small primary school in Mid Wales. In England, a director of education was asked to resign because her authority came bottom of the league tables on attendance when it was hardly her fault as she had only been in post for eighteen months and, to the author's certain knowledge, this authority had been experiencing similar problems for over twenty years. A headteacher in the north-east was forced to resign when she 'suspended' twenty truants and disruptive pupils prior to an inspection and their parents subsequently complained. And the number of these kinds of cases seems to be growing.

This is one reason why Jane Davidson, the Minister for Education and Lifelong Learning in Wales decided to abolish publishing league tables in the Principality after September 2001. It seems the adverse publicity and extra pressure exerted on professionals has become counterproductive.

Summary

This chapter sets the scene for the rest of the book by briefly describing key issues relating to the challenge of tackling truancy and other forms of school absenteeism. Included in the chapter is a consideration of the extent of truancy, current registration difficulties, professional issues, new initiatives in England, the growing problem caused by escalating familial breakdown, the 'pressure' of truancy, truancy and the UK, pupils' traits, teachers' attitudes, pupils' perspectives and attitudes, some reasons for not going to school in Scotland, and, finally, the cost of non-attendance.

Truancy and persistent school absenteeism are difficult issues which in some ways divide the teaching profession. Most teachers work exceptionally hard and often inwardly feel contempt for non-conformist pupils like truants. At the same time, schools, teachers and other caring professionals are doing more work and trying harder to reduce absence in schools than ever before. Notwithstanding, putting teachers in charge of attendance within a school when they do not want the role can be counterproductive. Handling truancy and attendance issues within schools is a skilled and delicate issue. Staff given this responsibility need help and support including appropriate professional development.

Chapter 2

Typical schools

This chapter will present two brief case studies of typical approaches used by secondary schools in order to combat absenteeism and truancy. The case studies are based on two of those schools involved with the author during session 2000 to 2001. The first case study focuses on a school in South Wales which has had serious attendance problems for over twenty-five years. Case study B is based on a large community school in south-west England which is becoming increasingly worried about its attendance profile as another Ofsted inspection looms.

Both case studies illustrate that many schools *are* trying really hard to improve their attendance rates. Often, however, they do not have the expertise to know how best to do so really effectively. Many schools are caught up in the daily reality of 'fire fighting' approaches because of the constant bombardment of new initiatives by government and LEAs to schools on so many different fronts. Typically, therefore, attendance is often raised up the agenda in a lot of schools, the nearer the timescale is towards its next inspection. In fact, it is a fairly well-known syndrome for schools to attempt or to actually improve their attendance rates close to an inspection only for them to deteriorate again shortly afterwards. As Ofsted have to include a section in their final report on schools with less than 90 per cent actual daily attendance, this tends to focus the minds of headteachers and their staff. Too many schools leave attendance issues too far down their agenda until it is too late.

Between Chapters 3 and 6 the text considers short-term solutions. From Chapter 7 onwards longer-term strategies are presented. Ideally, schools should utilise best practice from both approaches. Whilst the evidence shows that the two case study schools are doing their very best to improve attendance – and should be commended for doing so – they are all a long way from achieving ideal solutions. Readers should note that medium-term solutions as manifest by whole-school approaches have been considered in Chapters 9 and 10 of *Truancy and Schools* (Reid, 1999) and so have been excluded from this text.

Case Study A – Honeywell School

The author led a staff development event for all senior staff of 147 schools within a large LEA in September 2000. Within weeks of the event, one of the LEA's schools was placed in 'special measures' for a second time with poor school attendance the key reason given for Estyn's (the Welsh Ofsted) action.

Subsequently, the LEA and the headteacher and senior staff at Honeywell School thought it was almost inevitable that their school would follow suit. Their scepticism was partly borne of the realisation that their attendance rates were as bad, if not worse, than their peer school nearby which had already been put into special measures. In fact, the first school was located approximately three miles away and had a similar history to their own. The scepticism also developed because of a feeling amongst the staff that no matter what they tried and however hard they endeavoured to turn the situation around, little difference had been made to their overall attendance statistics. In this respect, the appointment of a comparatively new headteacher, whose experience was mainly obtained in another school within the LEA, had also made little difference. In fact, in private, the headteacher was prepared to admit that he was at his weakest on attendance issues as:

(a) he had never received any formal training on the subject;
(b) it was not his own favourite issue;
(c) he had come from a school which had a similar major problem of absenteeism amongst pupils albeit, he felt, for entirely different reasons;
(d) he had delegated responsibility for attendance matters to one of his deputies.

The staff in Honeywell School recognised that attendance was one of their main flaws, if not their weakest one, prior to their second major external inspection. The Estyn inspection took place in November 2000. The author's brief was to help and advise the school in preparation for their inspection to ensure that the school was advising Estyn that it was doing everything possible to overcome its attendance difficulties.

Honeywell School is located in South Wales on the outskirts of a major city. It currently caters for 780 pupils and, since its inception in 1976, has had major attendance problems. Ten years ago, the school had 1,670 pupils on roll but numbers have steadily been declining. In 1999, 18 per cent of its intake achieved five or more A to C GCSE examination passes; a reduction of 2 per cent on the previous year. Twenty-four per cent of the pupils are either statemented or classified as having other forms of special educational needs.

Honeywell School services a number of deprived residential areas, has a majority of its pupils from low socio-economic backgrounds and has a high proportion of its pupils on free school meals. A significant number of parents in the catchment area have exercised their rights by sending their offspring to other higher achieving schools.

In 1995, the school had an attendance rate of less than 80 per cent. The LEA recognised that Honeywell (and five other secondary schools in the area) needed to address this problem and that more could be achieved if schools worked together rather than in isolation. The LEA bid for Gest funding to tackle the problem. They then set up a working group made up of representatives from each of the schools and led by the charity 'Cities in Schools' (recently renamed 'Include'). Four years later, despite much hard work on the part of staff, the overall position had changed very little.

Organisation of the working group

As a result of a forthcoming inspection, the school established its own working party in 1999 to look at attendance and to present a plan on how to raise pupils' attendance levels.

The working party decided that their function should be two-fold:

1 to seek out and provide qualified and experienced experts to lead training days;
2 to provide a means of sharing good practice amongst themselves and with other schools who have worked their way through their problems.

In this way, the working group aimed to provide each part of the school with support and information to aid them in their efforts to improve their attendance rate. The school has been provided with three extra staff to facilitate their special and educational needs priority status. At the start of the financial year 2000/1, the school was in the 'red' to a sum of approximately £100,000. A new headteacher was appointed at the start of the 1999/2000 session.

The first task of the working party was to identify the causes of poor attendance in the school. This was done by pooling experiences and expertise. The main areas identified by the working party were: curriculum issues; bullying; basic skills; home–school relations; effective monitoring; rewarding good attendance.

The school's situation

In session 1995/6, the overall attendance rate was 77.8 per cent. In 1996/7, the attendance rate increased by 3.5 per cent to 81.3 per cent. In 1997/8, it again increased by 1.4 per cent to 82.7 per cent. In 1998/9, it decreased by 0.8 per cent to 81.99 per cent. In 1999/2000, it increased by 0.91 per cent to 82.9 per cent. The school's own target is to increase its attendance rate by 1.5 per cent to 2 per cent each year over the following three years.

The whole school attendance figures suggest that attendance in the spring term is often lower than the autumn and summer terms. More revealing however, are the data on attendance when analysed by year group. For example, in session 1995/6, the overall attendance of year 7 was 83 per cent. For year 11, it was 72.9 per cent. In 1996/7, there was a 14.7 per cent difference in the attendance rates of year 7 and year 11 pupils (86.9 per cent compared with 72.2 per cent). In the same year, there was a difference of 8.5 per cent between the attendance levels of year 10 and year 11 pupils. After a great deal of hard work, the school managed to raise the attendance of year 7 pupils in 1998/9 to 89.93 per cent, their highest ever level. However, for year 11 pupils, attendance remained poor at 74.42 per cent, which suggests that the internal procedures were being less effective for the older age pupils. In session 1999/2000, years 7 and 8 pupils recorded 86.33 and 88.15 per cent attendance respectively. For year 10, the attendance level was down to 78.98 per cent. The evidence suggested that there was an increasing attendance problem as the pupils became older and moved up the school. This was true for both girls and boys. These findings, which are commonplace in many secondary schools, imply that factors like the curriculum, teacher–pupil relationships and peer pressure are having a greater and more negative effect on pupils in years 10 and 11 than lower down within secondary schools.

There was a particular problem at the end of the winter term and after the summer examinations. Casual non-attendance accounted for the vast majority of absences. Attendance was also worse amongst the lower ability pupils. This information was obtained from a study of the registers and the results of a school-based questionnaire conducted with the pupils. The attitude amongst many staff at the start of the project was that they should concentrate upon those pupils who were in the classroom and wished to learn rather than upon the absentees. Some staff even thought their own teaching and learning situation was helped by the absence of some pupils.

Behaviour is another major concern of the staff. Some pupils do not behave well during the transitions between lessons, and individual incidents between staff and students are the norm. Some staff also experience difficulty in controlling pupils during their lessons. The author found that the behaviour of the pupils in the corridors between classes and during breaks to be amongst the worst he had witnessed during his career. Some pupils appeared to be playing a game whereby they kept bumping into members of staff as they passed alongside them. There was either a lot of clumsiness around or some of the pupils' actions were deliberate.

The curriculum

The first tasks were:

1 to raise staff awareness of the issues; and,
2 to persuade them to view absenteeism as a problem to be tackled rather than a situation to be ignored.

It was important that right from the beginning all staff were involved in trying to rectify the situation. The initiative was viewed as a 'whole school' problem rather than as a 'pastoral' problem. At the Curricular Heads meeting, the current attendance figures were produced and discussed. It was noted that the difficulties caused to teachers in mixed ability situations were much worse than in set classes. A wide-ranging discussion led to an acceptance of the need to try to rectify the situation. The Curricular Heads also agreed to co-operate with the Inset that the working group would provide. It was agreed that the KS4 curriculum needed to be more flexible and relevant especially for those pupils who were unable or unwilling to access GCSEs.

The working party identified two groups of pupils who were not catered for adequately:

1 Those pupils who were statemented MLD or EBD. For these, a developed 'Alternative Curriculum' was developed. A two-year course based on the core subjects Youth Award and the Duke of Edinburgh Award was introduced. This course has now been running for almost four years and the children who have completed the work have shown an attendance rate of 85–90 per cent over the two years and all have left school with some qualifications at COEA, GCSE, Youth Award or Duke of Edinburgh level. In the last eighteen months, a greater emphasis has been placed on improving the pupils' key skills to allow them to access further education.
2 Those pupils whose attitude to schooling was becoming or had become extremely negative leading them to miss school on a regular basis. Some of these pupils have also benefited from the school's latest initiatives.

Pupils with the worst attendance records were offered the opportunity to attend a 'Bridge Course' organised by Cities in Schools and paid for partly by the LEA and partly by the school. The number of places was strictly limited and became even more so over a period of time. Each group of ten, made up of pupils from two or more schools, was supported by a youth worker employed by Cities in Schools. The pupils undertook two days' work experience each week, organised and monitored by the youth worker, two days in an FE college and one day's personal activities and support including individual counselling and off-site activities.

This was a very successful course. Pupils attained average attendance rates of 85–90 per cent over the one-year. They all completed qualifications in key skills and many went on to attend the local FE college post-16 to follow vocational courses. Unfortunately, it proved to be a very expensive course and the LEA were unable to continue to fund the scheme over a sustained period. They have since replaced it with a less supervised and intensive programme. It has, therefore, been a less successful 'Access course' for year 10 and 11 pupils to participate.

Another problem is that this strategy could only benefit a very small number of pupils; a maximum of five year 11 pupils per academic session. The school, therefore, needed to widen the range of courses it offered at KS4 in order to try harder to accommodate a pupil's first choice. The school has done this by changing the way it organises the KS4 timetable and by offering GNVQ courses in 'Built Environment', 'Health and Social Care' and 'Business Studies'. The 'Built Environment' programme especially has succeeded in engaging pupils who had expressed a view that school had very little to offer that they considered valuable. Again, this has proved an expensive course to run. The school is hoping to offset the cost to some extent by co-operating with the college to provide a post-16 course in this field. If the college is successful, it will also help the pupils with progression.

Bullying

Bullying is a very real fear for a great many year 7 pupils and is closely linked to absence. The school recognised the need to provide bullied pupils with every assistance in overcoming their justified fears. After discussion with the pastoral team, it was felt that the best way forward was to work to increase the confidence of pupils in themselves and in the school. They needed to be convinced that they were equipped to deal with most of the problems that would come their way. Also, if they met a threatening situation they could not deal with, there would always be somebody to listen, understand and to take the appropriate action.

A head of year had carried out a questionnaire survey amongst the pupils which had indicated there was confusion over what constituted bullying, what would happen if they reported bullying, or, in fact to whom they should report it. Although pupils reported some evidence of physical bullying, they were particularly concerned about how to treat cases of verbal abuse and verbal bullying. A system of peer counselling was introduced. With the support of the year tutor, year 10 pupils were approached during the summer term. It was put to them that they probably understood the fears of the younger pupils better having previously experienced the same problems. Volunteers to act as peer counsellors during the next academic year were sought. They were asked to listen to the problems experienced by the younger pupils and to provide appropriate guidance. To help them, they were trained by a qualified counsellor so that they would feel secure in this work. They would also be supported by a member of the SMT and their year tutor and received regular debriefings to ensure that they were keeping to their brief. Counsellors and pupils alike were advised on the key issues and appropriate responses towards verbal bullying.

The school is presently in its fourth year of running peer counsellors' groups. The training for the first two groups was initially provided by Cities in Schools. Subsequently, it was decided that it would be more cost-effective to train a member of staff from each school in order to provide the appropriate Inset. The scheme has been developed to include the concept of year 7 buddies so that each new pupil has at least two older pupils with whom they can immediately identify.

The confusion over what constitutes bullying and how to cope with the pressures of a new school for year 7 pupils are addressed in an 'Anti-Bullying Day' which is run with the help of the head of English and Drama and the year 11 Drama Group. The day takes place early in September. It involves the form tutor in a central role to reinforce the message that these are the adults in the school most closely connected to the care and development of each individual pupil. A review of the school's Anti-Bullying Policy has recently been undertaken in order to incorporate all these changes and to flag up to the staff that this is an issue that can never be ignored.

The staff have also undertaken a full training day on bullying. A questionnaire from Sheffield University for use with year 8 pupils was obtained. The next stage is to find a way of collecting information from parents on their views on bullying in the school (without giving the impression that the school has a problem).

Basic skills

If pupils cannot access the curriculum they become disenchanted and lose the desire to progress. As a result, they begin to look for reasons not to attend school or they truant. As a school, the staff needed to reverse this trend and then prevent it from happening in the first place. The school therefore, organised several training days on literacy. Experts from all over the country were brought in to help to formulate the school's literacy policies. All members of staff attended these training days and a great deal of expertise was gained. To avoid this being seen as purely a problem for the English department, staff from outside the department were involved. As a result, the heads of English, Maths and Science started working together on the issue and have since delivered two training sessions to the staff of the school as part of the school's literacy programme. The school's English and Mathematics departments have also gained funding from 'The Prince's Trust' to improve their provision for study skills support.

Home–school relations

The school has spent a great deal of time looking at all aspects of the way it communicates and relates to the parents of their pupils. The main hurdle it has faced in all the work it has done since 1995 has been the unwillingness of a large minority of parents to accept that children who fail to attend school on a regular basis cannot hope to achieve their full potential. Unfortunately, a significant number of parents condone their children's non-attendance.

Therefore, a home–school agreement which is signed by all parents before their children start at the school was introduced. This agreement covers all aspects of the work carried out by the school and outlines what is expected from all parties, pupils–parents and the school. The wording was agreed after consultation between the headteacher and other members of the school staff. Again, if the process was to be repeated, an input from parents and pupils would be sought to make the agreement even more relevant to the needs of all parties.

A school-based analysis of recent correspondence revealed that the majority of letters to parents were sent either about bad behaviour or a child's lack of progress. Thus, the school decided to increase the number of positive forms of communication between the home and the school. The school now uses 'Praise Cards' to inform parents when their child has done well. Parents are also informed of any rewards their child has received. Regular mail shots to increase the amount of information the parents receive on the school are sent.

The school has worked with the year tutors to examine the way they correspond with individual parents and to examine how they conduct formal interviews with parents. The school policy revolves around the basic premise that everyone is working together to support and help the child. The school attempts to avoid any suggestion of blame or inadequacy on the part of the parents. This has not always been easy to achieve as some parents do come into school in a confrontational mood. Strategies for defusing such situations have now been developed.

The school's secretarial staff have also received training on how best to greet parents either on the phone or in person. It is equally important that these staff members convey the correct impression to visitors.

The main forum for contact between teachers and parents is the Annual Parents' Evenings. The school has experimented with different formats for these evenings and recently introduced some significant changes following feedback from a questionnaire about the organisation of parents' evenings given to all parents. Subsequently, the Year 7 Parents' Evening was brought forward to November when parents were invited into school to talk to their child's form tutor. The meetings took place in form rooms so that parents could see a part of their child's school life. These meetings proved very successful and the school's evaluation showed very positive feedback from parents and form tutors alike.

The school has subsequently developed this concept into a series of 'Year 7 Review Days' which takes place during November and in July. The school has taken this step to incorporate the idea of meeting individual pupil targets and action plans.

Parents' Evenings for the rest of the school are run on more traditional lines. The school is continually looking for ways to encourage more of the parents to attend, especially those from low socio-economic backgrounds. The next stage is to provide further training for all teachers on how to make the most of their parental interaction.

Effective monitoring

Being able to keep an accurate register of a form's and individual pupil's attendance is a skill expected of all teachers. Yet, most trainee teachers are never given any guidance on this aspect before they start teaching. The school has written its own comprehensive guide on the role of the form tutor which is given to all staff. This includes clear guidelines on how to ensure that a register is accurate. It also emphasises how to convey the importance of every absence being covered either by a note or telephone call from parents.

The school has introduced a policy of 'first day response'. This was initially conducted by a member of the SMT, year tutors and form tutors. However, funding has recently been found to pay for extra clerical staff to carry out this function. As a result, the number of unauthorised absences has decreased, although, worryingly, parental condonement of non-attendance is increasing.

The SMT have examined the different ways of registering attendance electronically. The school considers the very expensive 'EARS' system would be ideal but the cost is beyond their means. The school has, therefore, decided to introduce the Sims attendance module. The system was piloted in 1999/2000 with year 8 and the whole school started to use it in May 2000.

One of the inherent problems of this system is how to deal with poor punctuality. The school has two strategies to deal with this issue. First, it provides pupils with an easy way of 'getting their mark' when they are late for school. Second, it monitors lateness as closely as attendance and uses either punishments or support whenever necessary.

The Sims system does not monitor specific lesson truancy. Therefore, the SMT have introduced a regular routine of 'spot checks' carried out by themselves or one of the year tutors. When they have specific concerns over a particular pupil's attendance in their lesson, staff are also encouraged to consult the year tutor. All year tutors now have access to the Sims system and so checking on pupil attendance is a lot easier.

The school has given considerable thought to the ways in which long-term absentees can be re-integrated back into school. By working with the school's counsellor and EWO, the school has experimented with bringing a small group of such pupils back together to allow them to support one another through the process. Unfortunately, the success rate of the group was not good when compared with the time given to the work by the counsellor and the EWO.

Rewarding good attendance

Developing the concept of rewarding good attendance within the school proved controversial. Some staff felt that the school should not reward pupils for doing 'what they should do'. All staff however, already accepted the need to reward pupils for academic progress and positive behaviour. The SMT counterbalanced this view by carrying out an exercise on the school's existing reward system and incorporated rewards for good and improved attendance into the process. Thus, the staff were gradually able to accept the positive benefits upon attendance of utilising a reward process. The school also recognises pupils' achievements by publicising the name of every student who has achieved 100 per cent attendance each half term. Two notice boards within the school are used for attendance issues. On these boards, the names of pupils showing who has done well in any area of school life are published for anyone to see. This includes outstanding attendance.

As part of the SMT review of the school's reward system, pupils were asked to complete a questionnaire on their reaction to different types of rewards. At first, they were very concerned about the idea of being singled out in this specific way. They did feel however, that if their name was one of a group amongst other pupils they could cope better.

The school now awards certificates for good or improved attendance. These are given out in assembly by the headteacher. At the end of the year, any pupil with 100 per cent attendance is given a cash prize.

The school has discussed the possibility of running a lottery so that any pupil who gains 100 per cent attendance for a half term wins a ticket to the lottery which is drawn at the end of the year. The school started this scheme in session 2001/2.

The way forward

All of the above policies still have room for development and improvement. The school is considering the advisability of asking one of the school's governors to become directly involved in the work it does on attendance. The school is currently arranging for some of its pupils' parents to meet with a governor to talk over the importance of a good attendance record.

Parental attitudes remain the school's biggest hurdle. The school has to find more ways of getting the message across that school matters and that good performance is directly related to achieving positive academic outcomes.

Attendance is a permanent topic on the agenda on the senior pastoral staff meetings. The school also ensures that somebody from the school attends any relevant Inset or conference on the issue. Unfortunately, the LEA's working group on attendance no longer meets so it does not now have a forum to help it in this work.

Despite all these initiatives, the school's attendance has improved little. Therefore, the staff are asking themselves, what more can they do? They do not wish to be put in special measures but they were fearful that this might well happen.

In the event, after the inspection, the school's attendance figures were 'deemed unsatisfactory' by Estyn. However, 'in recognition of the progress' which the school has made, its efforts on attendance were judged by Estyn to be 'part of the school's overall drive to improve standards'. Honeywell had managed to escape being put into special measures so the staff now feel that their efforts have had a belated impact.

After visiting the school and holding discussions with a range of key staff and after inspecting Honeywell's internal documents, the author gave the school the following advice:

(a) To rewrite and update the school's policy document on attendance. This was weak and out-of-date. Although much good work was taking place it was not manifest by the school's policy document. After the old document had been reviewed and rewritten Estyn expressed pleasant surprise.

(b) To relate and integrate the school's policy documents on attendance, behaviour and bullying.

(c) To provide Estyn with individual examples of good practice in work with pupils in attendance cases.

(d) To ensure all members of the special needs unit and learning mentors were conversant with all attendance and behavioural issues and had been appropriately trained.

(e) To select three new short-term strategies from the lists provided in Chapters 3 to 6.

(f) To consider introducing a longer-term strategy as indicated in Chapters 7 and 8.

(g) To start involving parents more in school-based activities within the school either as helpers or as learners within classrooms.

(h) To consider a whole-school training day on improving school attendance before launching (e) and (f) above.

(i) To review the school's latest policy documents on attendance, behaviour and bullying in twelve months' time.

(j) To have a 'brainstorming' session on progress made in a year's time and to then consider implementing some further initiatives from the lists found in Chapters 3 to 6.

(k) To consider introducing an agreed alternative curriculum for disaffected pupils as from September 2001.

Case Study B – Seaside School

Staff in Seaside School have begun to realise that despite the number of internal initiatives with which it is trying to combat its pupils' absenteeism, the overall problem is not improving significantly and the range of related issues appear to be on the increase. The author was asked to lead a staff development day to advise the school on strategies with which they could hope to improve their overall attendance rates.

Seaside School contains approximately 1,250 pupils on two sites in a nice part of south-west England. Their overall rates of attendance during the last four years have been 87.8, 88.9, 90 and 91.1 per cent. In the current session, three out of five year groups have attendance rates in excess of 90 per cent. Only year 7 has previously achieved this in all recent years.

Across the school, 2,303 days were 'lost' due to family holidays alone. This accounts for 0.8 per cent of absences throughout the year and is broadly equivalent to fourteen pupils not attending school for a whole year. Unauthorised absence is gradually falling. By contrast, parental-condoned absence is on the increase.

In session 2000/1, the school began to appreciate that it is on the 'margins' as far as its next Ofsted inspection is concerned and this is now on the horizon. Therefore, after extensive internal consultation, the school has begun a large number of initiatives on attendance. These are:

1 A change of times for the school day, particularly to facilitate afternoon registration.

2 The introduction of a new electronic registration package. This has involved training for all staff and the implementation of hardware and software for electronic registration.

3 Specific attendance targets being set for each form and each year by the head of year which is appropriately monitored.

4 Specialised in-service training for heads of year and assistant heads of year on utilising attendance data.

5 The expansion of first day contact across an increased number of year groups to extend eventually to all pupils in the school.

6 Conducting a Prudential Sponsored Project on attendance in conjunction with the Police Liaison Officer.

7 Participating in a crime reduction project with the local council.

8 Reclassifying study leave/home study. For example, the week prior to half-term for year 11 pupils now falls into the criteria to count as full-time attendance and not as study leave which was previously equated with unauthorised absence.

9 Establishing a project to look at best practice in other schools. This has resulted in the school learning how to use opportunities presented by the new electronic system to inform parents more regularly about their children's attendance and absences.

10 All home school reports now include a summary of pupil attendance. In addition, separate letters are sent to parents on their child's attendance at the end of each term. These letters also comment on the pupils' attendance percentages.

11 Printouts of electronic registration by tutor group, year group and whole school are produced weekly and placed on the attendance notice board in the staff room.

12 The school has used grant money through the pupil referral unit initiative to fund its own full-time EWO for the first time.

13 The school has run staff development sessions on increasing pupil attendance and reducing unauthorised absence organised by an external consultant with follow-up activities planned.

14 The school is interviewing groups of persistent non-attenders to discover why they are missing (a) school; or (b) specific lessons.

The aim of all these fourteen initiatives is 'to raise pupil attainment by increasing their attendance; and, to ensure the school is above 90 per cent attendance and rising by the time Ofsted arrives'.

Summary

Case Studies A and B demonstrate the wide and diverse range of effort currently being shown by contrasting secondary schools to improve their attendance rates and reduce unauthorised absence. A great deal of dedicated hard graft is taking place by a range of professionals, including headteachers, senior staff, form tutors, education welfare officers, attendance support staff, learning mentors, staff involved in education action zones and other initiatives, and many more besides. Despite this, much more work remains to be done. As initiatives on attendance increase and improve, so it seems do the range of social impediments and familiar complications. Despite the excellent range of professional practice, teacher morale is being undermined as society continues to condone pupils who miss school and some parents continue to encourage their children to do so.

Chapter 3

Short-term solutions I

There are probably so many varied and different short-term solutions to truancy and absenteeism in use by schools throughout the United Kingdom that it would be almost impossible to mention them all. Many short-term solutions are unique to individual schools. Therefore, this and the next three chapters will focus on a consideration of some of the better known and more frequently used schemes. The solutions discussed in this and succeeding chapters are presented in tabular form in Figure 3.1 which, by itself, indicates the breadth and range of existing provision. Nearly 120 short-term solutions are listed in Figure 3.1. This chapter will focus on the first twenty of these short-term solutions; the remainder being covered between Chapters 4 to 6.

The short-term solutions considered in this and the next two chapters are most commonly applied at key stages 3 and 4. However, many of the solutions are equally applicable for use much earlier within primary schools. Evidence from some inner-city truancy patrols is reporting on the surprisingly large number of primary-aged pupils who are being picked up and returned to their schools.

Typically, most schools currently use a range of short-term measures to combat truancy and absenteeism; often the schemes with which they feel most comfortable. The majority of secondary schools currently utilise first day response as one of their key strategies. However, the remaining solutions shown in Figure 3.1 are less evenly spread around schools. Indeed, some of the ideas are fairly localised and used within specific LEAs, EAZs or by groups of schools. A typical secondary school probably employs between six and eight short-term solutions (see Chapter 2). A few use considerably more and many much less.

Short-term action tends not to provide lasting solutions to truancy and absenteeism. They are usually a form of deterrent. Several of the short-term solutions utilise monitoring, preventative and remedial techniques. In an ideal world schools should have a range of short, medium and long-term strategies in place. We will now begin to consider the first set of twenty short-term solutions in more detail.

1   First day response

First day response is now the normal official practice in the vast majority of schools and LEAs throughout the United Kingdom. It can be extremely time-consuming and labour-intensive. First day contact was originally introduced as a national response in England following adverse publicity in the media about two missing 10-year-old schoolchildren in Sussex, reports on child abuse cases, and pupils who had run away from home (often

1   First day response
2   Personal and social education programmes
3   Utilisation of colour-coded groups
4   Corrective schemes to overcome literacy and numeracy
5   Use of the Web, e.g. Plato concept = Independent Learning Systems
6   The use of classroom assistants
7   Mentoring programmes
    (a) adults/pupils
    (b) Connexions
    (c) sixth formers, younger pupils
    (d) able pupils with less able
    (e) parents with pupils
    (f) former pupils
    (g) provided by outside business: business link mentors
    (h) teenage sports leaders
    (i) the 'grey army'
    (j) mobilising the voluntary sector
    (k) undergraduates with pupils
    (l) young carers scheme
8   The use of role play
9   Incentive initiatives – whole school, year, form, pupil, etc. Positive reinforcement schemes
10 Use of at-risk registers/measures
11 Return to school policies
12 Reintegration strategies
13 Managing school transfers
14 Managing subject choices effectively for GCSEs/GNVQs
15 Improving special needs facilities
16 Second chance opportunities
17 Projecting achievement targets
18 Use of homework clubs and ICT
19 Summer school initiatives
20 Utilising pupils' common rooms and learning support centres
21 Breakfast clubs
22 After school clubs (ice skating, drama, etc.)
23 Work-related curriculum strategies
24 Key skills lessons
25 Appointing a home–school co-ordinator
26 Red lists – saving 20 pupils at a time
27 E-mail or text message support
28 Flexible tuition times
29 After hours support – tutors or clubs
30 Using local sports clubs
31 Presenting attendance certificates
32 Half-day rewards
33 Suggestion box schemes
34 Use of foundation programmes
35 Afro/Caribbean/Asian liaison officers
36 Student progress planners
37 Viewmaster – IT lesson initiative
38 Buddy system
39 Truancy Buster scheme
40 Closer FE–school links
41 Management of learning programmes scheme
42 Utilising external volunteers (e.g. Age Concern) to manage first day absence
43 Objective 3 funding
44 Improving the quality of registration time
45 Parental fines
46 New Labour's key policies on truancy
47 Truancy watch/Truancy sweeps
48 EWO interviewing pupil(s) and parent(s) in school time together
49 Establishing an attendance hot line with local shops
50 Spot checks
51 Creating a pupils' school council
52 Specialist pastoral training for staff on 'sensitive' issues
53 Provision of free bus passes
54 Using legal powers decisively
55 Use of security firms
56 Limiting school exit points and monitoring school transitions
57 Home–school, parent–pupil, pupil–school contracts
58 Developing strategies for punctuality and combating lateness
59 National advertising schemes
60 Formation of anti-truancy teams
61 Utilising paging systems
62 One-to-one experiences – case reviews
63 Inter-agency co-operation
64 Using specialist in-school projects
65 Utilising social workers in schools
66 Improved health checks
67 Appointment of specialist staff –
        Attendance support teachers
        Attendance support secretary
        Specialist counsellors
68 Special needs assistants
69 Extension of primary school practice
70 Compensatory programmes
71 School-based review
72 School-based questionnaires
73 Tackling social exclusion
74 Inclusive school policies: Social Inclusion Units
75 Using pupil panels
76 Governing body review on attendance
77 School trips
78 Use of stickers and badges
79 Personal congratulation schemes

80 Utilising the Internet	100 Use of external consultants
81 Attendance notice boards	101 Letters to parents
82 Attendance cups	102 'Premiership'
83 Attendance league tables	103 Truancy watch schemes
84 Attendance panel	104 Arrival and Departure Lounge
85 Pupils' photographs	105 Parental convoys
86 School newsletters – attendance section	106 Good and poor attenders 'runs'
87 Parents' evening on attendance or parental days	107 Truancy call
88 Detentions	108 Quiet room
89 End-of-day registrations	109 On-line registers/swipe systems
90 Business sponsorship	110 Phonemaster
91 Years 10 and 11 projects	111 Asthma clinics
92 Missing-from-lesson slips	112 Parental sit-ins
93 Attendance tribunals	113 Reduction in illegal working
94 Staggered start times	114 Pearson technology developments
95 Policies for habitual truants	115 The Scottish Shilling
96 'Catch up' units	116 Pacific Institute programme
97 Consistency of staff policies	117 Success Maker
98 Staff absenteeism	118 All the year round learning
99 Involving community police in school	119 Use of pupil referral units

Figure 3.1 100 plus short-term strategies currently in use in schools.

to London), the rise in day-time crime in shopping centres, the growth in the use of solvents, drug abuse and teenage prostitution. The pressure upon schools and LEAs to introduce first day response was effectively rubber stamped by the DfES as government policy in a series of statements and press releases during 1998 and 1999. Since then, schools and LEAs have struggled to come to terms with the various advantages and disadvantages of the scheme. Nearly everyone agrees, however, that introducing first day responses is helpful to all parties. It is in the management of the process that difficulties occur.

In fact, most schools, LEAs and education welfare officers now agree that first day contact with parent(s) and/or pupils is one of, if not *the* best, initial short-term solution. It has several merits. First, it expresses the school's concern to the parent(s) and provides as early a warning system to them as possible. Second, it strengthens the school's legal and procedural position in any subsequent action. Third, it facilitates early detection and helps with re-integration strategies. Fourth, it provides better insights into why a pupil is away from school (see later).

There are, however, some disadvantages. The scheme is notoriously time consuming and some parents are particularly difficult to contact. In former times, when every family had a known BT number, using the phone to contact parents was much easier than it is today with the vast array of telephone lines, numbers and local technological quirks! In truth, these difficulties alone can make the scheme so time consuming that in some secondary schools it is currently impossible for the 'office' to be able to make all the calls *and* contact every parent on each first (and/or subsequent) day of absence. This is especially true in large schools and those with high daily absence rates. The responsibility for making the calls also varies between schools often dependent upon local financial and administrative arrangements.

In far too many schools responsibility for making first day responses is left to a member of the senior management team (e.g. deputy head i/c attendance) and/or heads of year or form tutors. Whenever possible, the task should be undertaken in the first instance by 'office' staff with significant issues referred upwards. If no office staff are available to fulfil this task, then it should be the responsibility of a form tutor or class-room teacher (in primary schools) in the first instance.

First day contact does relieve many EWOs of this responsibility and enables them to 'free up' their time for more pressing business such as making home visits or court work. Unfortunately, the reason(s) given by the parent(s) for their child's absence can lead to schools referring cases to other external caring agencies, most notably social services, but often child guidance, education psychologists, the police and local medical centres. This, in turn, has led to an increased workload for individual EWOs and their local LEA offices, as absenteeism and truancy cases are notoriously fraught with related social, psychological and home background difficulties (Reid, 1985).

Nevertheless, some schools and LEAs are already convinced that first day response is the most natural and best short-term solution to the extent that in private some will question why it has taken so long to become normal practice. Equally, headteachers argue that whilst the advantages of the scheme are manifestly apparent, the downside is the extent to which their administrative support is overloaded. One school in the South Midlands, for example, has found it necessary to extend its phone lines from two to twenty to cope with the resulting pressure. People in authority should not underestimate either the amount of time or the subsequent stress which can be imposed upon office and other staff who make these regular calls. One attendance support secretary in a school in South Wales told the author that she is probably shouted at by parents on at least ten different occasions every day whilst making these calls. Another said she needed a second office to file the mountain of paperwork which had been collected from her daily checks and she simply had no filing time whatsoever. All her available time is spent on making the calls. In a typical comprehensive school of 1,200 pupils with a 90 per cent attendance rate, it is possible for an attendance support secretary/manager/teacher to be expected to make up to 120 calls a day and also to deal with the subsequent paperwork; all of which gives an indication of the scale of the problem. This is why some schools are opting out of first day responses and contracting these services to private companies as discussed further in Chapter 6 (see, for example, Truancy Call and Phonemaster Systems).

On the credit side, there is equally no doubt that schools are receiving better data on why pupils are missing schools and planning more meaningful individual and/or group solutions. Whilst the complexity of the reasons given for the absence are ever increasing, it has reinforced many schools' attention on parental-condoned absence (see Chapter 9). It is also generating better 'at risk' policies within some schools as well as leading to closer home–school contact and more informed liaison with appropriate external agencies.

First day response data is normally based upon pupils' registration details. Therefore, first day response is not as effective a strategy for identifying cases of post-registration truancy and specific lesson absence except in those situations where it is immediately detected and subsequent action taken.

2   Personal and social education programmes

There is an increasing recognition that schools, LEAs and parents could do more to prevent truancy. Raising awareness of the issues involved is one such approach.

Few schools currently include the topic of truancy, parental-condoned absenteeism, specific lesson truancy, etc. as a key part of their personal and social education programmes. An examination of PSE programmes in years 7 to 11 in selected comprehensive schools in England and Wales (Reid, 1999) revealed that popular topics for inclusion included: settling into secondary school, codes of behaviour, study skills, first aid, health hazards (AIDS, smoking, etc.), exam techniques, insight into industry, the changing body, sex education, gender, bullying (and/or bullying initiatives), records of achievement, the consequences of crime (shoplifting, joyriding), health and safety, alcohol abuse, child abuse, relationships, home–school responsibilities, dress sense, drugs, action planning in careers, youth enterprise, the community and local environment, equal opportunities, disabilities, religious toleration, ethnicity, meningitis, and so on. Quite a list! Yet, of all the schools' PSE programmes examined, only one included truancy on its contents list – and this only in years 10 and 11; far too late.

Truancy is an important issue for pupils to understand, because understanding can lead to rejection – the same theory as in educational programmes about drugs and alcohol abuse. When pupils are confronted with the realities of truancy – poor jobs in later life; lower wages; much greater likelihood of being on income support and housing benefit, links with criminality; social and psychological distress – they are much more likely to think twice about truanting. Enabling pupils to understand the short and long-term consequences of their action is important. Truancy education should start as young as possible – early in year 7 would be best in secondary schools. Truancy as a topic can be closely related to programmes on behaviour, discipline, disruptive behaviour, codes of practice and bullying, which are already key themes in many schools' PSE programmes. It will also bring issues within schools about truancy into the open rather than leaving them remaining hidden.

3   Utilisation of colour-coded groups

Many schools are beginning to be attracted by the ideas and principles which are considered in detail in Chapters 7 and 8 on long-term strategic approaches to combating truancy and other forms of non-attendance. Some schools therefore, are starting to utilise these concepts within their short-term schemes. For example, one school in Gloucestershire puts its at-risk and truanting pupils into the same colour-coded groups as outlined in Chapter 8 for monitoring purposes without attempting to implement the long-term accompanying schemes. So, persistent absentees are put into a red group and their attendance and progress are monitored daily and reviewed periodically. First day response, for example, starts with these pupils.

In another school in West Sussex, persistent truants are put into a red group. Less frequent absentees are put into a blue group. Occasional absentees are placed in a yellow cohort. Once again, the progress of all these pupils is regularly monitored and reviewed.

Another variant is to put troublesome pupils with severe behavioural problems into a red group. Disaffected pupils are located in a blue group. Non-attenders are placed together in a yellow group. Some schools then add a fourth layer by putting under-achievers into a green group. Pupils with health problems might then go into another colour coded group. Monitoring and reviewing procedures tend to vary school by school, partly dependent upon the size and scale of the problems.

4   Corrective schemes to overcome literacy and numeracy

Research shows that it is possible to boost pupils' literacy and numeracy problems in comparatively short periods of time by concentrated efforts. For example, a learning support department can introduce a corrective reading scheme aimed at raising basic literacy levels through the use of a daily structured group reading programme. Such programmes are designed to be positive and supportive for pupils. The need to attend on a regular basis is emphasised in these programmes. Success in a programme can also be linked in with a reward system.

One study found average gains in reading ages on the New Macmillan Reading Analysis Scheme of between eighteen months and two years over a three-month period across all four levels of the programme using a corrective reading scheme. There were specific cases of persistent absentees attending for the research programme who then missed the rest of their schooling. This must say something about *relevance* within the curriculum; not least related to pupils' aptitudes. As truants and persistent absentees tend to come from low educational backgrounds often with chronological reading and numerical ages well below their standard level, it is clear that boosting literacy and numeracy skills and enabling pupils to achieve is bound to reduce the longer-term pool of potential non-attenders.

5   Use of the Web: the Plato concept

Many pupils are fascinated by modern technology, not least the Internet. Schools are now beginning to use the Internet as a learning tool more and more. Some pupils who are turned off by traditional approaches to teaching become 'switched-on' when they use computers, computing software, e-mails, text messages and, probably most significantly, the Internet.

Private companies are also beginning to see the financial benefits for their organisations of becoming involved in applying learning solutions for schools or as part of a home support service. For example, one company has developed the Plato concept. The Plato concept is a supportive independent learning system. It operates at three levels. The pupils can follow the scheme at their own pace using the new technology. The first level is for responsive able pupils. The second is for average ability pupils. The third is for slower, less able pupils.

The Plato scheme can be used by regular attenders as a supportive learning scheme. Its best use, however, is probably to enable pupils to catch up with work they have missed. It is particularly effective, for example, in facilitating pupils who have been away ill from school for a long period of time or away on an overseas visit. It can be used as an effective re-integration strategy.

The Plato scheme provides a comprehensive coverage of all National Curriculum material with supportive materials. At present, schools pay for this science through the amount of time they buy. Some schools are currently asking supporting organisations (EAZs, parent–teacher associations) to help fund the provision. Some schools have reported that the scheme is very effective when working with truants and other similar cases. It can be helpful in enabling disruptive or potential excluded pupils to work on their own terms, preventing disruption to other classes. It reduces dependence on 'book copying' from other pupils in the same forms. It also encourages self-support and self-motivation. It can be especially effective for pupils who are temporarily experiencing serious breakdowns in their teacher–pupil relationships.

6   The use of classroom assistants

Many teachers are simply too busy to give pupils in need the attention they require. In primary schools, the use of classroom assistants in some LEAs is commonplace. Similar schemes are currently expanding in a major way within secondary schools. In some primary schools in, for example, Kent, there can be as many as six different classroom assistants in addition to the teacher. Typically, classroom assistants are used as a teacher's support, as mentors, as facilitators for pupils with special needs, etc. Equally, the number and range of classroom assistants used by secondary schools is growing rapidly. Many of these are being used as learning mentors (see Chapter 11).

Classroom assistants can be paid or unpaid, trained or untrained. They might be parents, mature (even retired) people, personal tutors, mentors or simply volunteers. The use of classroom assistants can be particularly beneficial for pupils who have reading, literacy or numeracy difficulties, special needs, behavioural problems, and those who need to catch up with missed work, such as truants.

The use of classroom assistants on a national basis at all levels of the education service could be especially beneficial in combating inequality, especially for those pupils who come from socially disadvantaged backgrounds. Since 1997, the creation of a pool of funded classroom helpers to facilitate learning has been one of the central planks of New Labour's educational policies.

7   Mentoring programmes

There are currently a whole variety of mentoring schemes in use in both primary and secondary schools throughout the UK. These mentoring schemes are growing significantly in importance to the extent that Chapter 11 is devoted to a consideration of the issues involved and a detailed analysis of some of the schemes.

The mentoring of truants and other non-attenders is also gaining increasing credence in the literature. There are a variety of mentoring schemes in practice. These include:

- peer mentoring;
- adult mentoring;
- school mentoring;
- parent mentoring.

Peer mentorship schemes often involve able pupils helping less able pupils with schoolwork and adjustment problems. Sometimes they involve older pupils working with younger pupils, e.g. sixth formers with years 7, 8, 9, 10 or 11 pupils. Peer mentoring schemes are often conducted as part of the normal, adjusted or alternative curriculum provision. Some peer mentoring schemes are undertaken full time. Others are part-time or for special times/periods during a school day/week.

Adult mentoring involves a grown-up working with a single or group of needy, difficult, disaffected or non-attending pupils on a full-time or part-time basis. Who this adult is varies considerably. It can be a student, teacher, parent, retired teacher or retired professional. In one sense, who it is does not matter. What matters, is that the scheme – notably the liaison between the pupil(s) and the adult – works.

School mentoring is when the LEA or institution makes special arrangements for an individual or group of pupils to attend a specially constructed curriculum (a form of alternative education) on or off the school premises. The mentor could vary from a specialist off-site tutor to qualified teachers who are currently not working full time. It is essential that schools vet these mentors thoroughly before placements begin. Teacher mentoring usually involves a full or part-time member of staff working with an individual or group of pupils. This can be done on a full-time, part-time or special times basis over a short or long-term period. The critical question is how and when to end this relationship and enable the pupil(s) to return to class and attend normally.

Parent mentoring takes place when a parent (often a mother or extended family member) takes responsibility for a child or group of children in or out of school to help with short or long-term learning, adjustment or behavioural problems.

The key to successful mentoring lies in developing a positive relationship between mentor and pupil. The aim is to provide the pupil with confidence, trust, a willingness to co-operate and learn and eventually, a desire to return to a normal full-time timetable or remain within a regular classroom on as equal a basis with other pupils as possible.

8   The use of role play

Some schools have found the use of role play, either in assemblies, in class teaching time, in form periods, or as part of the PSE programme, to be an effective means of preventing or combating such issues as bullying, extortion, racial or gender inequalities, indiscipline, violence, drug-related activity, as well as truancy.

Some schools produce plays and/or videos as part of this preventative work. An example is Mountain Ash Comprehensive School which produced an anti-bullying video as part of a project to improve school attendance, combat under-achievement and raise academic standards (Reynolds, 1996). It is believed that the therapeutic effects of this approach can be especially beneficial to pupils at risk, particularly those who are vulnerable to peer pressure.

9   Incentive initiatives

Positive reinforcement

There are currently so many variable incentive schemes in operation in schools in Britain that it is virtually impossible to list them all. For example, a school in Gloucester offers an annual prize of a mountain bike to the best school attenders based on a whole-school draw in assembly on the final morning of the school year. Any day's absence without good reason excludes a pupil from having his or her name entered into the draw. Some schools offer whole-school prizes. Others offer prizes by year or by form or house.

Many, if not most, schools now use various forms of positive reinforcement and rewards to promote good school attendance. A positive form of reinforcement and praise for pupils who attend school regularly – however this is done – can work wonders. A system of rewards and/or incentives will show the whole school community how highly attendance is valued and will demonstrate to pupils and their families that the school values and appreciates their efforts. Promoting this policy should be the responsibility of the entire school staff, not just pastoral staff and/or form tutors. Smith *et al.* (1994) suggest that pupils worthy of recognition include:

- 100 per cent attenders and other excellent attenders (over a term, a year);
- consistently good attenders;
- poor attenders who show a significant/any improvement;
- those from a year group with consistently good attendance;
- those from a year group who show a marked improvement;
- year 7 pupils who begin their secondary career with a good attendance record;
- the whole school.

Traditional forms of rewards include:

- letters to parents;
- personal congratulations from the headteacher, head of year or other senior staff;
- photo-display, featuring named pupils;
- stickers in homework diaries;
- regular features/presentations on an attendance notice board in school corridors/form or staff rooms;
- presentations at assemblies, parents evenings, etc. (for example, for the most improved attender in the year, form, school);
- linking attendance to a school's merit/credit/reward (for example, mug, crayons) system;
- the use of badges or special privileges.

More recently, some schools have begun to extend these schemes to include:

- monthly prizes for form, year for best attendance;
- termly prizes for best attendance;
- annual prizes for best attendance.

A number of organisations use former famous pupils or local celebrities to promote good attendance in a variety of ways. After travelling around the country promoting issues on attendance it never ceases to surprise me how many celebrities give up their time to help their former schools, other local schools and support educational promotional events. Spend time sifting through local papers and you may be surprised to see how many sporting, pop and cultural heroes give up their time to promote school attendance and related projects.

Rewards can include winning portable music systems, videos, televisions, radios, computers, etc. One school arranges for the best attending form in each year to be given an annual visit to Alton Towers. Similar schemes at other schools make the major prize a visit to Euro Disney, a week's holiday in France, or a trip to see England play soccer. Put like this, good attendance is fun and makes sense! Similar incentive schemes are run in many countries, most notably the USA. Some of the prizes on offer, for example at schools in Vermont, make efforts in the UK seem like small beer!

Lottery-type schemes

Some schools have begun lottery-type schemes to reward good attendance. Thus, every pupil, every form which makes 100 per cent attendance in a week/month/term/year enters a weekly/monthly/termly/yearly draw for a prize. Weekly prizes tend to be small. Monthly prizes a little bigger. Termly prizes are often quite significant whilst annual prizes are very significant to the extent that they would be valued by everyone. Paying for these schemes often requires ingenuity and extra funding activity on the part of school staff and/or parent–teacher associations.

In 2000, after the publication of *Tackling Truancy in Schools*, the author was attacked in the press by a spokesperson for the Campaign for Real State Education. It was suggested that the book was advocating the use of bribery to ensure that pupils attended school regularly which, after all, was the statutory responsibility of their parents. The book did no such thing. It merely reported neutrally on the widespread and differing use of a whole list of positive reinforcement schemes in British schools for a variety of reasons including encouraging attendance. In fact, encouraging attendance by using positive reinforcement schemes is, if anything, on the increase and numerous examples can be found of such schemes in LEA and school policy documents on attendance (e.g. Bolton). The fact that so many schools, LEAs and other organisations utilise the scheme in a variety of ways is surely testimony to the fact that the concept must have some merit and be deemed necessary and/or appropriate by a whole range of those in authority within the education service.

10   Use of at-risk registers

The use of at-risk registers by schools can help to identify potential truants at an early stage. Potential pupils included on such registers can be those with siblings who have previously or are actually truanting; pupils from one parent families; pupils whose academic performance is causing concern and whose progress is well behind; pupils with known serious problems at home and who may be involved with the social services, etc.

The identification of an at-risk register in primary schools can alert teachers to give special attention to their pupils with particular academic, social or psychological needs. In secondary schools, at-risk registers should be in use by the beginning of year 7 to be really effective. Thereafter, pupils remain on the register, or others are added to the register, depending upon personal progress and need. Pupils on the at-risk register should be carefully monitored throughout their school careers and appropriate action taken as necessary. Quite often, at-risk registers are used in conjunction with other short-term and longer-term initiatives (see Chapters 7 and 8) especially in respect of colour-coded schemes.

11   Return to school policies

One of the most difficult events for a truant is to be made to feel welcome or to be able to relax and re-integrate back into school in a meaningful way, especially after a regular or protracted period of absence. Therefore, schools need to formulate return-to-school policies. Some pupils who would like to return to school find that teachers inadvertently reinforce their truancy by making ill-judged comments or by singling them out for special attention in an unfortunate way. Making pupils who are already embarrassed feel even more self-conscious is not helpful and should always be avoided.

Smith *et al.* (1994) suggest that schools can apply the following guidelines that give out the right signals:

- Always ensure that the school keeps in touch with any pupil who is absent for long periods. (The child and his/her family still need to feel part of the school community throughout the period of absence.)
- Always make the child feel welcomed back (even if his/her past behaviour has been difficult).
- Never make sarcastic comments (a casual, 'Nice of you to turn up' or 'Had a nice holiday?' can in a moment destroy hours of careful preparation).
- Never leave a child feeling dumped in a corridor or outside an office. (There must always be someone to take responsibility for and know what to do with the child.)
- Always ensure that the child has someone/somewhere to go if things get difficult.

Pupils returning after a long absence cannot perform miracles. Renewing or remaking friendships, catching up in the classroom, readjusting to a structured day all take time and do not happen overnight. There may be hiccups. But throughout the process pupils must feel that the school is glad to see them and values their return.

12   Re-integration strategies

A number of Ofsted reports have recently been commenting on the fact that whilst schools tend to have appropriate attendance policies, very few have effective re-integration strategies. In practice, many pupils returning to school are often left to catch up on their own. If a person has been away because of truancy this is, to say the least, a strange policy and encourages further bouts of non-attendance.

Pupils tend to become absentees when they fall behind with their school work and are not coping well and making the required academic progress. Results from attainment tests show that regular absentees are two chronological years (often far more than two!) behind their designated literacy and numeracy benchmark.

Part of the Ofsted process on attendance is now to comment upon the suitability or otherwise of a school's process for re-integrating long-term absentees (whether for attendance, illness or for other reasons) back into school. Ideally, this involves helping recalcitrant and other kinds of pupils to catch up. Some schools have established social inclusion units to facilitate this process. Others use volunteers, mentors or learning assistants to help with this facilitating or catching up process. Some schools often attach responsibility for the process to their special needs department/co-ordinator. The Plato concept (see Section 5 earlier) is growing in popularity in facilitating pupils' re-entry strategies.

Either way, there is little doubt that facilitating pupils to re-enter school is both psychologically and academically helpful. Schools which do not offer this facility risk undoing much of the good work undertaken by the attendance support staff, education welfare officers, truancy patrols and others. Frequently pupils who find themselves after returning to school in a position in which they cannot cope tend to feel awkward and endeavour to absent themselves again as soon as possible.

13   Managing school transfers

Research shows that pupils are particularly vulnerable at times of making school transfers, especially at the age of 11, at the beginning of year 10 after selecting GCSE subjects, and when moving home or area, or at the beginning of each academic year as they move forms or classes.

Any change of school can be difficult for a child – whether it involves the move from nursery to infants, from infants to junior or whatever – but the transfer from primary to secondary school can be a particularly difficult time for some pupils as they face up to a number of new experiences. By developing effective links with primary feeders, schools will be able to facilitate the smooth transfer of the majority of pupils and to identify those pupils in year 6 who may appear likely to experience attendance and other difficulties at their secondary school.

Smith *et al.* (1994) have suggested the following guidelines should be used to facilitate the school transfer process to which the author has supplemented a few extra ideas. Most LEAs now have their own guidelines for use by schools on managing the transfer process effectively and Smith *et al.*'s are amongst the best. They stress the need for schools to realise that pupils are coming to a different learning, physical and social environment as well as the specific issues involved in the primary–secondary liaison itself.

A different learning environment

Secondary schools need to be aware that year 7 pupils may:

- experience difficulty adjusting to a much more complex learning environment;
- lack basic social and interpersonal skills;
- have special educational needs which have not yet been clearly identified;
- experience curriculum discontinuity;
- experience difficulty relating to several new teachers;
- experience difficulty working in a number of different classrooms;
- have a problem with a more structured timetable;
- find it difficult coping with the demands of homework;
- have had different learning experiences at their respective primary schools;
- miss their former friends, especially those pupils who come from small feeder primary schools.

A different physical environment

Secondary schools need to be aware that year 7 pupils may:

- be unused to moving around a large school for different lessons;
- lack basic organisational skills;
- be unused to using public transport to get to school;
- have difficulty adjusting to a large impersonal dining room;
- feel physically threatened to be amongst so many much larger and older pupils;
- sense a natural reduction in their self-confidence and self-esteem.

A different social environment

Secondary schools need to be aware that year 7 pupils may:

- be unused to relating to large numbers of adults and children;
- have to make new friends;
- miss the intimacy of primary school;
- be unused to the demands of wearing school uniform;
- now find it difficult accepting the fact that they are at the bottom of the school's structure (i.e. 'the pecking order');
- be early maturers (e.g. year 6 pupils whose voices have already broken);
- feel isolated and lost;
- be more vulnerable to bullying;
- feel sensitive to failure (e.g. inability to make a year group football team or a drama production because of the increased competition).

Any combination of the above factors may cause a year 7 pupil to experience difficulties in attending. It is vital that such difficulties are picked up and addressed sooner rather than later.

Effective primary–secondary liaison

This will involve:

- a clearly identified staff team responsible for maintaining links with feeder primaries;
- a clearly defined and regularly reviewed strategy to facilitate secondary transfer;
- systems to monitor and review the progress of all year 7 pupils;
- structured visits from primary schools in the summer terms – and follow-up meetings with primary staff;
- measures to ensure curricular continuity (purposeful liaison between year 6 and year 7 teachers);
- effective liaison with the education welfare officers attached to feeder primaries;
- special induction programmes for those year 7 pupils who come from primaries other than the school's usual feeder primaries (this may often be the odd one or two pupils – precisely those who may find secondary transfer a lonely and difficult time);

- getting the whole school involved in taking responsibility for assisting those newly joining the school;
- involving parents from the very beginning in the secondary school's policies and practices.

Smith *et al.*'s (1994) checklist provides a useful starting point from which staff in schools could subsequently 'brainstorm' the issues involved in managing the primary–secondary transfer phase appropriately. Of course, there is discussion within the DfES of beginning to experiment with all-through, all-phase schools from aged 3 years to 18. If this begins to happen, some pupils will no longer experience the primary–secondary change process in the same way.

14   Managing subject choices for GCSEs/GNVQs

Selecting subject choices for GCSEs and/or GNVQs is a sensitive time in school for pupils and for some parents. It provides clear evidence of their long-term academic potential. The process of selecting the right and appropriate choice of subjects for external examination requires both tact and empathetic advice and/or counselling. Too often vulnerable pupils are made to feel like 'dummies' and 'dullos' by insensitive management of the process or by, at its worst, callous remarks.

There is little doubt that in many schools the post-selection process and outcomes lead to a significant rise in non-attendance in years 10 and 11. This is partly because some pupils 'elect' to study subjects for which they are genuinely uninterested. It is also partly because some pupils are discouraged from taking subjects they would really like or prefer to take because of staff advice, timetabling restrictions or for other reasons. Or, in some cases, it is because the pupils realise that their chance of success in external subjects is strictly limited and would prefer not to be put through the whole process.

Since the introduction of league tables, the advice given to pupils and their parents by schools has been compounded by the wishes of some schools to appear as high in league tables as possible, especially on those tables which measure external examination performance. Thus, some schools prefer not to enter weak pupils into external examinations for which they have little chance of passing. One school in South Wales, for example, allows its pupils to take a maximum of eight subjects at GCSE rather than the previous twelve because it found it enhances their opportunity for a higher league table position.

Thus, staff in some schools would be better to encourage their weaker pupils positively to only take those few subjects in which they could do well rather than a lot of subjects when they are liable to fail the lot. Likewise, sensible timetable changes to give weak pupils more time in key subjects is another form of good practice. Now that the DfES permits weaker and disaffected pupils to spend more time on vocational subjects, and in alternative curriculum schemes, there is every chance that some of these longer-term problems can be dissipated.

Unfortunately, at the time of writing, some state schools are reluctant to allow their weaker pupils to attend relevant vocational educational programmes in FE colleges because of the loss of funding. Currently, if a pupil spends half his or her time in school and half in a college, both institutions claim half fees. Therefore, some headteachers are understandably reluctant to lose funding. It would be sensible for the DfES to address this problem by allowing both the school and the FE college to count each such pupil as one full-time equivalent. After all, the extra costs of this scheme are nothing when compared to the alternative – a long-term failing truant spending the rest of his or her life on income support and related benefits.

15 Improving special needs facilities

For far too long, special needs departments have been 'Cinderellas' within some state schools. There is now both growing support and funding to support special needs staff as part of the DfES's social inclusion policies.

Nevertheless, staff within special needs departments will often tell you that their individual and collective needs are for more time and resources. Improving learning outcomes for pupils with special needs often requires one-to-one support. With the advent of mentoring and learning support schemes, much more help is available than used to be the case. However, in some schools the number of pupils who require special needs support has also increased significantly. For example, in one large secondary school in Cardiff, 35 per cent of all its pupils require special needs, and this is no longer particularly unusual. Another, a specialist special needs school, has over 700 pupils. Imagine how much extra support this really requires. As many truants and persistent absentees throughout the UK also have special needs, you can begin to see the scale of the problem. For example, Beaufort School in Gloucester has been meeting this growing challenge by appointing approximately twenty learning support tutors to augment their seventy-five full-time staff, and this is typical of the situation in a very large proportion of secondary schools.

16 Second chance opportunities

There is a growing belief – fuelled by moves towards social inclusion and lifelong learning – that some school dropouts, disaffected pupils and educational failures can flourish if provided with relevant second chance opportunities. Following a three-year study of 384 pupils, including 128 persistent absentees, Reid (1985) reported that the majority of truants eventually regretted their actions as the consequences began to catch up with them. Evidence from early linked school–FE vocational projects suggest that many persistent absentees and disaffected pupils will attend when they see their programme as being relevant to their later world of work (Morgan, 1999; Reid, 2000).

Britain's first 'second chance' school was launched in Leeds in March 1998. The aim is to pioneer a helping hand scheme for the country's 45,000 plus young people who leave school each year without any formal qualifications whatsoever. Entry to the pilot scheme in Leeds offers priority to the most disadvantaged applicants in the 18–24 age range. Students include previously disruptive pupils, truants and dyslexia victims. The school's curriculum is strongly vocationally orientated and aspires to restore debilitated pupils' confidence as well as to build links with local employers.

Students are entitled to remain on benefit while studying on the basis that they are available for work. The curriculum has been tailored to link with the government's welfare to work programme for the young jobless.

Early evidence suggests that the scheme is being fairly successful. However, some of the students are relating better to their hands-on skills-based tutors rather than to conventional teachers. Providing one-to-one support in information technology appears to be especially popular possibly because of its long-term potential help to the students in finding meaningful and better paid work.

The scheme is currently being monitored by the DfES. If the outcome is judged to be successful, further regional centres in large urban areas of population are likely to be opened. The DfES believes that second chance schools for the young and disaffected can be partially financed through the European Social Fund Grant.

17   Projecting achievement targets

Staff in schools are becoming increasingly used to being set and meeting targets. Some of these targets are being set externally by the DfES, Welsh Assembly, Scottish Parliament and Northern Ireland Ministry of Education, often monitored by inspectors. Other targets are being set by senior management within schools for their own staff and pupils to meet. Often these targets are related to a school's own development plans. Sometimes these targets appear in the form of performance indicators and benchmarks. On other occasions, they are self-imposed.

Gann (1999) has written a useful book on the use of targets for schools by head-teachers and governing bodies. There are probably four stages in the process towards setting meaningful targets. These are:

How to form effective targets

- Express them as end results not as processes or activities.
- Express them singly: avoid combining targets.
- Make them precise, not too indefinite nor too complex.
- Make them practical and feasible, not theoretical or idealistic.
- Express them as clearly as possible, avoiding ambiguity.
- Select only those of real consequence: avoid trivialising the process.
- Aim to stretch the target holder personally or professionally.
- Tailor the targets to suit the person.
- Relate targets to the teacher's career plans where possible.
- Agree on targets to be realistic, not aiming too high nor too low.
- Agree on their being achievable within a stated time period.
- Allow opportunity to redefine targets if circumstances alter.
- Aim to set between four and six targets per year.
- Agree on the criteria for success.
- Encourage staff to develop through the challenge of high but achievable targets.

The steps towards good target setting

- Begin with a clear and written definition of what has to be achieved.
- Identify performance criteria on which the success of the tasks can best be judged, e.g. time, quality, quantity, cost, etc.
- Agree on performance standards which indicate what level of success will be considered satisfactory or good.
- Indicate a priority between targets where more than one is set.
- Confirm that you both believe the target to be feasible.

- Aim to develop trust, understanding and honesty about, for example, performance standards or your willingness to revise the target if conditions change.
- Fix a review date.

Types of target

- Personal targets – those related to the individual teacher's professional development or the teacher's personal development in so far as it has a bearing on school performance.
- Departmental targets – those required to be achieved by a whole department, pastoral group or other permanent work group.
- Project targets – those related to major temporary projects in the school usually involving problem solving or innovation. These are frequently interdepartmental or falling into areas not covered by departmental responsibility.
- School targets – those required to be achieved by the school staff as a whole.

How target setting helps to improve a school

- Makes forward planning for school, department and teacher, imperative.
- Gives teachers a clearer understanding of what is required and their managers a better indication of teacher workload.
- Improves communication throughout the school.
- Develops teacher participation, commitment and team working.
- Reduces teacher stress, conflict, fire fighting, duplication of effort and unnecessary work.
- Offers a more objective way to look at teacher performance: brings fairer reference writing.
- Brings out into the open problems with achieving targets.
- Brings staff development into the target setting of the school.
- Provides heads with a means of managing teacher performance.

One problem with target setting is that the targets rarely remain constant. As you begin to improve, so you need to improve still further. However, target setting is a useful tool for management in team building. Success breeds success.

(17a) Targets for nursery and infant schools

New Labour's initiatives designed to improve standards in schools have been focused on all phases of schooling, and begin with nursery, infant and primary education. The key ideas behind these targets for the early years are now presented, because they all have a knock-on effect and relationship with the antecedents of truancy.

Key principles

1 Good quality early years' learning opportunities, alongside childcare and support for family learning where appropriate.
2 A thorough assessment of children when they start primary school.

3 A concentrated drive to raise standards of literacy (with proper regard for oral expression) and numeracy, and develop positive attitudes to learning.
4 Smaller infant classes to support more effective teaching and learning.

Specific measures

1 The establishment of early years' forums representing the full range of providers and users of early years' education in their areas. The forums will review the services available, including the provision of advice to parents before children start school, and devise early years' development plans.
2 Improving quality and quality assurance procedures in schools by:
   (a) introducing common standards of regulation and inspection;
   (b) improving staff training and qualifications;
   (c) making better use of the role of parents.
3 Setting specific targets and standards for outcomes in early years' education. These desirable learning outcomes will emphasise early literacy, numeracy, personal and social skills and learning through play.
4 Introducing common assessment schemes for children starting school.

New Labour's view is that the better start pupils have when first going to school, the better will be their long-term educational achievements. The greater the number of pupils who succeed, the fewer who will fail, drop out or need to truant.

(17b) Targets for primary schools

Primary school education is arguably the most important, or one of the most important, phases in the long-term potential of human beings. Primary education is about more than literacy and numeracy. Yet, these core skills are at the heart of what is done in primary schools. They are also fundamental to all future learning. There is a clear correlation between under-achievement in primary school and failure in adult life as well as with truancy.

It is now considered essential that:

1 All primary schools regularly set and review their own targets for improvements in the basics.
2 Every school has a development plan.
3 Each school emphasises the importance of attendance and good behaviour for consistent learning to take place.
4 Every teacher understands the clear link between attainment and attendance.

For purposes of monitoring and accountability, national data on performance as well as for schools' own target setting should relate to agreed national targets. In this, there is a similar strategy in place for secondary schools. For example, local authorities and OHMCI are invited to focus attention on the performance of schools where results fall in the bottom 25 per cent following statutory assessments at 11 and 14. The aim is to promote better results and raise standards.

All primary teachers need to know how to teach reading and maths in line with proven best practice. Quite often, teachers find that a successful approach includes:

- dedicated time given daily to aspects of literacy and numeracy in which a balance of whole-class, group and individual teaching is used, under firm and rigorous teacher direction to enthuse and engage children;
- regular assessment of pupils' progress to enable the teaching to be tailored precisely to their stage of development;
- systematic teaching of phonics in reading as well as sentence and text level skills;
- constructive development of pupils' capacity in mental arithmetic and of applying mathematics in practical and lively ways.

Below are listed a series of other new initiatives which, taken collectively, should help to raise standards in primary schools, improve pupils' performance and, by so doing, help reduce the antecedents of truancy:

1 Local plans from schools should propose innovative new ways to raise standards, whilst at the same time improving levels of literacy and numeracy.
2 Time management needs to be improved in schools, e.g. finding ways of spending more time to help some of the most disadvantaged and under-achieving pupils such as truants.
3 Guidance should be provided on good practice in target setting for primary schools.
4 Guidance for teachers on administering reading tests within schools should be improved. Schools will be encouraged to analyse results systematically, setting targets for improvement and reporting results to parents.
5 Better guidance should be provided to governors. Governors should be involved in school standards and school improvement issues, including performance indicators, e.g. school attendance and pupils' overall reading scores by comparison with local and national norms.
6 Family literacy schemes should be supported and educationally worthwhile out-of-hours activities promoted to raise:
   - standards;
   - literacy and numeracy;
   - pupils' cognitive and non-cognitive skills;
   - community appreciation skills;
   - recreational and sporting achievement.
7 Using local training councils and other voluntary educational groups wisely.
8 LEAs giving priority to professional development activities within nursery, infants and primary schools.
9 Educational/business links for primary schools should be improved, thereby ensuring that more primary schools benefit from employer support.
10 Out-of-hours childcare programmes should be used wisely, e.g. in summer holidays.
11 Class sizes should be reduced for the youngest-age pupils. Research shows that whilst smaller classes amongst early age pupils do not guarantee good results, they can make a significant contribution. They enable classroom teachers and/or classroom assistants, parent helpers, student-teachers to spend more time with each child, to

identify individual pupil needs and difficulties early on, and to offer the help children need to master the basics.

Wragg *et al.* (1998) undertook a project aimed at improving literacy in the primary school. Their research reported that there are ten signs of a successful teacher in primary school. These are:

- a high level of personal enthusiasm for literature, often supplementing the school's resources with their own books;
- good professional knowledge of children's authors and teaching strategies;
- importance of literacy stressed within a rich literacy environment;
- progress celebrated publicly and children's confidence increased;
- teaching individualised and matched to pupil's ability and reading interests;
- systematic monitoring and assessment;
- regular and varied reading activities;
- pupils encouraged to develop independence and autonomy, attacking unfamiliar words, or teachers backing pupils' judgement as authors;
- a high quality of classroom management skill and personal relationships with pupils;
- high expectations, children striving to reach a high standard, whatever their circumstances.

(17c) Targets for secondary schools and attendance targets

Schools are obliged to meet attendance targets as part of the government's initiative to cut truancy. The initial target was for schools to reduce their levels of unauthorised absence by a third by the year 2002. This has been raised again in September 2001. The following methods are part of the process to cut truancy.

1 Home–school agreements. Under these schemes parents will be reminded of their responsibilities for ensuring regular and punctual attendance.
2 The launch of homework clubs.
3 Forcing schools to reduce their levels of truancy by one-third between Ofsted inspections.
4 Discouraging parents from taking their annual holidays with their children during school-time.
5 Providing pagers to the parents of constant offenders.
6 Introducing an electronic attendance system that marks pupils present at the beginning of every lesson.
7 Forcing schools to show their 'real' rates of truancy rather than 'fudging the figures' in order to improve their league table position.
8 Encouraging more truants to sit GCSE and GNVQ subjects, by ensuring they can make up for lost time through the use of classroom assistant or parent-helper schemes.

Briefly, other ideas for schools to consider include:

- reducing levels of physical and mental bullying within schools;

- establishing a family literacy scheme organised by the school at a time convenient for parents and their children;
- emphasising the importance to parents of good quality homework in raising standards;
- advising parents on the needs of their children when undertaking homework tasks (e.g. the need for a desk to write on; ensuring children can work in a different room from the television; providing adequate lighting);
- the use of home–school associations in every school;
- better support within schools in providing for pupils with behaviour problems;
- ensuring that pupils with behaviour problems do not interfere with the learning of well-behaved pupils – otherwise some may vote with their feet;
- stopping excluding pupils for truancy *per se*;
- providing a more welcoming atmosphere and an atmosphere where less-able and disadvantaged pupils feel able to approach and discuss their concerns with staff.

(17d) Attendance, literacy, attainment and target setting

There is little doubt that many truants have serious problems with literacy. Pupils with low literacy levels tend to perform poorly in formal assessments. They are also inclined to develop low academic self-esteem. Studies show that the reading scores for truants are often well below the levels for the average population of schoolchildren.

There are probably several reasons which account for the difficulties that truants experience. First, they often come from homes where there is little encouragement for schooling. Second, many truants are brought up by parents who were themselves truants whilst at school. Third, parents of truants often read less to their offspring in the early years. Fourth, the homes of truants are often overcrowded and not conducive to quiet reading, study or homework. Fifth, research shows that as pupils fall behind their peers in terms of literacy and numeracy levels, they are likely to fall further and further behind as they grow older. Sixth, as truants, by definition, tend to spend less time in school, they receive less help with their learning needs. Similarly, because truancy is a sign of school rejection, teachers are often understandably less enthusiastic towards truants than their other regularly attending peers. Teachers also tend to spend less time in discussion with the parents of truants on academic-related issues. Parents of truants visit schools and attend formal parents' evenings less than the parents of good attenders.

For all these reasons, truants tend to be located in the lower sets/streams within schools. Research shows that regular attendance is the prime requisite for ensuring positive long-term academic attainment.

(17e) The relationship between attainment and attendance

The Scottish Council for Research in Education Study (1995) reported the following correlation between attainment and attendance:

1 The best attenders tended to perform best in school.
2 As the level of absence increased, the level of standard grade award decreased – this was true for both mathematics and English language, but absence had a greater bearing on attainment in mathematics possibly because this is a sequential subject.

3 Boys and girls were almost equally affected by absence.

4 In general, for every 1 per cent rise in absence, standard grade awards for both English and mathematics dropped by 0.05 grade points.

5 The effect of explained absence was comparable in importance to the effect of unexplained absence.

6 Absence rates between schools showed considerable variation.

7 Apart from absence, there were no other factors affecting attainment.

8 Primary and secondary school staff believed that missing school would lead to poor performance.

9 Primary teachers were concerned that lasting habits of non-attendance might develop from early irregular attendance.

10 Despite evidence to the contrary, teachers tend to believe that apart from attendance, social and personal factors also affect pupils' performance at school.

11 Secondary teachers were more concerned about the effects of absence on learning than primary teachers.

12 The truants themselves realised that their absence might make them fall behind and get lower marks; they also felt uneasy about the consequences.

13 Truants felt that when they returned to school, staff did not want to help them, and some secondary teachers agreed with this sentiment.

14 Primary and secondary staff thought that good attenders were not much affected by truants or truant behaviour – but good attenders would have less of the teachers' time if they had to spend more time with truants.

15 Most good attenders feel unaffected by truants and truant behaviour.

16 Some primary teachers thought failing how to fit into society was as important an effect for truants as falling behind in work.

17 Headteachers thought high truancy rates gave schools a poor image.

18 Truancy was a major problem in only a few schools.

The findings of the Scottish Council for Research in the Education Project (1995) which undertook research into the causes of truancy in selected primary and secondary schools accords well with the work of Reid (1985, 1999, 2000). The authors also reported that:

1 Primary teachers believed that truants' parents gave regular school attendance a low priority compared to family demands.

2 Secondary teachers agreed with this. They also thought some parents passed on the opinion that education was unimportant to their children.

3 They believed this view would be stronger in areas of high unemployment.

4 Secondary school staff also tended to think that truancy was motivated by a dislike of some subjects, a perception that some of these subjects were irrelevant, as well as these pupils having difficulty with their school work.

5 Less often, they thought reasons for playing truant included peer pressure, personality clashes between pupils and teachers, intimidation by the size of secondary school, bullying, school phobia and other psychological problems.

6 Primary pupils thought being bored at school and not liking subjects were understandable reasons for staying away.

7 Many primary pupils reported they would consider staying away from school if their mothers asked for their help.
8 Truants in secondary schools said they truanted because they were bored with school. Some of the 'good attenders' said that if subjects were made more interesting and more choice was available, truants would be more likely to attend.
9 Primary pupils who played truant were most likely to spend the time at home.
10 Secondary pupils who played truant were most likely to gather together and talk.

Finally, the study reported that:

1 In general, primary staff were less affected by pupils' truancy than were secondary staff, because their experience of it was more limited.
2 When truancy was encountered in primary schools, headteachers reported greater administrative burdens. Classroom teachers reported frustration in going over old ground, and an extra workload as they tried to tailor lessons to the needs of returned pupils.
3 In the secondary schools, the main effect of truancy on guidance and subject teachers was the stress of the added workload it brought, caused by the need for more complex classroom management and difficulties with lesson planning. As with the primary staff, teachers found it frustrating to go over old work.
4 Headteachers in both primary and secondary schools were aware that high truancy rates would give a school a poor public image, but for most the problem of truancy was not great enough to cause undue concern.
5 Although truancy was not a major problem in most of the schools which took part in the study, the degree of frustration and sense of added workload reported by staff who had to cope with it emphasises the value of reducing the incidence of truancy wherever possible.

18   Homework clubs, ICT and truancy

Homework guidelines

In theory, the development of homework clubs provides an opportunity for disadvantaged and under-achieving pupils to have every chance to develop their learning skills and academic performance. The guidelines on homework clubs provide practical advice for parents and teachers about how much time children at different ages and stages should on average spend on reading with their families and on other forms of homework. For younger children, the emphasis is very much on reading and less formal tasks, whereas formal homework will usually come into play for older primary and secondary pupils. The lottery-funded study support centres are designed to offer facilities for homework, sports and arts in environments which are connected to 8,000 schools throughout the UK.

Research has suggested that more than two out of five 10-year-olds previously received no regular homework. By contrast, more than half this age group spend three nights or more watching television. The DfES guidelines provide teachers and parents with sensible and realistic benchmarks on the amount of homework different age groups at

Year	Reading	Other home activities
Reception class	10 mins	10 mins
Years 1 and 2	20 mins	10 mins
Years 3 and 4	20 mins	20 mins
Years 7 and 8	45–90 minutes per day	
Year 9	1–2 hours per day	
Years 10 and 11	$1\frac{1}{2}$–$2\frac{1}{2}$ hours per day	

Figure 3.2 Recommended daily home learning-based activities.

Source: DfES, 1998.

Note
For younger-age children, other home activities could mean reading and sums with parents/carers. This would then become more formal homework as the child grows older.

primary and secondary levels might be expected to undertake. Homework policies should also be incorporated into home–school agreements.

The DfES consultation documents suggest that the recommended time for daily home learning-based activities are as shown in Figure 3.2. The homework guidelines are intended to give parents a clear idea of what is reasonable to expect at different ages. At the time these were issued in 1998, parents had been responding positively to TV advertising which encouraged more reading at home by parents with children. The homework guidelines are also part of new home–school agreement guidance, which is being issued to schools to encourage improved co-operation between teachers and parents – and which will also tackle standards, truancy and discipline issues.

Homework clubs

Plans were announced in November 1998 by the DfES to ensure that over 6,000 schools in England have homework and study support centres by 2001: £220 million was made available – including an extra £80 million from the year 2000 from the Standards Fund. Ministers had already pledged £180 million across the UK (£140 million in England alone) for the New Opportunities Fund from the National Lottery to provide out-of-school hours learning opportunities. The new centres, targeted at children aged 7 and over, will provide them with a quiet place to do homework, as well as offering sports and arts activities and access to computers.

The then Secretary of State for Education was quoted at the launch as saying:

> Homework is an essential part of every child's education. It is right that parents should have a clear idea of what it is reasonable to expect for their children so that where no regular homework is given, they can discuss this with teachers. But it is also essential that we provide the space and facilities to enable youngsters to do homework where it is difficult to study at home. Study centres will also improve access to sport, arts and computers for youngsters. The extra money we are announcing today – and the partnerships we are developing with football league clubs – will widen that access to many more children. I am very pleased that we

have already got 29 football clubs on side. Clubs like this one at West Ham United are right on target when it comes to getting youngsters motivated to do their homework, and helping raise standards of literacy. Homework is one of many areas where partnership between parents and schools is essential. Homework does more than just reinforce what goes on in schools during the day, it also helps develop important skills like independent learning and enquiry, as well as self-discipline. These are skills that will remain relevant throughout a person's life. Good schools have always had clear, well thought out arrangements for homework.

Playing for Success is part of New Labour's drive to expand study support and out of school hours' provision generally. The study support centres offer programmes focused on improved literacy, numeracy and IT skills mainly for 7–14-year-olds who are disaffected or likely to become so. Other clubs which initially signed up included: Barnsley, Blackburn, Bolton, Bradford, Charlton, Crystal Palace, Derby, Everton, Huddersfield, Leeds, Leicester, Liverpool, Manchester City, Middlesbrough, Newcastle, Norwich, Nottingham Forest, Port Vale, Portsmouth, QPR, Reading, Sheffield United, Sheffield Wednesday, Stoke, Sunderland, Swindon, West Bromwich Albion and Wolves.

The development of a national grid of homework clubs interfaces closely with other new learning and technological developments. These include:

- ICT for work on literacy and numeracy targets;
- the 'interchange of pupils' between schools and other learning centres, including the provision of master classes to stretch gifted (and under-achieving) pupils to their full potential;
- home learning schemes via the Internet or other ICT links;
- the sharing of teaching materials and best practice in teaching and learning with neighbouring schools;
- ensuring equality of access, notably for those in rural areas, those with special needs and those in areas of deprivation, by removing barriers to learning;
- the development of summer schools;
- extending school sporting opportunities for all;
- improving and developing the work of the Education Action Zones, which support literacy and numeracy schemes, homework and study revision clubs, and family learning, together with housing, health and social services initiatives locally.

It is still too early to speculate on the positive effects which the development of homework clubs, ICT and the other initiatives will make on truancy. At the very least, they are bound to impact on the cycle of disadvantage, under-achievement and disaffection on which truancy thrives.

19   Summer school initiatives

The first major expansion of the summer school initiative was launched by the DfES in 1999. By then, 1,200 schools were already participating. Of these, 900 were literacy schools. The other 300 were numeracy summer schools. Summer schools were then providing additional lessons for over 40,000 pupils.

At the same time, the DfES launched the National Grid for Learning by initially providing £105 million to help schools develop their content and infrastructure in new technology particularly in the use of the Internet. The hope is to enable pupils from deprived backgrounds, including those attending summer schools, to have direct access to the new technologies.

Simultaneously, universities and colleges throughout the UK have been asked to promote schemes with schools, especially those located in deprived areas, to wider access and participation rates in higher education to New Labour's target of 50 per cent. A large number of innovative local schemes have resulted in these initiatives. Amongst the most popular are providing 'taster' classes for pupils, providing short-term stays in halls of residence and providing one or two weeks' study skills support during July or August.

20   Utilising pupils' common rooms and learning support centres

An increasing number of schools are beginning to discover the advantage of providing pupils below the age of years 12 and 13 with common room facilities. Unfortunately, at present, far too many schools are constrained by a lack of space. However, as pupils now mature much earlier than fifty years ago, they appreciate being treated as physical adults much sooner than previous generations. Social pressures upon adolescents are much greater and have a more significant impact upon their attitudes and socialisation processes.

Schools which provide common room facilities for pupils in years 9, 10 and 11 report a marked improvement in pupils' behaviour and attitudes towards responsibility. It appears therefore, that pupils appreciate and respect the extra recognition. At present, there is no firm evidence that such privileges lead to an improvement in school attendance. However, as peer pressure and poor teacher–pupil relationships are two of the prime reasons for institutional absenteeism, it seems probable that such a correlation is likely.

Similarly, more and more schools are beginning to discover the benefits of providing learning support centres for pupils. The range of facilities within these centres varies from school to school as do accessibility and usage. Typically, learning support centres facilitate pupils' academic needs. These normally include assistance with study skills support such as literacy, numeracy and writing (e.g. how to prepare and write an essay). They also often include access to a computer, e-mail, the Internet and word processing skills. As so many non-attenders experience serious or minor deficiencies with basic skills, such schemes can only benefit needy pupils and help contribute to a reduction in absenteeism and truancy. Interacting with specialist teachers, learning mentors, ICT tutors and special needs assistants can also only be beneficial.

Summary

This chapter has provided details on the operation of twenty of the most popular short-term solutions in many schools including some of the best known schemes. The following three chapters continue to develop this theme including considering some of the lesser known ideas. In Chapter 4, we will now consider a further twenty-nine potential solutions.

Short-term solutions II

This chapter continues to present and discuss a further range of short-term strategies currently in use in schools. The precise ideas now considered are numbers 21 to 49 shown in Figure 3.1. Therefore, nearly thirty different short-term strategies are now considered.

I Breakfast clubs

The concept of school breakfast clubs has been gaining in momentum since around 1998. The idea is to encourage pupils to arrive at school early, often up to an hour before the official start of the school day. Early arrivals are then usually given a free breakfast such as cereal, bacon and egg and a bread roll. In some schools however, pupils do have to pay either a subsidised or the full cost of the food. Apart from the socialisation benefits of having additional contact with peers, most schools then arrange the early arrivals into groups based on need often in different rooms along a corridor of the school. In one school, for example, one room is allocated for help with homework, another for ICT needs and a third for catching up with back projects. A number of schools now use breakfast clubs as a means of facilitating literacy and numeracy skills.

Some schools particularly find that breakfast clubs are popular with pupils from deprived and disadvantaged backgrounds. They also assist parents who themselves make early morning starts to work especially when both parents are in full-time employment. They can therefore, be popular with business-orientated families.

The concept of breakfast clubs is both preventative and remedial. It is preventative because it facilitates pupils' needs especially their learning needs. In this way, it is envisaged that it helps to reduce absenteeism including specific lesson absence and parental-condoned truancy. It is remedial because breakfast clubs often help pupils to overcome specific difficulties such as facilitating re-integration following a long-term or short-term illness.

The organisation of breakfast clubs around the country is largely *ad hoc* although most conform to the above description. However, exceptions and alternative schemes abound. For example, one school uses breakfast clubs to organise extra lessons for gifted pupils in maths, science and modern languages. Another uses them to help their potential athletes with training within school. A third uses its breakfast club to assist the school's swimming club. A fourth has an 'open' breakfast club policy. Under this scheme, all early arrivals are entitled to a free breakfast rather than standing around in the cold and rain. Its purpose is entirely social rather than educational. The idea is make sure the pupils are being looked after as soon as they arrive on the school's premises.

2 After-school clubs

Once again, the organisation of after-school clubs varies from school to school, often dependent upon the individual or group skills and interests of the staff involved. Typically, most schools continue to offer the provision of coaching for a certain number of sports such as soccer, hockey and netball. In recent times, there has been a tendency for the number and variety of sports offered to be more diverse than a generation ago. For example, some schools now offer specialist clubs for surfing, ice skating, volleyball, tennis, etc. rather than the usual range of soccer, rugby, hockey, netball and, possibly, athletics. The broader the range of sports clubs offered, the more likely it is that increasingly numbers of pupils will take advantage of the opportunities. Some schools now link specifically with local sports clubs who provide the specialist coaching themselves.

Similarly, many schools offer a range of cultural, aesthetic and recreational activities apart from sport. Typically, these might include music and drama clubs, dance tuition, chess, travel, subject-related activities (e.g. history clubs) and many more. The provision of ICT clubs is an area that is rapidly growing.

As with breakfast clubs, the concept of after-school clubs is preventative but they are also developmental. Pupils with interests in outside school activities tend not to become absentees. There is little doubt that some pupils who might otherwise opt to miss school attend regularly because of their involvement with after-school clubs.

3 Work-related curriculum strategies

Effective alternative curriculum prográmmes at key stage 4 can make a vital difference between success and failure, between social inclusion and social exclusion for the students involved. The programmes could also have positive effects on families, schools, the organisations' participation rates and, as a result, on local communities.

This was a key finding in research conducted by the National Foundation for Education Research (NFER) which revealed that these programmes have enormous potential for re-engaging young people in learning and ensuring they are on the right road to post-16 success. The NFER was commissioned by the Local Government Association, using its Educational Research Programme, to undertake a project designed to explore and describe the characteristics of alternative curriculum programmes for pupils at key stage 4 (Cullen et al., 2000). Its aims were to assess the degree to which they were effective in helping young people to view mainstream education and training more positively, and in opening up clear progression routes to post-16 education, training and employment.

At key stage 4, pupils commonly follow a programme of GCSE courses. Normally, there is a range of these available. However, they are mostly academically orientated – a feature that renders them inappropriate for a small minority of pupils. Disaffection, lack of interest, truancy and under-achievement are all too common a reaction to the curriculum in years 10 and 11. Hence, many schools across England and Wales have chosen to offer at least some of their students something a little different during their last two years of compulsory schooling.

For example, as well as attending school for part of the time, some students also go to further education college, gain experience on a long-term work placement, or learn new skills with a training organisation often involved in personal-development activities run by youth workers.

The report written by Cullen *et al.* (2000) revealed that:

(a) Overall there was evidence that 'freeing up' the curriculum at key stage 4 was welcomed by schools and generated developments which had a wide range of perceived positive outcomes.
(b) Teachers, tutor providers, parents and other professionals, cited many examples of individual triumphs and of the way that the lives of individual young people had been turned around by involvement in these programmes.
(c) In all cases, the main feature was that a greater range of long-term life chance opportunities had been made available to the young person concerned. This was largely because his/her attention had been focused on what he or she could do within an environment that was prepared to meet such young people at least halfway, and show that it had room for them.
(d) The research data also indicated that the LEAs had the potential to play a pivotal role in enabling schools to give some of their pupils access to alternative curriculum programmes at key stage 4, both as mediators of national and local policy initiatives and as key members of local partnerships.
(e) The NFER research found that alternative curriculum programmes seemed to be most effective when they developed locally, linking in to local networks, resulting in mutual benefits. Government policies and initiatives, as well as the work of other national agencies and organisations, could energise existing local work and stimulate the creation of new programmes.

The researchers summarised a range of key factors associated with the effective provision of alternative and work-related curriculum programmes. These included:

- A supportive school context: effective relationships between alternative programmes and the regular curriculum; supporting structures within the school.
- A supportive local context: the identification of, and effective communication with, organisations willing to work with schools including support of the LEA.
- Selection procedures: the selection of pupils to participate in alternative programmes: criteria and processes for selection, equal opportunities issues.
- Sustaining collaborative partnerships: gathering information and providers and pupil participants, matching pupils with appropriate placements, off-site support.
- Encouraging and acknowledging achievement: alternative accreditation at national, local and institutional levels, celebrating achievement.
- Monitoring, review and evaluation: the collection of evidence, criteria for success, analysing costs and benefits, assessment outcomes.

In addition, the research revealed that it is critical that the transition of young people who have thrived under the conditions of alternative programmes at key stage 4 is well managed so that their progression remains positive. This may present severe challenges both in terms of resources and imaginative constructions of support arrangements. But, unless these challenges are addressed, all that these alternative programmes will have done will be to have postponed these young people's longer-term social exclusion. A more detailed consideration of alternative curriculum strategies can be found in Chapter 10.

4   Key skills lessons

The provision of extra key skills lessons for less able pupils is commonplace in many of today's secondary schools. The extent and availability of the support available varies from school to school and is often dependent upon resource constraints including staff and room availability, the provision of information technology and the number of pupils involved. In some schools these are not small numbers. For example, in one school in south-west England with 894 pupils on roll, 524 are considered to need extra support with literacy, numeracy and key skills. The provision of key skills is also a growing burden on schools, especially those encouraging and supporting large numbers of children of recent refugees.

Schools vary in the number of learning support staff with which they are provided as well as the roles these staff are given within schools. Some learning support tutors assist classroom teachers. Others provide specialist help either to an individual pupil or a range of individuals. Some learning support tutors are key skills specialists. Others are used as mentors.

The provision of specialist or extra key skills lessons is mainly preventative. However, it can be both therapeutic and pastoral. The nature of the work involved can be very demanding. It is not known the extent to which extra key skills support helps deter absenteeism. It is certain, however, that this form of extra support can be nothing but positive.

5   Appointing a home–school co-ordinator

Over a wide range of staff development events for both teachers and education welfare officers with which the author has been involved for several years, one of the issues which constantly recurs as requiring better management is home–school communication especially in cases of non-attendance. Few schools currently manage this process well although the introduction of first day response in cases of non-attendance has considerably improved the situation. It has certainly reduced the number of cases in which the truancy was unknown to the parent(s) as well as the school. It has also caused severe inconvenience to some parents and in some schools has served to reinforce those who believe that parental-condoned absence is the single largest category of unauthorised absence.

In recent years, some schools have improved home–school liaison by appointing attendance secretaries and/or attendance support teachers, often in addition to support from education welfare. Despite this, given the large number of non-attendance cases within certain schools, and the attitudes of certain parents towards absenteeism (see Chapter 9), individual cases continue to cause friction and other difficulties. Thus, the position of a lot of schools in dealing with parents involved in non-attendance cases remains delicate – to say the least. Many education welfare officers refer to this issue as the 'hard hat' syndrome!

Consequently, some schools are beginning to combat these communication difficulties by using grant money which is being made available under schemes promoted by the DfES to appoint specialist home–school co-ordinators. Some schools are so desperate for help that they even use their own money or funding supplied by their LEA. The appointment of these staff helps to free up time for education welfare officers and pastoral staff from administrative chores thereby enabling them to concentrate on case-work and other therapeutic issues. Some education welfare officers have been so bogged down by paperwork that their specialist field skills have been too little or rarely used which, in turn, has reduced confidence in their professional skills in certain quarters.

6   Red lists

The use of red lists is considered in a different context more fully in Chapters 7 and 8. In this specific short-term context, the term 'red lists' is often used as a means of identifying and supporting certain categories of needy pupils such as those requiring specialist study skills support or those who need daily monitoring because of problems with their health, behaviour, attendance or bullying.

A typical use of a 'red' list is to identify say, twenty pupils who are most at risk throughout the school. The pupils could be a risk to others or be at risk to themselves. Some schools use specialist lists for each year/house group. The daily monitoring reports of these pupils are given priority and followed up immediately when needs arise. Pupils on the red lists are thus the first to be followed up for first day absences.

This form of daily monitoring tends to be at its most effective when comparatively small numbers of pupils within a school are at risk or have specialist support needs. In schools with very large numbers of pupils with behavioural and/or attendance problems, the use of red lists can sometimes be counterproductive.

7   E-mail or text message support

Many schools are starting to encourage their staff and pupils to communicate on mutually beneficial issues through the use of e-mail or text message support. This form of communication is probably most used in connection with homework. However, its application across the full range of schools' learning and social networks is growing.

Paradoxically, the pupils least likely to benefit from such initiatives are those from poor homes who cannot afford the equipment. Or those who do not attend school regularly; precisely the two groups who require encouragement and support the most. This is an issue which politicians and the DfES are known to be thinking about.

8   Flexible tuition times

Some schools are beginning to experiment by offering pupils (and/or parents) the choice of flexible tuition times. Staff in some schools have indicated that they would prefer to start the school day much earlier and to finish at lunch-time or in early afternoon as in some European countries. In schools where early starts have been tried, headteachers have reported a slight rise in absenteeism and a considerable rise in lateness. They can also cause difficulties with the accuracy of attendance registers. One school in Gloucester, for example, brought forward its school-start time for an experimental period only to return to its regular time because of the growth of lateness and associated administrative difficulties. These included problems with pupils catching buses at the earlier time – especially during hours of darkness in winter.

Another form of experimentation is to allow regular non-attenders to come to school for negotiated parts of the school day rather than to miss school altogether. Some schools are beginning to adopt enlightened approaches which enable absentees (and sometimes other categories of at-risk pupils) to choose the part of the curriculum for which they will attend. Normally, these absentees select core elements of the curriculum such as literacy and numeracy classes (including maths and English), ICT and other favoured subjects. Some schools are trying to organise this form of negotiated curriculum alongside vocational opportunities including links with business and/or local FE colleges. Obviously, some traditionalists dislike any form of negotiated curriculum. They perceive it either as weakness or 'giving in' to deviant and other non-conformist groups. Clearly, your support or otherwise for schemes like a negotiated curriculum depends upon your own point of view.

As moves begin to change the school year, possibly to five or six terms, significant changes in attendance patterns may also occur. On the one hand, shorter terms could enhance attendance. On the other, given the likely 'hike' in travel costs by travel firms in the new shorter school holiday periods, there could well be a significant rise in parental-condoned absenteeism due to the taking of family holidays during school time. It would be no surprise if extending the number of school terms per year leads to a significant rise in pupils' absenteeism.

9   After hours support–tutors or clubs

In one sense, after hours tutor/tutorial/learning support clubs are the corollary to break-fast clubs at the other end of the school day. Whereas staff or pupils in some schools prefer breakfast clubs, others prefer after hours tuition support. Again, it depends on your preference. Comparatively few schools offer both breakfast clubs and after hours support. After hours support appears to be more popular amongst younger age groups and in primary schools.

There is no commonly agreed formula for the nature and organisation of after hours learning support clubs. Some offer support to any interested pupils. Others target specific groups of needy pupils. Conversely, some schools use after hours (and/or lunch-time and/or breakfast clubs) to support the needs of their particularly gifted pupils. After hours clubs can be particularly beneficial to pupils who have missed a lot of schooling for one reason or another or those who are in the process of being re-integrated due to attendance difficulties. Similarly, after hours clubs are especially helpful with children of recent refugees or for those who require other forms of linguistic help. After hours clubs can be supported by the efforts of Afro/Caribbean or Asian liaison officers. Learning support after-school clubs are normally organised by a member of staff often under the aegis of the special needs department, head of year or a learning support tutor and/or mentor.

10   Using local sports clubs

The use of local clubs to provide specialist sports tuition for pupils is increasing significantly. This development can be supported by sponsorship either locally or organised on a regional or national basis. With the growth of specialisms within schools, encouraged by New Labour's announcement in February 2001, a number of schools are likely to seek specialist sports status. Achieving specialist sports status will prove popular amongst some categories of pupils and parents which, in turn, should help prevent some pupil absenteeism.

11   Presenting attendance certificates

The presentation of attendance certificates either in assemblies or during open or parents' evenings has become a normal part of everyday school life. In some schools, the presentation of an attendance certificate is seen as sufficient reward in itself. In other schools, attendance certificates are associated with a wider 'reward' system.

Being presented with an attendance certificate can have certain rewards within and outside school. For example, Burger King has teamed up with Morriston Comprehensive School, Swansea, to reward pupils with good attendance. Pupils who regularly attend school gain merit points. If, and when, they collect enough points, they are awarded with a Burger King voucher which can be used in any Burger King restaurant. The school utilises the slogan 'Good attendance wins fast food for eager pupils'.

Many teachers support the use of attendance certificates on their own merit. Staff tend to see the awarding of attendance certificates as a form of positive reinforcement especially for certain categories of pupils who are unlikely ever to achieve significant academic success. Also, the promotion of attendance certificates sends out the clear message to pupils that their attendance matters. In circumstances where pupils' attendance contributes to form, subject, year group or whole-school prizes, this is literally true!

12   Half-day rewards

Another scheme which is prevalent in some schools will also not win support from too many traditionalists. Some schools agree or 'barter' with their regular non-attenders to a less than full timetable. Unlike flexible tuition times, half-day 'rewards' are a fixed concept.

Half-day rewards are generally agreed in two forms. The first is for pupils to attend either morning or afternoons only throughout the week. The alternative is for pupils to be allowed to attend alternate mornings or afternoons throughout the week. Sometimes the half-days include attendance at non-conventional lessons such as the provision of specialist literacy, numeracy and ICT support or being helped by a learning support tutor or mentor.

Protagonists of the scheme believe it is better to allow pupils flexibility to attend for regular half-days rather than for a pupil to become a hardened truant or one who causes the school serious time-consuming worries as a result of persistent and erratic absences. The idea is to re-integrate the pupils back into full-time schooling after his or her confidence has been restored.

13   Suggestion box schemes

The use of the suggestion box scheme originates from the United States and from initiatives on bullying such as the Childline movement. The use of suggestion boxes in schools can be widened to include a whole range of problems that put pupils at risk. It is imperative that such schemes follow these principles:

(a) The box should *not* be placed at the end of a long corridor.
(b) The box should not be placed outside the office of the head, deputies, heads of year, etc.
(c) The ideal location is in a quiet spot close to a busy part of the school that all the pupils tend to use. This means that the pupils can easily gain access to the box while, at the same time, not drawing attention to themselves.
(d) The information given should be anonymous.
(e) Staff should not overact when/if the box is used for trivial and/or different purposes from the ones intended.

In schools where suggestion boxes have been used, the following outcomes have been found:

(a) The boxes can be more or less frequently used, often dependent upon the amount of publicity given to their use.
(b) The boxes tend to be used more by years 7 and 8 pupils rather than by older age groups. However, when the boxes are used by older-age pupils (including year 12 and 13 students) the issues can be serious. For example, the use by a pupil to indicate that her friend is pregnant and needs help, or that a pupil is not really a truant but is being abused at home, or that a pupil is staying at home to comfort the mother (following a separation and/or divorce) or because the mother needs company and/or protection.

Suggestion boxes are unlikely to help in trivial cases of non-attendance. They can, however, be crucial in potential or actual serious cases. Many pupils exhibit deep concerns about their friends in need or trouble but are reluctant to speak to staff in authority about them. Suggestion boxes, appropriately used, can form a convenient half-way house. They are most useful in potentially the most serious cases and can be life savers, e.g. when a person is truanting because of the severity of his or her bullying.

The opportunity to help alleviate such problems surely outweighs any negative arguments against the usage of suggestion boxes. But, for whatever reason, the use of suggestion boxes can be unpopular with some teachers. In several cases reported through the use of suggestion box schemes, it has been found that some suspected truants and/or long-term absentees were not truants or absentees at all. Rather, they have been victims of abuse, parental neglect or family break-ups as well as other serious issues like solvent abuse.

For example, in one school which implemented the scheme the following anonymous feedback was given to the school for action:

(a) Details of a 14-year-old girl was reported by a friend because she had become desperate as a result of becoming pregnant. Up until that point, despite being four months pregnant, the only person to be aware of the situation was her best friend who was torn between loyalty and deeply felt distress for the potential long-term consequences.
(b) Details of a 12-year-old Asian boy who was being seriously 'victimised' by classmates and other pupils within and outside school.

(c) Details of a 13-year-old girl who developed a large lump on her leg and feared she had cancer.

(d) Details of a 12-year-old who spent most of the time living at home on her own following the break-up of her parents' marriage.

14   Use of foundation programmes

Research shows that there is often a considerable gulf between pupils' attainment and achievements in primary schools at the point of their secondary school transfer. Often these divides are not due to innate intellectual differences but to major differences between primary schools' own outcomes even in homogeneous areas, or weak or very good teaching (by subject or across the board) or is due to a wide range of other local, social and educational factors.

Some secondary schools are beginning to find that the use of foundation programmes can help all pupils in year 7 to start from the same baseline. For example, using the first six weeks of year 7 to ensure pupils are ready to advance into the National Curriculum by providing all their new intake with the same lessons and testing. Therefore, all pupils are assessed using the same baseline. Alternatively, using periods of time in year 7 or later to boost pupils' reading and/or literacy and numeracy levels. Some educationalists believe that the start of each new year should re-commence with a two-week foundation programme based on pupils' individual and collective needs. Thus, setting is based on pupils' real abilities rather than on data obtained from primary schools. Pupils put into lower sets than they really deserve tend to become alienated and disaffected from school. Some even graduate to truancy.

15   Afro/Caribbean or Asian liaison officer(s)

Some schools with largish numbers of ethnic minority pupils, more particularly some of those with considerable numbers of children of recent refugees or asylum seekers, are beginning to find the appointment of an Afro/Caribbean or Asian liaison officer helpful. Not only does this facilitate improved home–social communication, it also prevents specialist staff from being immersed in another set of administrative burdens. Home–school communication in certain cases requires an ability to speak a pupil's 'mother tongue' or first language.

The appointment of specialist Afro/Caribbean or Asian liaison officers can be seen as another form of mentoring and, in some cases, of learning tutors' support. The provision of specialist English language tuition for ethnic minority pupils with language difficulties is a growing phenomenon within some British schools. The establishment of good home–school relationships, and the provision of specialist language support for pupils (and, in some cases, for their parents as well) is regarded as key in enabling ethnic-minority pupils to settle quickly, in establishing a social rapport within their schools and local communities and in helping their early learning needs to be quickly and accurately identified.

Sometimes schools refer to the above initiatives by another term, namely language skills classes. Either way, the aims are the same.

16   Student progress planners

The use of student progress planners is already good practice within many schools. Student progress planners are closely allied to target setting, records of achievement, the National Curriculum and attainment tests. Student progress planners are particularly helpful with less able and disadvantaged pupils such as school absentees. Meeting progression targets can ensure that a potentially at-risk pupil makes satisfactory progress and, by providing detailed personal attention, does not graduate to occasional or persistent non-attendance.

17   The viewmaster scheme

The viewmaster scheme is a novel approach which utilises information technology and is normally organised by the ICT department. The concept is to enable pupils to view outlines of their forthcoming lessons by visiting an ICT laboratory within school. Under the scheme, teachers put their future lessons online six or more weeks ahead of teaching them. Interested pupils can then look up the content of their next or future lessons. The idea is to fire up the pupils' interest in learning and make them wish to attend their forthcoming lessons. This is partly because they can look forward to the ensuing lessons but also because they can see the future directions which their lessons are taking. Rather than allowing only the teachers to be aware of the content of a subject's curriculum, the pupils also become empowered. Thus, the viewmaster scheme is considered to have a deterrent potential.

18   Buddy system

A 'buddy' system is another form of mentoring. Buddy systems were originally developed in the United States. There are many different kinds of buddy system. Typical buddy systems include:

(a)   an able with a less able pupil;
(b)   an older with a younger pupil;
(c)   an indigenous pupil with a peer from an ethnic minority background;
(d)   a 'buddy' teacher with a difficult pupil, a slow learner, an irregular attender or a pupil from an ethnic minority background.

The key idea of the buddy system is to enable needy pupils to achieve their learning targets, homework, and be able with confidence to ask for help from a 'friend' without fear of rejection.

19   Truancy Buster scheme

'Truancy Buster' schemes are another innovation introduced by New Labour. Under the package, schools that dramatically cut their absenteeism and truancy rates are entitled to enter for a one-off 'Truancy Buster' award. Schools that win the awards are free to use the money in any way they wish.

The Truancy Buster initiative was launched as an integral part of the School Standards Fund social inclusion scheme. Of the £137 million made available in 2000, £10 million is set aside for on-site support units for disruptive pupils; the so-called pupils' sin bins! As part of the same scheme, LEAs in England are entitled to bid for £37 million to fund schemes to reduce truancy.

From 2002, all excluded pupils will be entitled to alternative full-time education. Many of these excluded pupils will then be sent to off-site pupil-referral units where, since 1997, the number of available places has increased to over 1,000.

The Truancy Buster scheme was introduced partially because of the clear correlation between absenteeism and exam performance. At schools with very low absence rates (less than 0.1 per cent of half-days missed) nearly three-quarters of pupils achieve five good (A*–C) GCSE passes. At those with the highest rates of absence (more than 2 per cent of half-days missed), just 28.6 per cent of pupils get five good passes.

Truancy Buster rewards are intended to encourage schools to implement innovative schemes on attendance. The DfES seems particularly delighted when Truancy Buster initiatives lead to a corresponding fall in youth crime as reported in, for example, York through the endeavours of their truancy watch schemes. At Montgomery High School in Blackpool, one of their truancy initiatives is for local shopkeepers to alert the school by phone when suspected truants are seen. The school then sends appropriate staff or police to apprehend the truants and make them return to school.

20 Closer FE–school links

Closer FE–school links can help deter absenteeism in a number of ways. First, they can ensure that needy pupils receive a tailor-made curriculum through the utilisation of relevant components of a school's and an FE college's curriculum. Often, local FE colleges have greater strengths and resources in vocational subjects (e.g. bricklaying, hairdressing and ICT) than many secondary schools. By extending an opportunity to disaffected and less able pupils to gain more vocational choice, often allied to suitable work placements, a lot of potential absenteeism can be prevented.

Second, local FE–school schemes can help clear some 'unwanted' and potentially disruptive pupils from secondary schools. Thus, keen learners and regular attenders are liable to less disruption of their normal teaching.

Third, some FE colleges are better geared to cope with pupils who are unruly within schools and who fail to make regular attendance. The vocational nature of the curriculum means that some pupils who are disenchanted with school see it as a fresh start. Owing to the vocational nature of the teaching, some pupils also see it as having more relevance to their long-term employment needs.

21 Management of learning programmes scheme

The management of a learning programme scheme is another linked to closer FE–school partnerships. Under these arrangements, FE colleges and schools agree a management programme for ensuring the pupils supported by the scheme make satisfactory progress. Sometimes schools and FE colleges hold regular meetings of their respective management teams for the learning programmes schemes to ensure individual and collective pupils' progress.

Since the DfES's announcement in 2001, it is likely that certain pupils and secondary schools will be entitled to follow more vocational programmes rather than the full National Curriculum. Equally, it seems likely that vocational learning programmes will be introduced into some more state schools. The long-term effect of enabling some secondary schools to become 'specialist' schools in, for example, the arts, science or technology is still unproven as are its likely outcomes upon attendance and truancy.

22   Utilising external volunteers

The organisation of attendance issues within some schools is a daily grind and headache. Therefore, some schools are using volunteers to undertake the task. In parts of Hull, for example, volunteers from Age Concern are managing first day absence in order to take the load off weary staff. In some other schools, the task is performed by volunteer parents or organised as part of a Rotary Club initiative.

23   Objective 3 funding

Some schools are applying to the EEC for funds under the Objective 3 scheme. Weaver School in Northamptonshire, for example, is part of a scheme to help the skills and motivation of the local workforce to raise prosperity across the EEC. Project LA081 – known locally as the Re-Engagement project – has raised £1 million for the county. Of this sum, £80,000 has been given to Weaver School; £40,000 is for within-school improvements, and the remaining £40,000 is to facilitate out-of-school provision.

24   Improving the quality of registration time

The issue of form periods and registration time is another constantly recurring matter within a number of schools. All kinds of changes have been tried by some schools. These include using form periods for PSE programmes, self-signing-in schemes, computerised registration, specialist pupil registration numbers, the shortening of registration time or form periods to a minimum, the postponement or abandonment of afternoon registration/form periods, the use of swipe cards, etc. None of these schemes have proved ideal. One of the problems with swipe cards, for example, is that they do not detect specific lesson absence or post-registration truancy (unless electronic devices are placed on all school exit points).

Staff in schools continue to suggest that the wise use of quality time during form periods can be exceedingly beneficial. It enables pupils to identify with a key member of staff; more especially within larger schools. It enables form tutors to observe changes in pupils' behaviour (fretting, victimisation, tearful moments) which often signal greater problems. It also enables pupils to confide in an appropriate teacher 'counsellor' provided a trust relationship is in place. Research suggests that form tutors are the first point of contact for 'needy' pupils and often preferred to heads of year and/or department who, in some schools, are seen in administrative and/or managerial roles. Equally, utilising form tutors effectively can prove to be one of the best (and, most certainly, the first) line of defence in attendance cases.

25   Parental fines

On 19 October 2000, New Labour announced increased fines for parents whose children truanted. The maximum fine per parent was raised from the existing £1,000 to £2,500.

In support of the raised fines, the government produced the following statistics:

(a) 75 per cent of children who are out-of-school have an adult with them.
(b) Many young offenders can barely read and write probably because they spend so little time in school.
(c) The Metropolitan Police has reported that 40 per cent of all street robberies are committed by 10 to 16-year-olds, many of whom are truanting at the time.
(d) Research evidence shows that persistent truants are heading for failure in school and later life, and are more likely to be on income support, to be homeless and to end up in prison.

The government therefore, introduced new laws making non-attendance an arrestable offence which will force parents and guardians of absentee pupils to face the courts.

Despite this, many schools, education welfare officers and LEAs are reluctant to take non-attenders and their parents to court. There are several reasons for this situation. First, many truants and their parents come from poor social and economic backgrounds and already have serious social, financial and related housing problems. Second, the profiles presented in court by the social services often militate against conviction, which can be soul-destroying to schools and EWOs alike and, to some recalcitrant parents, seems like a victory for them. Finally, even when the fines are imposed, magistrates rarely use the maximum sum and tend to give much lower amounts (e.g. £40). Again, given the burden of administration involved, this also seems counterproductive to schools and EWOs. Even then, the vast majority of fines remain unpaid despite often being allowed to be paid on a monthly basis (e.g. 50 pence a week or £2 a month).

In the latter circumstances, magistrates are reluctant to impose prison sentences because it can have the effect of breaking up the family or causing a child or teenager to be put into care. Hence, more magistrates are beginning to use parenting orders in truancy cases which mean that parents are forced to attend good parenting classes or undertake community-based activities.

26   New Labour's key policies on truancy

New Labour's key first-term policies for tackling truancy between 1997 and 2001 were:

(a) fines for parents increased to £2,500;
(b) police given powers to return pupils to school;
(c) 'Truancy Buster' cash rewards for schools;
(d) mentors to advise and help truanting pupils;
(e) truancy to be cut by a third between September 1998 and September 2002;
(f) schools with poor truancy records to be set targets and to be subject to more rigorous inspections by Ofsted with the possibility of facing further repercussions from Ofsted if they fail to meet their agreed targets;
(g) funding to enable truancy sweeps to take place especially in inner-city areas.

27 Truancy sweep schemes

Truancy sweep schemes are another part of community-based action against non-attendance. Under truancy sweep schemes schools, LEAs, police and other community groups can work together on truancy initiatives. The new police powers to take truants found in public areas back to school or wherever specified by the LEA have strengthened truancy prevention activities.

Truancy sweep initiatives can be supported by:

- leaflet campaigns for parents (useful where parents condone absence);
- publicity in local shopping centres or on buses, such as 'truancy-free zone' posters in shops and information packs for retail staff;
- pupil pass schemes;
- truancy hotlines; and
- advertisements in local newspapers.

For example, in the north-east of England, six LEAs (Darlington, Gateshead, Newcastle, North Tyneside, South Tyneside and Sunderland) worked with Northumberland Police and Nexus (operator of the Metro underground system) to sweep an area to pick up pupils either truanting or encouraged by their parents to be out of school. The education welfare officers and community police officers were clearly briefed. Teams were provided with mobile phones, telephone numbers of schools in the area and up-to-date lists of excluded pupils. Parents had been pre-warned by a leaflet drop.

During the day, 156 children and young people were stopped in the Whitley Bay and Wallsend police command areas: 80 per cent of pupils were with a parent. Forty truants *per se* were identified; six of these were returned to school using the recent police powers under section 16 of the Crime and Disorder Act, 1998.

Thus:

(a) the sweep made clear to parents that condoned absence was unacceptable;
(b) the 'word' went around and fewer pupils took time out for weeks after;
(c) specific instances of crime were tackled;
(d) two cases of child protection arose because of the day's events.

28 EWO interviewing pupil(s) and parent(s) in school time together

Another tactic which is growing in credence since the introduction of the larger parental fines for truancy, and as a result of the truancy sweep schemes following the Crime and Disorder Act of 1998, is for letters to be sent by EWOs from schools or LEAs which require parent(s) to be interviewed with their non-attending child together during school time. This can cause major inconvenience to a parent(s) especially when they need to make arrangements for 'cover' at work. It also prevents the waste of unnecessary time by EWOs. It is not unusual for an EWO to have to visit the same house on five or six occasions before they find someone at home.

29 Attendance hot line

Some schools and LEAs are now introducing attendance 'hot' lines as part of truancy watch/sweep initiatives. Under these schemes, local business people, shopkeepers and voluntary organisations are notified of a specialist hot line to school or the LEA on which to report suspected truants or prevent potential criminal activities. Previously, for example, shopkeepers have not known what to do when they found organised groups of truants/potential shoplifters within their vicinity. This was one of the main recommendations of the Lewis Report (1995).

Summary

This chapter has considered another twenty-nine potential short-term options to combat non-attendance. In the next chapter we will consider many more. All these schemes show that the options available to schools to help them to reduce truancy and other forms of non-attendance are continually increasing. While some of the ideas are fairly novel or unusual, most are readily implementable and simply make good practical sense.

Chapter 5

Short-term solutions III

This chapter continues presenting and considering a further range of short-term solutions to truancy and absenteeism within schools. The specific ideas discussed are listed in Figure 3.1 numbers 50 to 75.

I   Spot checks

The use of spot checks is not a new phenomenon. It has been one of the most consistently used policies within schools for at least the last half century. Spot checks are particularly effective in combating specific lesson absence and post-registration truancy. Detecting cases of specific lesson absence and post-registration truancy is a weakness in many schools. It is also a significant weakness in existing official statistical returns on attendance.

Most schools undertake spot checks randomly. These are often targeted at known points where pupils 'skive'. Such places often include the toilets, unused rooms, bicycle sheds, 'blind spots' within schools (e.g. at the foot of very tall buildings) or at points close to the school gates. Typically, for example, these places are regularly used by pupils who are members of the smokers' union or by early 'courting' couples.

Staff would be wise to undertake spot checks within an external radius close to school boundaries as well as within schools. But, often this does not happen. Early evidence from truancy patrols suggests that a high percentage of absentees remain in places (e.g. local parks) close to their schools. This appears to be especially true in cases where pupils fear or know that their parent(s) will not condone their absence.

2   The creation of a pupils' school council

The creation of a pupils' school council can be an effective way of ensuring that the vast majority of students are 'on board' and support current school policies. Gaining the support of pupils is one of the best deterrents to absenteeism which thrives on peer pressure. Reid (1985, 1999) has reported that poor teacher–pupil relationships, adverse peer relationships, unfavourable school climates and aspects relating to the curriculum are four of the main 'causes' of truancy and absenteeism.

Using school councils within secondaries can be a salient experience in itself. Many staff may be surprised to find how naturally 'right wing' many pupils are and feel towards their non-conformist peers such as truants. Pupils often take the view that if they can conform to a school's rules, then they cannot see why others should be allowed to get away by breaking them.

School councils can take many forms within schools. Some involve only years 12 and 13 pupils and may or may not have a role within the rest of the school. Some school councils are, for example, related to a school's prefect system. Other types of school councils include either the election or appointment of a small number of pupils by year, house or by form normally to serve for a fixed-term period. Often, the number of pupils serving on a specific council is determined by the size of a school and its year groups. Clearly, most schools seek manageable units.

Some school councils are allowed to conduct their own business freely. Others are more shackled by having constraints imposed upon them. Effective school councils often elect, for example, a pupil governor while some elect the head boy and/or head girl. It is useful to place such issues as attendance, truancy, behaviour (including a pupils' code of conduct or pupils' charter) and bullying as regular items on the agenda of school council meetings; at least on an annual basis. This is another way of ensuring that pupils know that their attendance matters and the issue is treated seriously by all those employed in the school's mission.

School councils are known by a variety of different terms throughout the UK. Some are called school unions. Some are known as school trusts. In fact, alternative titles abound. Their main utility is to ensure that pupil-sensitive issues are treated seriously by staff (e.g. pupils' facilities within schools, Christmas parties, school discos, the form of school dress and the dress code, canteen matters, voluntary work, vocational placements, school attendance policies). Therefore, pupils feel part of the school's community and valued as individuals. It is perhaps surprising, therefore, that only a minority of schools continue to implement school councils.

3 Specialist pastoral training

Far too many teachers within schools are involved in pastoral work at a variety of managerial levels without ever having received any specific training for their posts. The National College for School Leadership in Nottingham is beginning to ensure that future heads and deputy heads have been trained appropriately. By and large, however, professional development has always been more readily provided for senior staff within schools rather than for the rank and file. Similar training deficiencies are equally apparent within the education welfare service.

It is increasingly starting to be recognised that all staff teaching within schools require key training on certain 'common' issues. These include such topics as truancy, absenteeism, bullying, disruptive behaviour and, worryingly, drugs. Few staff receive such training on their initial teacher education programmes.

Even more worrying is the ever increasing complexity of related issues in truancy cases. Evidence is mounting that few cases of truancy are ever single issue problems. Nor are these cases solely related to educational issues although school-focused problems *often* provide the specific trigger point. Typically, education welfare officers report that dealing with a specific truancy case can lead to a great deal of further social work involving the whole family. Frequently, truancy cases are referred to local social service departments. Significantly, cases of truancy occur more often in some of the most deprived parts of the UK. The complexity of cases within large urban, inner-city areas is well known and the whole list of social, education and psychological factors involved in truancy and school absenteeism have been considered elsewhere in *Truancy and Schools* (Reid, 1999).

Similarly, the range of sensitive issues on which teachers can suddenly find themselves in the front line also appears to be on the increase. These can include aspects of racial conflict and other forms of inter-pupil tensions, the use of the 'morning after' pill, sexual and child abuse, pupil harassment and bullying (within schools and externally within local communities) and, of course, the supply and use of drugs as well as many more. Yet, few teachers have any specialist training on any of these matters. How many teachers understand, for example, the law of strict liability in drugs cases (*Sweet* v. *Parsley*, 1968)?

Consequently, an increasing number of schools are feeling a need to broaden the range of their school-based professional development activities to help inform teachers of their responsibilities, duties and rights as well as the rights of their pupils. Paignton Community College, for example, now arranges specialist training on key pastoral issues on a termly or annual basis as needs arise. During one day in December 2000, no fewer than five 'sensitive' topics were covered because of the proliferation of non-standard pastoral activity within the Torbay region. And their situation is by no means unusual.

4   Free bus passes

Many schools are leading activists in the fight for the provision of free bus passes for all included within a three-mile radius of a school's location. The provision of free bus passes reduces the range of excuses which can be used for non-attendance. For safety reasons, some schools now ensure or encourage buses to disembark pupils within the boundary of the school.

Unfortunately, studies on bullying suggest that poor or tense relationships amongst pupils travelling to and from schools can be an area of serious concern and a number of cases of serious victimisation can be found in the literature (Sharp and Smith, 1999).

5   Using legal powers decisively

LEA's legal powers to enforce attendance are:

- school attendance orders;
- prosecution for irregular attendance;
- parenting orders;
- education supervision orders.

The law

LEAs need to co-operate on any attendance problems, and where many children attend school in neighbouring authority areas they should have standing arrangements for co-ordination to prevent truancy. Early warning of attendance problems will normally be to the LEA where the pupil attends school, but any necessary legal action is the responsibility of the LEA where the child lives.

School Attendance Orders (sections 437–443, Education Act 1996)

A School Attendance Order (SAO) gives an LEA powers to help it ensure that children attend school. An LEA must serve an SAO on the parent of a child of compulsory school age who fails to prove the child is receiving suitable education, and where the authority believes the child should attend school. The attendance order specifies to the school (or Pupil Referral Unit) that the child should attend. Failure to comply with an SAO is an offence, unless the parent can prove the child is receiving suitable education outside school. The Order itself has a specified legal format. The procedures allow for:

- consultation with the school which is to be nominated (or another affected LEA);
- parents to choose a school, other than the one named by the LEA, as the school to be named in the school attendance order;
- appeals by such schools and LEAs to the Secretary of State for a direction if there is disagreement; and
- aligning school attendance orders with statements of special educational needs.

Format for a school attendance order

This is normally set out as follows:

As you [name of parent] of [address of parent], being the parent of a child of compulsory school age in the area of the Authority, have failed to satisfy the Authority in accordance with the requirements of the notice served on you under section 437 (1) of the Education Act 1996 by the Authority on [date of notice] that [name of child] is receiving suitable education, either by regular attendance at school or otherwise:

And as, in the opinion of the Authority, [name of child] should attend school:

You are required to cause [name of child] to become a registered pupil at the following school:

[Insert full name and address of the school and omit the whole or part of the following words as the case requires]

being the school [specified by the Authority] [selected by you] [determined by a direction of the Secretary of State for Education and Employment] [as the school to be named in this Order] [specified in the statement for the child under section 324 of the Education Act 1996].

Failure to comply with the requirements of this Order is an offence unless you can prove that [name of child] is receiving suitable education otherwise than at school.

Signed [name of officer] of [name of Authority] Education Authority.

[Dated].

School attendance orders are not intended for pupils who attend irregularly. For these, LEAs should consider prosecution or applying for an Education Supervision Order.

Prosecution for irregular attendance (section 444, Education Act 1996)

If a pupil of compulsory school age fails to attend school regularly the LEA can prosecute a parent unless the parent can show that:

- the pupil was absent with leave agreed by school staff;
- the pupil was ill or prevented from attending by any unavoidable cause;
- the absence was on a day exclusively set aside for religious observance by the religious body to which the parent belongs;
- the school is not within walking distance of the child's home and the LEA has made no suitable arrangements for:
  - the child's transport to and from school;
  - boarding accommodation at or near the school; or
  - enabling the child to attend a school nearer their home ('walking distance' is defined in section 444(5) of the Education Act 1996).

The law also recognises the special position of traveller families. LEAs must judge whether and when to prosecute on a case-by-case basis. Sometimes prosecution will be a last resort. In other cases it may be right to begin prosecution at a much earlier stage to prevent problems worsening.

Continuity of learning is critical to educational progress, so LEAs should adopt a rigorous stance on truancy. A block of prosecutions could help prove to parents how seriously the LEA regards truancy and condoned unjustified absence. LEAs should make sure local magistrates are aware of truancy issues including problems with parentally-condoned unjustified absence.

On conviction, the offence carries a fine up to a maximum of level 3 on the standard scale; currently up to £2,500 a parent for each absent child. The same penalty applies to convictions for failure to comply with a school attendance order.

Parenting orders

Magistrates may impose a Parenting Order if this would help prevent further pupil absence. The Order will require parents to attend counselling or guidance sessions for up to three months. It may specify other requirements, for example, ensuring the child is escorted to and from school for up to twelve months (Education Supervision Orders, section 36, Children Act 1989; see also section 447, Education Act 1996).

An Education Supervision Order (ESO) makes the LEA responsible for educating a child of compulsory school age. LEAs may apply for an ESO instead of, or as well as, prosecuting parents for poor attendance or failure to obey a school attendance order.

ESOs should ensure that such a child receives full-time education suited to their age, ability, aptitude and any special educational needs, and that both parent and child are given sufficient support and guidance. A supervising officer is appointed to work with the child and family. ESO proceedings are 'family proceedings' as defined by the Children Act; this means the child's welfare is the main consideration.

An ESO normally lasts one year or until the young person reaches 16. ESOs may be extended for up to three years if an LEA applies within three months of the expiry date, and may be extended more than once.

Unfortunately, far too may LEAs, schools and EWOs continue to fail to use their legal powers on attendance cases decisively. Natural caution is compounded by:

(a) the leniency of some local courts;
(b) the lack of training received by some magistrates and their clerks on attendance issues;
(c) the complexity of the prevailing 'social' and wider familial issues including the perspective and report of the local social services department;
(d) time delays and administrative and bureaucratic complications.

Many cases take far too long to come to court. This is not only counterproductive, it can make for much more additional and often unnecessary work as the pupil's and his or her family's circumstances change. In 2001, it took on average six months for an attendance-related case to reach court. In Scotland, this period rose to nine months on average.

6   Use of security firms

Some schools currently use security firms to patrol main entrances and boundary perimeters before and/or during and/or after the end of the school day. Such schemes can be expensive. They are often costed at the expense of the remaining teaching and support staff in the school. Unfortunately, violence at the point of entry to schools is not unknown as the Stephen Lawrence murder epitomises.

There is no doubt that the use of security firms can reduce the amount of specific lesson absence off the school premises. Another tactic used by some schools is to ensure that the exterior boundaries are secure through, for example, the building of high walls and/or secure fences around the entire perimeter of the school. Such schemes can be helpful; but they are also a last resort and an indication that the school is failing in its intention to reduce its truancy.

7   Limiting school exit points and monitoring school transitions

Some people never learn. Unfortunately, the same can be said for some schools. It never ceases to amaze some people just how lax some schools continue to be over the control and management of their official and unofficial exit and entry points. In some schools, despite all the recent adverse publicity in the media (partly following the Lisa Potts case and Dunblane) far too many pupils appear free to come and go as they wish, facilitating specific lesson absence and post-registration truancy. Equally, well-known 'truancy holes' (unofficial exit points!) remain unattended within some schools. Some of these truancy holes have been in operation for generations! One truancy hole at a school in Swansea has been used by its pupils for the last twenty-five years. Who's kidding who?

8   Home–school, parent–pupil, pupil–school contracts

The government has suggested introducing home–school contracts for all pupils at some point in the future. Every school had to have its own home–school contract scheme in place by September 1999. The aim is to encourage parental, pupils' and schools' responsibilities. Whether and how such contracts can be made legally binding is a question requiring further research. In any event, the use of such contracts can only be helpful.

Pupil–school contracts can be equally helpful. Although a number of schools already have such contracts, they tend to be in their infancy. The use of home–school and pupil–school contracts is thought to have considerable potential in the fight to reduce truancy. However, this thesis has never been properly tested or evaluated.

9   Developing strategies for punctuality and combating lateness

Smith *et al.* (1994) have written a useful guide on *Attendance Matters* for schools as part of a Hertfordshire School Attendance Project. They suggest that:

> Lateness on the part of teachers or pupils can lead to indiscipline and truancy. In both instances, it gives the wrong message. Repeated absences at the beginning of a school session can amount to failure to attend regularly for the purpose of section 199 of the 1993 Education Act. In addressing lateness schools must:

- have a clearly defined and consistently applied policy on lateness. This must be precise in terms of the times when registers will close and the sanctions that may be applied;
- publicise this policy in school and communicate it to parents;
- balance any sanctions with positive encouragement;
- praise and acknowledge punctuality;
- praise and acknowledge latecomers who improve;
- ensure that teachers set a good example by arriving punctually for lessons;
- follow up the reasons for lateness and be alert to any emerging patterns or problems;
- set in place systems for effectively monitoring lateness – latecomers should sign a late-slip or a late-book;
- never cover for lateness (if a pupil is absent when the register closes he/she should be marked absent – to leave a gap in the register and then to mark a pupil down as present when/if he/she eventually arrives is to disguise any difficulty which that pupil might be experiencing and to delay any support which might be offered).

Smith *et al.* propose that a school policy on lateness should:

- be firm but fair (an approach which tends to be over-punitive may well have the effect of discouraging the latecomer from attending at all);
- balance sanctions with positive encouragements;
- bear in mind the school's geographical setting (the vagaries of public transport, etc.);
- consider how far the responsibility for pupils failing to arrive punctually rests with them personally or with their parents.

Smith *et al.* provide the following definition for lateness:

> Lateness will be defined as any arrival ten minutes later than the bell for the start of the session. A pupil arriving more than ten minutes late will be given a late mark. More than three late marks in a week will result in a detention.

10 National advertising schemes

The DfES has become increasingly concerned in recent years about rates of absence from schools. In particular, it is seriously worried about the role played by some parents in condoning their children's absence. Therefore, it has been decided to promote some national advertising schemes to remind parents that it is their legal responsibility to ensure that their children attend school regularly. At the same time, reminding parents of the possible consequences for them of failing to fulfil their statutory obligations.

11 Formation of anti-truancy teams

The formation of anti-truancy teams is an alternative to truancy sweeps organised by the police. Anti-truancy teams are considered to be more informal and less threatening to pupils and parents alike.

Teachers and social workers in Milton Keynes are an example of an anti-truancy team. They take part in a scheme which could serve as a model for cross-departmental co-operation in the organisation of services for children. The Close to Home Project follows repeated demands for such integration. Teams of social workers, youth workers and teachers go out into the community from their school base. The intention is to reduce truancy and exclusions. The teams also include careers staff, educational psychologists and education welfare officers. They operate in the catchment areas of two local secondaries, the Leon School and the Sir Frank Markham Community School.

The youth offender teams in the Crime and Disorder Bill, 1998, require schools to work with social services, probation officers and the police. Up to 70 per cent of young offenders have either been regular truants or have been excluded from school or both (Reid, 1986).

12 Utilising paging systems

The concept behind paging systems is to enable schools to alert parent/s to the fact that their child has failed to register, participate in post-registration truancy or has otherwise left the premises without permission. Informing parents in this way helps schools fulfil their statutory duties while, at the same time, putting indirect pressure onto the parent/s who are often inconvenienced by the notification – especially if they are at work. It can help parents and schools tackle truancy together in those cases where parents are conducive to the educational needs of their children.

Unfortunately, each pager is relatively expensive, and many schools cannot afford to equip all parents, or those whose children truant, with them. It may be that if this scheme is to work, some form of government help will be necessary. Teachers generally consider this scheme to have short rather than long-term benefits.

13   One-to-one experiences/case reviews

The use of specialist one-to-one sessions is becoming increasingly popular within some schools. The general process is as follows. A non-conforming pupil, such as a seriously disaffected student or a persistent absentee, is asked to attend an in-depth review session with relevant staff. The procedure and process is not dissimilar in some ways to the typical case study reviews which are commonplace within the social services field.

During these one-to-one experiences, it is normal practice to review a pupil's attendance, behaviour, academic progress and related matters. Often, it is possible to agree future preventative strategies. These can include the use of a report card system in which the pupil is required to report daily, twice daily or at the start of every lesson to a designated member(s) of staff.

Another popular approach is to make a particular teacher have daily responsibility for a pupil whilst in school. This member of staff is then expected to report on a regular basis in writing or in person to the senior management team, heads of year meeting or the appropriate managerial meeting within school. It is intended that the fostering of a closer relationship between a teacher and the pupil will have a range of social and academic beneficial effects including an improvement in attendance.

Sometimes, decisions are made to significantly amend a pupil's individual timetable. It is not unusual for some disaffected pupils to be expected to follow up to 50 per cent of a normal timetable with the remaining time being spent in special needs, in vocational programmes or with a specialist learning support mentor sometimes following an *ad hoc* approach.

Individual variations of these types of practice abound throughout secondary schools. In certain circumstances, individual one-to-one schemes and case reviews lead to exclusion after every alternative has been deemed to fail.

14   Inter-agency co-operation: joined-up professionalism

Too many cases on truancy are mishandled due to inter-agency conflicts, rivalry and/or poor communication. Within schools it is essential to effect and maintain high levels of attendance. Schools need to develop a whole-school policy on attendance. Such a policy will be:

Owned by everyone
Teachers, pupils, parents and governors all need to be involved in drawing up such a policy. A policy devised by just one or two senior staff may be ineffective. Any policy must be periodically reviewed and all parties concerned periodically consulted.

Communicated to everyone
Pupils and parents must be periodically reminded of the school's expectations regarding attendance and punctuality. Governors should be kept informed of the policy and how it is working.

Understood by everyone
Pupils and parents must be clear as to those explanations for absence/lateness which are acceptable/unacceptable. They must also clearly understand what will be the

consequences of any unauthorised absence/lateness. Lines of communication and dele-gated responsibilities within schools must be clearly established. Staff must be clear as to what is classified as authorised/unauthorised absence.

A clear whole-school policy on attendance, together with effective systems for monitor-ing and promoting attendance, can help create a school ethos which:

- values and contributes to high levels of attendance and punctuality;
- reduces levels of authorised absence and lateness;
- reassures parents and the wider community;
- prepares children for the time-keeping discipline of adult life and, most importantly;
- enables children to take the fullest advantage of the educational opportunities which school has to offer them.

Whilst the ultimate responsibility for ensuring that children attend school regularly rests with the parents, schools can do a great deal to encourage and support parents to meet this responsibility.

Teachers are in the front line in having to deal with difficult pupils. But neither the causes nor the effects of truancy and exclusion can be understood solely in educational terms. Schools often find themselves having to deal with problems that should have been dealt with by families, or by other public agencies. Similarly, when schools fail to keep children on their premises, or exclude them, the costs spill over onto other agencies and onto the wider community.

The costs of truancy and exclusion?

Educational under-achievement

The most obvious impact is, of course, on education itself. Truants are more likely than non-truants to leave school with few or no qualifications. The Youth Cohort Study (1998) showed that 38 per cent of truants reported that they had no GCSEs, compared with 3 per cent of non-truants. Of those who had truanted, only 8 per cent obtained five or more GCSEs at grades A to C, as against 54 per cent of those who had not truanted in year 11.

Unemployment and homelessness

Like others with low qualifications, those who miss school are more likely to be out of work at age 18, and are more likely to become homeless. For example, over three-quarters of homeless teenagers in one Centrepoint study were either long-term non-attenders or had been excluded from school.

Crime

The most striking link is with crime:

1 According to the Audit Commission (1996), nearly half of all school-age offenders have been excluded from school; and a quarter truanted significantly.

2 Home Office research shows that truants are more than three times more likely to offend than non-truants. One study found that 78 per cent of males and 53 per cent of females who truanted once a week or more committed criminal offences (Social Exclusion Report, 1998).

3 A sixth-month study by the Metropolitan Police found that 5 per cent of all offences were committed by children during school hours; 40 per cent of robberies, 25 per cent of burglaries, 29 per cent of thefts and 20 per cent of criminal damage were committed by 10 to 16-year-olds.

4 In 1995–6, the Metropolitan Police arrested 748 excluded children, some of whom had committed between 20 and 40 offences before arrest.

5 There is evidence that the sentencing of those who have truanted or been excluded is severe: one study showed that pupils who have a poor attendance record were much more at risk of a custodial sentence than those with more positive reports.

Exclusion and truancy have costly effects, whether those costs are borne by the police, courts and prisons, by the social security budget or by the victims of crime. The government is already substantially overhauling the system for dealing with young offenders. Tackling exclusion and truancy at an early stage as possible is one way of attempting to stop youngsters being drawn into crime in the first place.

Who is responsible?

Both nationally and locally, responsibility for dealing with the problems associated with truancy and exclusions is fragmented. In Whitehall, DfES has the main responsibility for policy on truancy and exclusions, but the Department of Health also has a key interest, notably through social services, as does the Home Office for the crime and criminal justice aspects.

Several departments run specialist funds to support exclusion and truancy projects. DfES runs two: the Standards Fund, of which in 2000 some £22 million went to attendance and behaviour projects, and New Start, which aims to bring together multi-agency programmes for young people aged 14 and over who are disaffected and at risk. Other projects are funded through the Single Regeneration Budget, on which DETR leads. The Home Office and the Department of Health also sponsor projects through mainstream funding. In addition, local projects may get funding from other sources, whether private, charitable trusts, the lottery, business or the European Social Fund.

At a local level, responsibility is divided between schools, local education authorities and the police. It is simply not clear who is responsible if overall levels of truancy and exclusions suddenly rise as the appropriate professionals, not least the police and education welfare service, are already grossly overstretched.

The professionals who look after children who may truant or be excluded are required by law to produce a range of strategic 'plans' including Children's Services Plans, Behaviour Support Plans, Education Development Plans, Youth Justice Plans, Drug Action Strategies. The purpose of these plans is to focus on particular problem issues. But the number of them runs the risk of duplication and a lack of co-ordination. And some children have as many as eight different professionals dealing with them, not always communicating with each other as clearly as possible.

A complex set of interrelated problems have not and continue not to be well managed by government and local education authorities. Responsibility has been divided and dispersed without sufficiently coherent policies to prevent behavioural problems, and to deal with them when they do arise. 'Joined-up problems' of this kind were one of the main reasons behind the setting up of the Social Inclusion Unit which has begun to undertake some extremely important work.

15 Utilising specialist in-school projects

The utilisation of specialist in-school projects is in some ways a variation on the ideas contained in Section 13 of this chapter on one-to-one experiences and case study reviews. Some schools, by way of an accommodation for their disaffected pupils, negotiate special in-school projects as an alternative to attendance at regular lessons in order to prevent them from dropping out of school altogether.

Sometimes these projects involve time spent in vocational activities out-of-school. For example, one school in the South Midlands utilises a scheme which enables underachieving and disaffected pupils to undertake work-related projects during school hours. These include projects on the following themes: preparation for citizenship, preparation for adult life including parenting skills; preparation for financial management; preparation for work. Undertaking these projects normally involves work placements. Included in these work placements are the local 'cottage' hospital, the LEA, motor manufacturers, large stores and various voluntary and charitable organisations.

16 Utilising social workers in schools

There is a growing view that large secondary schools and some primary schools require full-time social workers to be based in schools. The rationale for this view includes:

- a history of poor inter-agency communication between social services and education/ schools;
- the fact that some teachers spend too much time on social work (note: not pastoral care) issues;
- the avoidance of duplication which, in cases of truancy, often comes to a head in court cases;
- the belief that teachers and social workers operating together in cases of social need and deprivation are likely to achieve more than when working apart;
- the belief that both sets of professionals will see the wider picture in individual cases.

Too often cases involving social workers are blighted by issues about confidentiality.

One danger in this approach will be to possibly demean the role presently played by existing education welfare officers/social workers. The alternative view is that it would enable the EWO services to focus specifically upon attendance issues. There is currently a lot of interest in the idea of appointing or attaching social workers to schools in Scotland and the idea has been seriously considered by the Scottish Parliament.

17   Improved health checks

Data obtained from school-based studies indicate that a small proportion of pupils are inclined to miss school for comparatively minor health, social or psychological reasons. Sometimes, regular health checks with a school nurse can help to identify and overcome problems. Examples of such problems include head lice, itches, rashes, embarrassing facial or skin traits, irritable bowel syndrome, asthma as well as many more.

Increasingly, the number of pupils prone to stress and stress-related problems, especially teenagers, also seems to be on the increase. Some protagonists believe that levels of stress amongst some pupils have increased since the advent of the National Curriculum, attainment targets and more regular testing within state schools.

18   Appointment of specialist attendance staff

Unfortunately, some schools have too little education welfare time allocated to them. Some are also not in a position to buy in this support on a full-cost basis. In fact, the provision of education welfare officers to schools is not evenly distributed throughout the UK. Some schools are relatively generously provided. Increasingly, however, these appear to be fast becoming fewer in number.

The appointment of specialist attendance staff within schools has both advantages and disadvantages to the education welfare service. The significant advantage is that it frees up the education welfare officer to concentrate full-time on the major attendance cases. The disadvantage is that it can lead to role conflict, duplication and a reduction in the influence of specific education welfare officers or of the service locally.

This position is a consequence of a long debate within the education welfare profession. The professional associations for educational welfare have long since argued that their conditions of service and training should be equated with social workers. However, responsibility for education welfare resides currently and historically within education departments inside LEAs. Headteachers' professional organisations too, argue that they prefer EWOs to focus on educational issues (i.e. attendance *per se*) rather than upon whole family-related matters. Headteachers wish to see an improvement in their attendance rates and in facilitating non-attending pupils back into schools. For them, this is their EWO's prime role.

The reality therefore, is that many, if not most, EWOs are spread too thinly on the ground. Their individual caseloads equally tend to be far too high; often close to impossible. Hence, headteachers become frustrated and can decide they need to appoint their own attendance support staff who are directly responsible to them. The process has been exacerbated by the increasing moves to delegate more and more autonomy to schools including fuller financial management. Moves are afoot which will probably lead to some or all of existing education welfare being put under the daily management of local schools although possibly, still within local education authority control. The introduction of the Connexions Service in April 2001 in some ways posed another type of challenge for the education welfare service.

Some secondary schools continue to have full-time education welfare officers. Often, these are increasingly only in the larger schools, or those in inner-cities or in areas with severe social derivation, or with significant histories of absenteeism, or those containing a number of pupils from ethnic minorities which may or may not include children of recent refugees.

A high proportion of secondaries only have partial EWO support perhaps for half a week or for two or three days a week. A few get as little as half a day or one day per week; a quite ridiculous situation.

Equally, the position with EWO provision for primary schools differs from LEA to LEA. Some LEAs provide full-time EWO support for the larger primary schools. In many LEAs, however, EWO support for primary schools, especially smaller primary schools, is minimalist. This is particularly unfortunate given that there is clear evidence that the earlier the interventions take place in attendance cases, and the younger the pupil, the greater the chance of success. It is in this current climate that the arguments for further devolution of the education welfare service to schools have been flourishing.

Attendance support teachers

The responsibilities of an attendance support teacher also vary from school to school, and from LEA to LEA. However, the duties of the attendance support teacher are to improve the attendance in the school and to ensure attendance and related issues are given a much higher profile in the school and within the local community. The specific functions of the post will involve further development of the management systems in the school to:

- ensure attendance of pupils is correctly monitored;
- ensure prompt follow-up action to deal with absenteeism and lateness;
- tackle specific attendance problems and to have strategies in place to address the difficulties, e.g. re-integration programmes, appropriate support groups, perhaps a governors' attendance panel;
- promote good links with parents;
- foster good links with other agencies;
- further develop the links with the community;
- ensure that the transition from the primary to the comprehensive school is less traumatic for pupils and to acquire knowledge on the pupils who may require additional support before and after this period;
- provide advice and support for pupils returning to school after long periods of absence;
- reward good attendance;
- liaise with the following to ensure that the above strategies are being dealt with efficiently and effectively by:
  - the headteacher and the senior management team;
  - the heads of department;
  - the heads of year;
  - the special education needs co-ordinator;
  - the education welfare officer;
  - other agencies that may be involved with pupils experiencing attendance difficulties;
- provide in-class support where necessary;
- provide in-service training where appropriate;

- be able to communicate effectively and sensitively, both orally and in writing, to a wide range of audiences;
- have a sound understanding of why some children do not attend school regularly and of how some of these difficulties can be overcome.

Postholders are normally directly responsible to the headteacher. The skills required for the post tend to require:

- an understanding of the current legislation for dealing with the attendance of pupils at school;
- an understanding of the current issues related to the attendance of pupils at school;
- a vision of how these current issues might be addressed.

Attendance support secretary

In some schools, to download one or more senior managers, appointments are increasingly being made of a full-time attendance secretary to provide the administrative support and back-up on attendance. This appointment often frees EWOs to spend all their time on home visits. It also enables staff in schools to deal with re-integration and prevention in the knowledge that the paperwork on attendance and truancy is in good hands. Attendance support secretaries also often handle first day responses.

Specialist counsellors

Comparatively few schools employ specialist counsellors. However, in certain seriously deprived inner-city regions in which pupils in schools face a multitude of social and deprivational issues, the appointment of specialist counsellors to advise pupils is beginning to make a comeback. Schools which opt to employ specialist counsellors should ensure that they have been appropriately trained, are suitable and empathetic when dealing with pupils and understand their role boundaries. Communication skills are all important.

19   Special needs assistants

Like learning mentors, special needs assistants are an integral part of the staff of most secondary schools and are also utilised in a large number of primaries. The titles of these appointees tend to differ from school to school, region to region. For example, other terms used to describe special needs assistants include classroom assistants/helpers, literacy tutors/specialists, learning support tutors, along with several more.

Special needs assistants tend to work alongside an individual or group of pupils either within regular classrooms, in special need units or in purpose-built designated areas. Often, these special needs groups contain a number of absentees and/or disaffected pupils.

There is little doubt that the complexity of special needs issues within many schools is proving increasingly difficult to manage. At the same time, there is a lot of superb support being provided for pupils with special needs which, in turn, can only be helpful in combating absenteeism. In some parts of the country, the growth in the number of pupils with special needs is becoming an increasingly worrying situation and may or may not be related to the continued growth in familial breakdowns as morals within society spiral downwards.

20   The extension of primary school practice

Most pupils spend longer in primary than secondary schools. They forge early friendships with peers from the same locations. Too often, secondary schools undervalue these links. Care should be taken at the point of primary–secondary school transfer to ensure that friends have the opportunity to sit and be together in the same forms and, in at least, some teaching classes.

There is no reason why, at the point of primary–secondary transfer, that pupils from the same classes within primary schools should not be kept together as a whole unit. Thus, they might form the whole or part of the new secondary form tutor group.

Some pupils become unhappy very quickly in schools when they are split from their friends. Research shows that peer group unhappiness is one of the prime causes of truancy. It should be remembered that in out-of-school hours, pupils visit and/or play with their friends rather than their class peers. As pupils grow older, especially in adolescence, having close friends becomes increasingly important.

21   Compensatory programmes

Many truants are educational failures. Therefore, existing National Curriculum and attainment target guidelines are not always suited to their needs. Few truants, for example, are competent modern linguists. Theoretically, protagonists argue that time spent on subjects in classes which are meaningless to lower achieving pupils would be better spent in remedial or compensatory programmes on such issues as literacy and numeracy, work placement schemes and in preparation for adult life classes.

Schools are beginning to become involved in local neighbourhood, community and anti-social exclusion programmes. Often, these are focused on the local school or in deprived locations nearby. These opportunities can provide pupils, their parents and neighbours with specialist second chance or specifically targeted programmes to meet their local needs.

22   School-based review

Schools should regularly review their attendance policies (Reid, 1999, Chapter 9) and practice including the effectiveness of all staff engaged in the process. Ideally, the review should be carried out annually rather than immediately prior to the next Ofsted or Estyn visit.

The school-based review process follows distinct states. These are:

(a) the initial school-based review;
(b) brainstorming to develop strategies to improve attendance;
(c) formulating coherent staff development programmes.

These three stages may subsequently lead to the initial steps the staff will decide to take which, in turn, will lead a strategic plan to combat absenteeism. Finally, after a school has developed and introduced its plan and evaluated it, prevention strategies will be needed to ensure that absenteeism is firmly under the control of staff.

Planning a whole-school approach to reducing truancy (perhaps to meet the government's targets for schools to reduce truancy by one-third) can be fun and provide an interesting and varied agenda for one or more professional development day.

Initial school-based review

The purpose of initial school-based review is to:

- analyse what management systems are already in place to manage attendance;
- have a clear understanding of the roles and responsibilities of staff in the school;
- understand the roles of the support agencies;
- formulate an agenda for action.

Developing strategies to improve attendance

This can be carried out by:

- using the SIMS (or other software package) attendance module to record and monitor attendance;
- ensuring that there is a quick follow-up action to absenteeism and that the appropriate methods are employed to re-introduce pupils back into full-time education;
- involving governors, teachers, parents and support agencies in attendance-related issues;
- improving communication links with parents;
- liaising with feeder primary schools to identify potential absentees;
- developing a support system to support pupils with literacy difficulties;
- devising an anti-bullying policy and programme for pupils;
- rewarding good and improved attendance.

Coherent staff development

This is achieved by:

- regularly discussing with the SMT, procedures and processes in relation to any new strategies;
- the delivery of in-service training on attendance-related issues;
- providing the necessary support and staff development for NQTs and students on the initial teachers' training course.

First steps

The first and most important step is the recognition that there is a problem. The next step is to raise the profile of attendance in the school. This is done by:

1 delivering in-service training on attendance related issues to all members of staff;

2 introducing or reviewing the use of the SIMS (or other form of computerised package) attendance model into the school to record and monitor attendance;

3 ensuring that the form teacher is the key person in monitoring the attendance of all members of their form;

4 involving governors, teachers, parents and support agencies in attendance-related issues within the school and outlining their rights and responsibilities in relation to the role they play with pupils in the school;

5 ensuring that there is quick follow-up action to absenteeism and that the appropriate methods are employed to re-introduce pupils back into full-time education;

6 providing in-class support for pupils who experience difficulties in basic skills; ensuring that pupils who missed school for various reasons – authorised or unauthorised – have the opportunity to make good the work they have missed;

7 encouraging staff to produce work that is differentiated;

8 devising an anti-bullying programme throughout the school;

9 improving communication links with parents and providing transport and childcare facilities for parents' evenings;

10 making home visits if necessary;

11 producing a booklet for new staff and supply teachers on the monitoring of attendance in the school;

12 rewarding good and improved attendance;

13 improving links with the feeder primary schools and identifying potential absentees.

Planning stages

The aim of the school is to:

1 improve the recording and monitoring of attendance;

2 identify actual and potential problems early;

3 understand the functions of outside agencies and work together in a partnership;

4 successfully re-integrate pupils after long periods of absence;

5 improve links with parents;

6 create an ethos in the school which encourages success and achievement, a good attendance record being part of this;

7 have awareness and sympathy for problems which some pupils face, while at all times ensuring they have full access to the opportunities that can enhance their lives and raise their self-esteem within the community.

Prevention

To prevent absenteeism schools need to ensure:

1 all pupils have accessibility to the curriculum;

2 support is provided for pupils who may be experiencing difficulties;

3 all pupils are encouraged to succeed and an ethos prevails which is conducive to learning;

4 all pupils feel safe and there are strategies in place to minimise bullying and deal with it effectively if an incident arises;

5 all parents are well informed of what is expected of them in relation to their child's attendance at school;

6 all children know:
  (a) they are part of the school community;
  (b) they will be missed if they are absent from school;
  (c) their parents will be contacted to identify the reason for absence;

7 excellent and improved attendance is acknowledged and rewarded.

23 The use of school-based questionnaires

A lot of schools have begun to implement measures to prevent and combat truancy based on their own assumptions. Research constantly shows that truancy is a multi-causal phenomenon. Each truant is unique. Whilst there are similarities between categories of truants, the causes can vary regionally and locally. Schools, too, vary considerably in the extent of their attendance and truancy problems. Some schools have major difficulties; others only minor problems. It can be extremely helpful therefore, when schools are able to obtain precise information on the causes of truancy within their own schools.

One way of achieving this is to obtain direct information from the pupils themselves. This can be achieved through the construction of questionnaires for use with:

(a) whole-school cohorts;
(b) whole-year cohorts;
(c) whole-subject cohorts;
(d) form groups.

Sometimes, it is sensible to obtain information from the whole of years 7 to 11 first and subsequently break down this large cohort into smaller units for more detailed secondary questionnaires. Interviewing a sample of good and bad attenders in addition to, or separate from, the whole-school questionnaires is another sound approach.

With today's technology, it is comparatively easy to obtain school data on such variables as:

(a) Specific lesson absence. Is it the same lessons being missed? Is it always the same group of pupils? If so, why? What does this information tell you about the quality of teaching of this subject within the school? If, for example, there are two teachers of chemistry in a school and one always has a high attendance rate and the other does not, what does this imply?

(b) Teacher absence. Evidence is beginning to mount that teachers who miss school frequently tend to lower pupils' confidence sometimes causing them to either drop out or become specific lesson absentees.

(c) General patterns of absenteeism, daily, weekly, termly, yearly by form, group, year and subject.

These data can be used at staff meetings and reviewed periodically as part of the school policy on attendance. The information can also be fed back to staff and used as part of appraisal processes. It can also be used at parents' evenings and with governors. The details can also be put up, for example, on a special school attendance notice board in the staffroom.

On a technical point, it is wise to:

(a) Keep survey questionnaires simple and limit the number of questions. For young pupils a few questions may be enough. For years 9 upwards, questionnaires should still be kept to a maximum of twenty questions.

(b) Be careful to ask for information in simple English. Remember that less able as well as able pupils will be completing the instrument. Make sure the meaning of the questions is clear. Set out the format of the questionnaire in an easy-to-read, well spaced-out style.

(c) Use only a few essential independent variables, e.g. gender, age, form, year, etc.

(d) It is usually better to let the pupils complete the form anonymously. They will give you more meaningful data if you do so.

(e) Decide in advance:
   (i)   what information you require;
   (ii)   what use you will make of the data;
   (iii) how you intend to cross-tabulate the independent variables with the dependent variables, e.g. the link between age, gender, subject with pupils' views on their curriculum, teaching or aspects of school life.

Reid (1999, Chapter 10, pages 198–204) has provided a sample questionnaire on attendance for use in schools with appropriate findings for discussion based on data obtained from a school in South Wales.

24   Tackling social exclusion

Tackling social exclusion was perhaps at the core of New Labour policies on education between 1997 and 2001. New Labour's thesis is as follows:

Social exclusion wrecks lives and wastes resources. This is the mantra of the Social Exclusion Unit (SEU) that gives us all pause to take stock. The SEU is right, of course. Its first three reports – on truancy and exclusion, rough sleepers, and neighbourhood renewal – show a consistent pattern of cause and effect. They identify individuals and communities who are cut off from mainstream services and social networks.

People who are socially excluded are less likely to have ready access to public services and find those services more difficult to use. They are more likely to lack basic literacy and numeracy skills, to be unemployed or in low wage employment and to suffer disproportionately poorer health. Some may become involved in drugs misuse and crime; many more will be victims of crime or lead lives restricted by the fear of it.

The real tragedy is that lives need not be wrecked, nor resources wasted on repairing the damage, were we systematically to apply what we already know. The SEU in its reports – and the government in many of its White Papers – have gathered together many examples of public, private and voluntary sector interventions, and of community, self-help, caretakers and neighbourhood wardens, for example, which have increased local surveillance, reduced crime and brought neighbourhoods back into good repair. Adult mentors and work-based curricula for 14-year-olds have played their part in greater staying-on rates and higher educational attainment and rates of employment. Local authorities have brokered agreements with key commercial services to have them return to socially excluded communities.

So the question for public sector managers is not 'How can we tackle social exclusion?' but 'Why aren't we doing so?'

Work being done shows that a major barrier to tackling social exclusion is that people who hold the responsibility often don't have the power to act. Many organisations now have designated posts focusing either on the overall issue or on key parts of it such as community security, educational attainment and regeneration. The problem is that these posts are generally on the edges of organisations and, despite the efforts of very able staff, they can easily become detached from the organisational mainstream. There is little chance for people in these posts to make much headway, for instance by achieving major turnarounds in the use of mainstream budgets and services.

Part of the problem originates from the way government works in vertical departmental 'silos'. At the national level, this is something that the SEU, actively chaired by Tony Blair, tried to change. Examples of early successes include the immediate amendment of education legislation to include recommendations from the truancy and exclusions report and the publication of joint health and social services priorities, underpinned by an explicit aim to treat the two sectors as one.

Locally, too, there is much that can and is being done. Early studies identify seven key areas for action and, more importantly, show how they must be linked together to ensure a coherent and effective joint attack on the problem. They are:

- *the identification of positive social outcomes*: enabling people to see that life can be different and to identify what they want from it – the essence of community planning;
- *community self-help*: recognising the abilities and resources of people who are socially excluded and enabling them to use these to rebuild social networks, restore community confidence and make effective use of democratic processes;
- *the restoration or remodelling of private sector services*, such as stopping whole areas being 'redlined' and so being unable to get insurance cover, and connecting people to the informal networks through which many employers recruit;
- *the improvement of public sector services*, such as targeting and siting services to increase access and providing community leadership to help communities and excluded individuals to gain a voice and get a response from key organisations;
- *collaborative community and organisational action*: working through zones, partnerships, joint service management, one-stop shops and pooled budgets to ensure services dovetail with one another and with local communities;
- *the regearing of local public sector management*: rethinking the way public services are planned, commissioned, provided, managed and quality assured to provide a consistent, mainstream focus on building social cohesion.
- *regional, national and European action*: using the appropriate levers to bring about local change and working with others to create a favourable policy environment within which to tackle social exclusion.

25   Inclusive school policies: Social Inclusion Units

Since 1997 all schools, colleges and universities have been asked to ensure that they have inclusive policies in place for pupils and higher education students alike. There have, therefore, been a whole host of local and national ideas promoted to widen access, increase participation rates, monitor and extend equal opportunities especially for ethnic minorities in order to ensure that educational opportunities are available to as many people as possible. The issue of boys' under-achievement in schools in certain subjects and the influence of 'laddish' behaviour have, for example, been two subjects which have been much discussed.

In order to facilitate these policies, some schools have begun to establish their own social inclusion units. Sometimes these units have been linked to other recent initiatives such as summer school programmes, breakfast clubs and after-school clubs and learning mentor schemes.

Sometimes too, in another development, special needs departments and/or units have been retitled social inclusion departments/units partly because the latter titles are considered to be more empathetic and descriptive of their work. A third movement is to create social inclusion units available for all pupils from deprived catchment areas (often pre-determined by postcode analysis) irrespective of pupils' abilities. Often, these type of social inclusion units concentrate on literacy and numeracy skills such as oracy or providing information technology support. Finally, some social inclusion units are providing reintegration programmes for long-term absentees from school irrespective of the reasons for their non-attendance.

26   Pupil panels to tackle truancy

Experiments have begun with pupil panels made up of children who regularly skip school in an attempt to tackle truancy levels in Britain. The original scheme was co-launched by Unison (the Union for Education Welfare Officers) and the National Association of Social Workers. Initial panels were set up in London, Scotland and the north-west of England with a view to reporting their findings to the government's Social Inclusion Unit. It was hoped that the panels would provide more light on why pupils miss school and how they spend their time when they are truanting. Their findings suggest that the main reasons for missing school include:

- bullying;
- pupils finding school to be boring;
- a dislike of certain subjects.

It is widely believed that peer pressure is another cause of truancy. Thus, their findings accord well with other studies.

Whereas, in the late 1950s, the average age of all kinds of truants was 14 or 15, it is now between 12 and 13. Some pupils as young as 7 deliberately stay away from school. Perhaps we should all ask why the age and onset of truancy are ever decreasing.

The concept of pupil panels could be extended locally to schools in the following ways:

- by using pupil panels of good attenders to advise non-attendees on how to overcome their problems;
- by mentoring frequent absentees with good attenders to help them overcome their educational problems. This may prove particularly helpful in cases where absentees could be successfully re-integrated back into school provided they are able to catch up with outstanding school work;
- using pupil panels of absentees to advise individual schools on:
  - why they miss school;
  - what would make them return to school on a regular basis;
  - what changes schools could make to help them overcome their particular difficulties.

Summary

This chapter, the third of four on short-term solutions, has considered twenty-six further initiatives to combat truancy and other forms of absenteeism from schools. Some of the initiatives considered in this chapter have involved long-standing schemes; others are fairly new and unusual. We will now conclude the four chapters on short-term solutions by considering the remaining ideas in Chapter 6.

Short-term solutions IV

This is the final one of four chapters on short-term strategies currently in use in schools to combat truancy and other forms of absenteeism. It concludes the first part of the book as thereafter the contents focus on longer-term solutions and new emergent issues. The issues presented and discussed in this chapter are listed in Figure 3.1 numbers 76 to 119. They take the number of potential short-term solutions to almost a hundred and twenty. By their very title and nature, some of the ideas considered in this chapter will only require a minimum of discussion as most will already be well known to staff in schools and the education welfare service. Therefore, they are described using a 'potted' format. Some of these schemes, however, may well be new to some readers; not least some of the concepts based on developments in information technology.

I   Governing body review on attendance

In schools which have a significant attendance problem, the involvement of the governing body can provide a welcome stimulus. The sudden interest in attendance issues by the governing body is one of the best ways of concentrating the minds of headteachers and other senior members of school staff. Some governing bodies already regularly review a school's policy document periodically. This can be a useful exercise in itself as governors can often bring insights into issues from the wider 'world of life' and business and help 'tighten' key sections.

Another growing and influential trend is to require senior staff to make and/or present an annual report on attendance to the full governing body. Again, discussing outcomes and measures taken to combat non-attendance in detail can be a helpful stimulus to school staff in ensuring that all of them are actively carrying out their own roles effectively. There is nothing worse than governors discovering that maths or religious education, for example, tends to have a higher and disproportionate number of absences when compared with other subjects. The question 'why' is just around the corner.

A third development is for the governing body to appoint one (or two) of their number to take special responsibility for attendance and attendance-related issues. The delegated governor will often involve himself or herself in school-based attendance issues as well as in overseeing the annual report and policy document on attendance. Not all headteachers welcome such 'hands-on' involvement but those who have tried it report that it can be particularly effective. Some schools follow similar practices on matters like bullying, behaviour and exclusion.

Finally, in a few schools, governors are directly involved in promoting school attendance issues at, for example, parents' evenings or by serving on attendance panels or governing body attendance panels (see Chapters 4, 7 and 8).

2   School trips

School trips are frequently used as incentives for good attendance. For example, some schools allow all pupils to participate in end-of-term or end-of-year school trips (whether free or partially subsidised) provided they have been regular attenders. The lure of a trip to Alton Towers, Thorpe Park or Euro Disney is a key strategy of many schools' attendance policies.

3   Use of stickers and badges

The use of stickers and/or badges is another form of promoting improved school attendance. Stickers in subject or homework books have been used as a form of praise or reward for pupils, especially younger age pupils, for generations. Similarly, the use of badges on pupils' lapels to denote achievement and/or improved attendance is another version of the same concept. Often these stickers are used to promote 'reward' schemes within schools in a whole variety of ways.

4   Personal congratulation schemes

Another form of praise or reward is the use of personal congratulation schemes. Under such schemes, pupils who show a marked improvement in attainment or attendance are rewarded by a visit to meet senior staff within school during which they receive personal praise. Sometimes, during these sessions they may share a cup of tea or be given a packet of sweets, a can of coke or special badge (see above). Some teachers believe the use of personal congratulation schemes to be the single most effective way of promoting and encouraging achievement and attendance. Some schools use local celebrities to bolster their scheme such as well-known sports stars or actors.

5   Utilising the Internet

Another growing reward is to allow improving or better attending pupils to be given more access and use of a school's Internet facilities. More and more pupils are beginning to thoroughly enjoy surfing the net. For those pupils without these facilities at home, it can provide a real treat.

6   Attendance notice boards

Attendance notice boards are normally used for positive reasons. They serve to show gains (and sometimes deficits) in the individual attendance of pupils, forms, year groups, subject areas and whole school. They can be used to depict differences between the attendance of boys and girls, year groups, subject groups, etc. Sometimes attendance notice boards are used to highlight particularly encouraging improvements amongst individuals or groups through the display of pupils' or whole-form, subject or year group photographs (see number 10 later).

7 Attendance cups

The acquisition of an attendance cup can provide a boost to pupils within schools. These attendance cups are frequently awarded during whole-school events such as assemblies or school prize evenings. Attaining the attendance cup can lead to special rewards for the winners. These may include the freedom not to wear school uniform to school for a week at the end of the summer term, going on a special trip (perhaps to the cinema and/or for a meal, to a pop concert or theme park) or receiving individual vouchers or spending tokens (at, for example, HMV Stores).

8 Attendance league tables

Just as local schools and LEAs feature in regional attendance league tables, so many schools now choose to monitor their own internal patterns through the use of league tables. These may be placed on school attendance notice boards or on special notice boards within the staff common room. Thus, teachers, like their pupils, can see how their forms and teaching groups are performing against their peers.

One risk of such a policy is it does tend to highlight those teachers who continually suffer higher absence rates than their peers including, where there are good internal tracking systems in use, specific lesson absence and post-registration truancy. Clearly, these data can be used by senior staff during appraisal interviews and for other purposes such as performance-related pay.

9 Attendance panels

The use of specialist attendance panels to consider individual cases of pupils' absences has considerable merit. Attendance panels are normally composed of a member of the senior management team (often a deputy head in charge of attendance), relevant head of year, form tutor, education welfare officers and, sometimes, others as deemed relevant.

Attendance panels will meet at set times to either meet regular and/or occasional non-attenders on their own or with a parent(s) either during school time or afterwards. Attendance panels will continue to monitor the progress and attendance of those pupils they have seen. Improvements will be noted and commended. Failure to improve will often lead to prosecution and the use of other kinds of deterrents. Attendance panels reinforce to parents and pupils alike that a school cares about attendance issues and that their attendance matters (see also Chapter 8).

Within certain schools, senior management teams now carefully scrutinise staff attendance as well. Frequent staff absence is often a sign of stress, personal problems or being unable to cope. An interview between a headteacher and an absent member of staff can sometimes lead to helpful resolutions of key or sensitive issues (see also number 23 later).

10   Pupils' photographs

The use of pupils' photographs for outstanding achievement is commonplace in many schools. Such achievements might be winning a scholarship to Oxbridge, playing for a county team or winning an international cap. Increasingly, schools are using pupils' photographs to reward significant academic progress. Some schools are also beginning to use the same concept either for making 100 per cent attendance or as a means of promoting significantly improved attendance. Often, these are located on designated notice boards.

11   School newsletters: attendance section

Another growing idea is to include a special section on attendance in school newsletters sent to parents and around the local community. These columns can be used to high-light the achievement of form tutor groups, whole years and the school. It is not a good idea to reinforce the achievement of individual pupils in this way.

12   Parents' evening on attendance or parental days

Over recent decades traditional parents' evenings, especially for potential year 7 pupils prior to transfer to secondary schools, have tended to emphasise curricula available, choice and options. This has been particularly true prior to pupils nominating their GCSE choices before starting years 10 and 11.

More recently, some schools have combined these sessions to ensure that parents and pupils understand and comply with school policies on such issues as bullying, behaviour and attendance. Sometimes, covering a range of issues can make parents' evening over-long. Therefore, some schools are holding more than one event. Or, they are alternating parents' evenings between curriculum and behaviourally focused functions. Some schools believe there are major benefits accruing from stressing school policies on attendance (and other issues) and making compliance a condition of entry to a school. Many schools now send parents a copy of the school charter or handbook prior to pupils start-ing at the school. Alternatively, they send copies of key policy documents to homes following discussion at a parents' evening.

Some schools, also or alternatively, hold parental days in addition to or instead of par-ents' evenings. In a small number of cases, some schools hold parents' evenings (nor-mally by year group) for everyone. Specialist parental days are then held for targeted groups only. Targeted parents often include parents of bullied or bully pupils when key issues are often confronted head-on, sometimes involving an external speaker or expert, with supporting materials which may or may not include the use of video, role play or a presentation by pupils. They also might include the parents of regular or the most persistent absentees. The agenda normally stress the consequences of their children's actions for them as well as the educational consequences.

13   Detentions

Detentions have long been in use to combat pupils' non-attendance. Detentions can be used in a variety of ways. First, they can be helpful by enabling pupils to catch up with their backlog of course work. Second, they are meant to be a deterrent against similar repeat behaviour. Third, they show the conforming majority that deviant behaviour will not be tolerated.

Unfortunately, in the case of persistent absenteeism, the use of detentions can be counterproductive. As schools try hard to re-assimilate their absentees back into the fold, placing them in detention tends to make them feel victimised and awkward amongst their peers and so, often inadvertently, re-encourages the precise behaviour which the detention is trying to overcome.

14   End-of-day registrations

Another fairly recent innovation in some schools is an end-of-day registration period. End-of-day registration periods have tended to be introduced in those schools that have serious problems with post-registration truancy and specific lesson absence.

End-of-day registration periods can also have the effect of shortening a school's teaching day. Some schools regularly now use a morning registration period and an end-of-day registration period thereby forgoing the form period at the start of the afternoon sessions. A small minority of schools alternate between afternoon and end-of-day registration periods, using the latter as a kind of spot check.

15   Business sponsorship

Many, if not most, secondary schools are currently involved with business sponsorship of one kind or another. However, typical business sponsorship, even in an era allowing for lottery grants, is small beer when compared with some states in America. For example, in some schools in Vermont prizes for achieving 100 per cent and regular attendance are almost unbelievable. Illustratively, regular attendance in one middle school in Vermont entitles pupils to an all-expenses-paid trip to a summer camp with full involvement in all social, recreational and sporting activities. This trip is fully funded by the local business community who vie, through adverts in the local paper and on the local radio, to be associated with the scheme. Being involved in school-related activities and holding positions in parent–teacher associations is highly sought after and prestigious in some states and can even affect the ups and downs of local business interests.

It is not known exactly how many local businesses are involved in attendance-related initiatives in the UK. Certainly, some schemes do exist. Reid (1999) has previously reported on some, particularly the Aiming Higher Certificate which was then sponsored by the Hong Kong and Shanghai Bank. The Education Action Zones in England are also, of course, partially funded by business.

16   Years 10 and 11 projects

Specialist projects in years 10 and 11 are undertaken in a variety of ways. Mostly, they are undertaken to supplement a particular GCSE or GNVQ. A lot of less able pupils take fewer GCSEs or GNVQs than their peers in many schools although, perhaps surprisingly, this is not always the case. However, in certain cases, one-off projects in years 10 and 11 are undertaken independently of the National Curriculum. They can either be specialist one-off schemes or taken as part of alternative education programmes.

Years 10 and 11 projects focused on attendance are meant to have both a learning and therapeutic effect. They help pupils with attendance difficulties learn about the consequences of their action. They can also be therapeutic in the sense that understanding leads to prevention and can resolve the mental turmoil involved in being a truant.

Some schools, perhaps too few, undertake group projects into such issues as drug abuse, alcoholism, bullying and truancy either as a part of a PSE scheme or as part of a certificate of education of one kind or another.

17   Missing-from-lesson slips

It is normal practice in some schools to use missing-from-lesson slips. These are routinely used when pupils need to attend medical or dental appointments or, for example, externally provided music lessons.

However, some schools now operate regular daily checks along the lines first described by Reid (1982b) in his article on school organisation and persistent school absenteeism. This process works in the following way.

A school introduces daily attendance checks at the start of every lesson often supported by spot checks in corridors, toilets and known truant-haunts. Each form tutor provides a designated class/attendant monitor with a list of known absentees (or, alternatively, of all those present) dependent on a school's internal organisation at the start of each school day. These are then retained and carried by the form monitors on specially prepared sheets and shown to the subject teachers at the beginning of each lesson. A second roll call then ensues based on the subject teacher's own register. Any missing pupils not accounted for are reported and chased up on at once. The original registration sheets are then collected at the end of the day. It then becomes the job of the pastoral heads of year working in conjunction with the EWOs to ascertain all the reasons for the pupils' absence. Regular feedback and reports are subsequently given to form teachers and the whole staff.

Originally, the concept and ensuing policy grew out of need. However, it is also a way for the staff to communicate their general concern for their pupils' welfare as well as to enforce good attendance habits. Moreover, staff as a whole are made aware that non-attendance at school can be an early warning signal to a vast array of potentially serious problems and that each member of staff, from the form teacher upwards, has a crucial role to play in the school's pastoral care system.

18   Attendance tribunals

Some schools organise their own self-styled 'attendance tribunals'. These are regular dates which are set for meetings with the parent(s) of irregular attenders. Their purpose is to review the attendance and academic progress of their child and to provide as much in-school support as possible.

Some attendance tribunals only involve one or two key staff such as a head of year and education welfare officers. Others involve more senior staff including headteachers and a deputy. Generally speaking, parents tend to prefer dealing with one or two members of staff rather than too many.

19   Staggered start times

Some schools have experimented with staggered start times as a means of improving attendance without any clear body of opinion emerging. Consequently, some schools take a pragmatic view – either officially or unofficially. They encourage pupils to attend, whether latecomers or truants, to some extent during the school day at their own convenience. The theory is that some schools prefer to see their pupils attending for part of a day rather than not at all.

20   Policies for habitual truants

Some senior management teams within schools have prepared their own policies for dealing with habitual truants. These have come about partly for reasons of consistency as well as to ensure that each case follows all appropriate procedures. The main influence however, has been the dismay felt by education welfare officers and senior staff within schools following inconsistent and/or lenient sentences passed by magistrates' courts. In some serious attenders cases, often compounded by known home background and social circumstances highlighted in case reports from social services, magistrates dismiss actions *sine die*. This can be soul-destroying to an EWO who has put in many long hours of work before the school and LEA take the case to court.

Therefore, in order to ensure equitable treatment for all pupils within a school, some EWOs and LEAs now prefer to take their own sanctions against habitual truants. Since 1 April 2001, pupils are no longer allowed to be excluded solely on the grounds of truancy. Therefore, many schools now prefer to use alternative curriculum solutions including the appointment of full-time learning mentors in cases of pupils with prolonged or habitual truancy. It is becoming recognised that truants returning to school require specialist approaches.

21   'Catch up' units

'Catch up' units facilitate re-integration strategies for pupils who have been away from school for a while either for illness, non-attendance or for other reasons. The aim is to ensure that individual pupils catch up with the learning and course work which they have missed as soon as possible. In this way, the pupils concerned do not feel awkward or disadvantaged and should have no school-based learning reason for starting to miss school again.

22   Consistency of staff policies

One of the issues within a lot of schools is the need to ensure that school policies are interpreted in the same way by all staff towards pupils. This is not always the case. For example, in one class a teacher will allow pupils to eat sweets. In another, he or she will not. One teacher may reinforce the 'rule' that shirts are not worn outside trousers; another will not. These inconsistencies affect pupils' behaviour within classrooms.

The same is true with attendance. While one teacher may be very concerned when a pupil misses his or her lesson, another may not care less. Many teachers simply take the view that if pupils wish to miss their lessons it is simply one less to teach and one book less to mark. It is a vital part of devising school policy documents that *all* staff agree with and approve the policy. And that the policy is carried out consistently across the school.

23   Staff absenteeism

There are several suggestions in the literature, but no firm research, that staff absenteeism fosters pupil absenteeism. Increasingly, staff absences are monitored by senior management teams within schools. However, pupils 'learn' when and which staff are more likely to be away. They soon discern when staff are prone to intermittent attendance on, for example, a Monday or a Friday.

At professional development events, many staff from schools have claimed that their internal league tables show a correlation between staff and pupil absence. They also suggest that irregular staff attendance can be linked with lower pass rates in external examinations and with differences in pupils' performance at attainment targets set for key stages 3 and 4. At conferences it is not unusual for delegates to cite differences between able and less able and 'strong' and 'weak' teachers and teaching styles as a key factor in schools' attendance rates.

24   Involving community police in school

Many schools, more especially primary phases, are becoming inclined to involve their local community police in school-based activities. At first, they used to act as advisers on such issues as road safety, joyriding and drugs. Increasingly, however, their role is being broadened to include such issues as the consequences of truancy. The community police will advise on the law about attendance at school as well as on the role of truancy patrols and for truancy watch schemes.

Police are increasingly being called into schools to deal with fights between pupils. Some of these fights have been found to be connected with bullying. Some are racially motivated. In Swindon, for example, fights between pupils are leading to assault charges being made in serious cases. Some inner city schools in London decided to ask for a permanent police presence in the spring of 2001 following a series of incidents involving rival gangs. A few schools around the UK now utilise full-time police officers in the related fight against drugs and drugs-motivated crime.

25   Use of external consultants

Some schools, especially those with a long and consistent history of non-attendance, are beginning to involve external consultants in reviewing their school attendance policy documents and practices (see Chapter 2) and in organising tailor-made staff development events on attendance and related issues. Teachers often find it beneficial to be involved in these activities when external trainers are involved as it helps facilitate new ideas and discussion. Given the increasing attention by Ofsted towards attendance issues, schools are beginning to realise that they can no longer accept attendance rates of say, 80, 85, or 90 per cent. Many staff within schools are deeply worried about the effects that non-attendance is having on the overall performance of their schools; not least those in special measures partly or fully because of poor attendance.

26 Letters to parents

Writing to parents to inform them when their child is failing to attend school regularly is a normal part of most schools' attendance policies. Increasingly however, schools are beginning to write to parents specifically to let them know when their child starts making improved attendance.

Some schools now monitor individual pupil attendance as part of their internal league table or attendance notice board analysis. Therefore, it is much easier to detect those pupils whose attendance is rising or falling and requires parental notification.

27 'Premiership'

Some schools attempt to put 'life' into their internal league tables on performance and attendance by constructing their own football-related divisions including promotion and relegation and even, in some cases, utilising play-offs. Top attending pupils, form tutor groups, subject groups and year groups are placed in the 'premiership'. Those whose attendance or academic performance are causing concern find themselves in the third division. At the end of the year, those in the premiership or at the top of the premiership win prizes (e.g. special free school trip). Those at the bottom, of or in division three, undertake forfeits (e.g. school litter parties). This is another way of retaining pupil and staff interest in attendance and performance issues. It can be fun. It can be highly motivational as it leads to 'reverse' peer pressure; pupils putting pressure on their classmates to attend in order not to lose them a sought after prize and prestige.

28 Truancy watch schemes

Truancy watch is similar to neighbourhood watch schemes. Just as in neighbourhood watch the idea is crime prevention with neighbours reporting to police any suspicious circumstances, so in truancy watch schemes locals (parents, shopkeepers, any member of the community) will report suspected truants on a local hotline either to the school or to a nearby truancy patrol. Clearly, this is also helpful in the fight against juvenile crime.

29 Arrival and Departure Lounge

One school in the Home Counties has established an 'Arrival and Departure Lounge'. The concept is that all pupils arriving late to school, or at any time during the school day, are channelled to the lounge. Similarly, any pupil who needs to leave school early (e.g. a medical or music appointment) has to leave via the exit from the lounge. The arrivals and departure lounge is staffed by a full-time receptionist who can call upon the services of appropriate staff for support when help is needed. The school considers the concept has seriously helped to reduce specific lesson absence and post-registration truancy.

30 Parental convoys

Some schools are asking parents of regular attenders to fill their cars up on the way to school by collecting irregular or erratic attenders including truants. Apart from the obvious environmental benefits, it places a subtle form of pressure on both the irregular attender and his or her parent(s). Some schools are reporting that this scheme is working very effectively and has had a significant effect upon reducing unauthorised absence.

31 Good and poor attenders 'runs'

Good and poor attenders 'runs' are a related concept to parental convoys. In this case, schools arrange for good attenders to 'call' for poor attenders and either walk together with them to school or ensure they catch the same school bus. Similarly, some schools are finding that this scheme is working very effectively for them.

32 Truancy call

Truancy call is a scheme run by a private company based in Birmingham which looks after a school's first day responses for them. The scheme is managed in the following way. Truancy call is an electronic system. Within minutes of the scheme being informed that a pupil is away from school, the company is able to contact the parents immediately and provides direct feedback to the school. The school should discover very quickly whether a parent is aware that their child is absent.

Thus, once the registers are taken, details of missing children are clicked into the system. The automated service then calls parents using a screening system to ensure only the parent receives the message. It keeps redialling (up to early evening) until contact is made.

Once the system makes contact, it asks the parent if they are aware their child is absent from school. If they are, it asks the parent to record the reason why their child is away. It also offers an option to be connected to the school.

The recorded reason given by the parents for their child's absence is then stored automatically back into the system. A form tutor/attendance secretary (or whoever within a school is given this responsibility) can then listen to and mark the reason for the absence and the date the pupil is expected to return. In the case of parental-condoned absence it provides the school with a timed and dated response from the parents providing the reason for their child's absence from school.

The system can also cope with specific lesson absence and post-registration truancy. If a pupil registers and then goes missing, a simple click onto the system will result in a specific call informing the parents of this occurrence and will request an immediate response.

33 Quiet room

Some schools use a 'quiet' room to put either disruptive or other categories of pupils for designated periods of time. In some schools these rooms have been given the nickname of 'sin-bins', 'coolers' or, presumably in recognition of Tom Hanks, 'Castaways'. Some schools however, are providing quiet rooms for other purposes. These include assisting pupils who are being bullied to carry on with their school work or to enable 'returners' to catch up with their school work. Some schools also use quiet rooms to place: (a) potentially disruptive pupils thereby excluding them from certain lessons; (b) specific lesson absentees on the premise that it is better to give them set assignments rather than have them 'skiving' around the school; (c) pupils whose personal relationships with individual teachers have irreparably broken down.

34   On-line registers/swipe card systems: e-registration schemes

In March 2001, the government announced an extra £11.25 million to enable pupils in some schools to be required to clock in and out of lessons on-line as part of a scheme to cut truancy and post-registration absence. The DfES has suggested that the use of electronic registration can reduce truancy by up to 10 per cent over a two-year period. Teachers are able to trace which pupils are absent by using only a few clicks on the computer, enabling them quickly to follow up suspicious cases with their parents.

Initially, the money is to be given to 500 schools in England with some of the worst attendance records. The money will pay for swipe card systems, electronic hand-held registers and equipment to scan written records.

35   Phonemaster

A school in Scotland became the first in the UK in September 2000 to introduce and use American telecommunications technology to combat rising truancy. The phone-master system is linked to a network of computerised class registers. The system is similar in design to the truancy call process described earlier in number 32.

36   Asthma clinics

A school in north-west England found a strong correlation between pupils who suffer from asthma and erratic and irregular attendance. It was discovered that monitoring the attendance and health needs of these pupils on a daily basis helped a great deal. They persuaded their local general practitioner's practice to hold regular asthma clinics within the school. Subsequently, it was shown that the attendance of the school's asthmatic pupils improved significantly.

37   Parental sit-ins

Some schools are beginning to experiment with parental 'sit-ins' for pupils experiencing such problems as attendance, bullying and behavioural difficulties. Under the scheme, a parent or close relative is invited to attend some or all of his or her child's lessons until such time as the parent, the school and the pupil collectively agree that the issue has been resolved. Involving parents in lessons appears to have a positive benefit on other pupils as well as those who are being targeted especially from the perspective of improving classroom behaviour.

38   Reducing illegal under-age work

A TUC/MORI Survey (2001) reported that 485,000 schoolchildren are working illegally. Of these, over 100,000 of the children admit to playing truant in order to

	National	London	South East	South West	North East	North West	Eastern	East Midlands	West Midlands	Yorkshire	Wales
% of children working during term-time	22%	18%	23%	24%	10%	19%	31%	24%	21%	25%	26%
% of children working in last summer holidays	20%	17%	17%	25%	14%	16%	22%	23%	19%	20%	29%
% of children working before 6 a.m.	23%	22%	22%	27%	23%	20%	29%	16%	23%	26%	20%
% of children working after 8 p.m.	45%	43%	47%	48%	46%	49%	43%	42%	33%	45%	54%
% of children who were often or sometimes too tired to do homework or schoolwork because of job	29%	14%	27%	28%	22%	36%	24%	39%	23%	32%	46%
% of children playing truant to do job	10%	11%	6%	13%	7%	9%	5%	14%	15%	9%	4%

Base: Except for points one and two, all those with a term-time or summertime job.

Figure 6.1 Percentage of pupils working during term-time by region.

Job type	National	London	South East	South West	North East	North West	Eastern	East Midlands	West Midlands	Yorkshire	Wales
Baby sitting	38%	49%	43%	27%	34%	45%	30%	44%	28%	38%	38%
Cleaning	14%	13%	18%	8%	5%	21%	7%	17%	19%	10%	16%
Office work	5%	13%	7%	6%	–	3%	3%	4%	2%	6%	11%
Factory work	2%	1%	–	–	–	3%	2%	3%	–	1%	5%
Farm work	4%	–	7%	4%	5%	6%	4%	1%	1%	4%	3%
Gardening	8%	8%	8%	5%	5%	8%	9%	3%	15%	2%	10%
Milk round	3%	–	5%	1%	–	2%	4%	1%	–	3%	6%
Paper round	39%	23%	33%	25%	33%	51%	51%	41%	60%	33%	32%
Shop work	15%	19%	16%	20%	11%	16%	15%	11%	11%	13%	19%
Market stall	4%	3%	5%	5%	–	6%	4%	4%	3%	1%	–
Catering	13%	6%	21%	23%	14%	13%	10%	11%	5%	9%	9%
Other	22%	40%	24%	17%	50%	12%	22%	14%	12%	25%	15%
Not stated	4%	–	3%	5%	–	2%	3%	4%	4%	5%	21%

Base: All those with a term-time job.

Figure 6.2 Type of illegal work amongst school-age pupils by region.

undertake paid work. Figures 6.1 and 6.2 provide the percentage of pupils working during term-time by region.

Class struggles, a survey of 2,500 schoolchildren in England and Wales, reveals nearly half a million children are working illegally. It is against the law for any child under 13 to do any kind of paid work, but the survey shows that one in four – 289,000 – say they do. Thirteen-year-olds are only allowed to do paid jobs linked to 'cultural, sporting, artistic or advertising work' and even then only with a licence from their local authority. But over 35 per cent of 13-year-olds (196,574) said they were either working during term-time or had worked in the last summer holidays. The vast majority worked as baby-sitters or had paper rounds, both of which are illegal.

On top of this, many more children are working longer hours than they are legally allowed. No one under 16 is allowed to work before 7 a.m. or after 7 p.m. But almost half (45 per cent) of the working children questioned said they worked after eight at night, and 23 per cent said they worked before six in the morning.

The MORI survey of 2,500 schoolchildren shows that illegal school-age working has not declined since the last TUC survey four years previously, despite the introduction of the European Young Workers Directive, designed to tighten working time and ensure paid work did not have a negative impact on students' school work. The survey's key findings are:

- one in ten children admitted to playing truant in order to do paid work; boys are more likely to skive off school for this reason than girls (12 per cent as opposed to 5 per cent);
- one in four children (25 per cent) under 13 admit to doing paid work either during term-time or in the summer holidays; just over a third of schoolchildren (36 per cent) do some kind of paid work; the older children are, the more likely they are to have a job; almost half (44 per cent) 15 and 16-year-olds are working;
- children are also working illegal hours: although, according to the European Young Workers Directive, no one under 16 is allowed to work before 6 a.m. or after 8 p.m., almost a quarter (23 per cent) have worked before 6 a.m.; 45 per cent said they worked after 8 p.m. – although a significant number of these would be babysitting, which is not illegal;
- term-time working negatively affects a significant proportion of schoolchildren – 29 per cent of respondents said they often or sometimes felt too tired to do home-work or school work;
- the most common jobs are baby-sitting (37 per cent) and paper rounds (35 per cent), followed by cleaning (19 per cent) and working in a shop (16 per cent); girls are most likely to have jobs as baby-sitters and boys are most likely to have paper rounds;
- although one in ten (11 per cent) schoolchildren say they earn more than £5 an hour, most are paid much less; around a third (31.5 per cent) earn £2.50 an hour or less; nearly one in five (17 per cent) of those working in term time get less than £2 an hour.

Whilst not all of the European Young Workers Directive has been brought into force, some key parts were introduced in June 2000, including:

- children under 16 should not work more than two hours on a school day or twelve hours in any school week;
- during school holidays, children under 15 cannot work more than twenty-five hours a week and 15-year-olds have a limit of thirty-five hours.

According to the TUC poll, 30 per cent or 320,286 children with term-time jobs said they did more than two hours a day. One in ten reported working more than five hours a day.

Local authorities have responsibility for enforcing these rights, but the TUC believes councils are not doing their jobs properly. The TUC would like to see more spot checks in workplaces to ensure unscrupulous employers are not taking advantage of school-children.

Clearly, effective monitoring of illegal under-age working and taking the appropriate subsequent action ought to help reduce truancy and other forms of non-attendance. For example, Terry was found to be a persistent truant with severe behavioural problems at the age of 14. A school investigation found that he began his daily routine at 5 a.m. by going out on a milk round. He often arrived late to school. After school, he undertook a paper round. Then, he used to go and help on odd jobs at a nearby local shop under-taking chores such as stacking and replacing goods on shelves. After undergoing a thorough medical examination, his GP reported that he was 'physically and mentally exhausted; too tired to attend school'. After stopping the early morning shift, Terry gradually was re-integrated back into school and his behaviour started to improve.

39   Pearson technology developments

Originally developed in the United States, Pearson is one of several new Internet com-panies which is beginning to specialise in educational products. The reality is that there will soon be wired classrooms and diagnostic gadgetry which could spell the end of the trusty blackboard and chalk and old-fashioned worksheets. The potential of the Internet means that each pupil can be taught on their own terms, in their own way and in their own time.

The new technology means that it will be much more possible to extend the school day, be more flexible about timetabling and be under the more watchful eye of parents. Pearson's software, for example, will be able to link schools and homes, enabling parents to look at attendance records, test results, homework assignments as well as the curricu-lum. Tests and homework will be able to be marked on-line. But installing the software and hardware will not be cheap. In fact, it will be very expensive. Moreover, some exist-ing school buildings may not be suitable for the enterprise.

Similar ventures are being launched in the UK. They include learn.co.uk, a Guardian Newspaper Limited backed venture, Schools.net and R.M, the latter specialising in the production of white interactive technology friendly boards which can be linked to PCs within the classroom and be responsive to a range of software.

40   The Scottish Shilling

In exchange for promising good attendance and application to their studies, senior school pupils are being offered up to £40 a week to stay on at school. In 2001, the original pilot scheme first trialled in East Ayrshire was extended to Glasgow, Dundee and West Dumbartonshire. Early reports suggest that paying older pupils to attend school is not only improving students' academic performance, it helps to create a better positive school ethos and encourages more pupils to stay on at school to take their Highers.

41   Pacific Institute programme

This is a specific course designed to build confidence and self-esteem. Programmes vary according to the user's ability. Each unit is sub-divided into: (a) an overview of the project; (b) video activities including energising games in which the teacher/mentor acts as the facilitator; (c) task achievement including the setting of self-orientated goals; (d) putting self-talk into words through affirmations.

The Pacific Institute programme is especially useful with 14 and 15-year-olds, particularly for those with low self-esteem. The Pacific Institute project has been found to be feasible for work with groups of up to thirty children. The project really makes you believe in yourself. In fact, the project can also be used with teachers in schools in, for example, an all-day activity in raising team awareness and levels of professional self-esteem.

42   Success Maker

Success Maker is another software package. It can be used throughout the secondary age range. It is especially effective in raising standards of literacy and numeracy for pupils in years 7 and 8. For example, in Mountain Ash Comprehensive School pupils in year 7 receive one lesson per week in maths, one lesson a week in English and one lesson a week in either maths and/or English. The school utilises sixty individual workstations for the project and these workstations have been especially wired up for the purpose. The original cost of establishing the scheme was £250,000 which came from a specific one-off grant. Staff in the school believe the project is a great success.

43   All-the-year-round learning

The Oak Tree Education Trust in Liverpool launched an initiative to educate and endeavour to return truants back to the mainstream. The Trust caters for some of the most difficult pupils in Liverpool. Some of their intake are persistent truants and suspended or excluded pupils.

The Trust operates by first approaching the youngsters in their homes and seeks to establish a home–school contract with their parents to co-operate with their educational rehabilitation. The school operates an all-year-round policy. It even stays open during half-term and summer holidays, when attendance is voluntary. Surprisingly, many of the disaffected youngsters turn up voluntarily because they have begun to enjoy learning.

44   The use of pupil referral units (PRUs)

Pupil referral units (sometimes called progress review units) are often used by schools to place their disruptive or disaffected pupils for short periods of time, sometimes to allow for a 'cooling-off' period. Some PRUs are located on school sites. In such cases, these units are often locally referred to as either 'coolers' or 'sin-bins!' More frequently, however, PRUs are specialist units located at convenient points within LEAs, often catering for pupils from a number of different schools.

PRUs specialise in improving pupils' behaviour in the short or long term and in facilitating their pupils with individual learning needs support programmes. The aim of the units is to return pupils to their former or alternative schools wherever possible. A number of pupils referred to PRUs have histories of attendance problems as one of their symptoms. However, some PRUs themselves experience difficulties in ensuring that pupils placed with them also attend on a regular basis.

Summary

Chapters 3 to 6 have provided almost 120 different short-term ideas for combating truancy – and other forms of non-attendance. These confirm the range and variety of schemes on offer at almost every level. They include some of the latest technological ideas, schemes involving parents, the police and other caring professionals, in-school and out-of-school solutions, as well as a whole host of innovative schemes which are already helping to reduce truancy and other forms of non-attendance in schools throughout the United Kingdom. Hopefully, these four chapters will provide a valuable resource for readers to consider. We will now move on and consider some longer-term and more strategic solutions in Chapters 7 and 8.

Chapter 7

Long-term strategic approaches I

The PSCC scheme

The next two chapters are especially important for those teachers and education welfare officers who work in schools with a history of serious, long-term attendance problems. The discussion is particularly relevant for those schools that have received adverse criticism on attendance in a recent inspection or may be fearing the worst from a forthcoming inspection. Finally, the contents will provide significant ideas and challenges for those staff who work in schools that are either at or towards the bottom of league tables on attendance or have been put into special measures (or even failed an inspection) partly or totally because of attendance issues.

Implementing long-term strategic approaches to combat poor attendance is a relatively new idea. The author first began working with schools on longer-term strategic approaches for reducing absenteeism during his teaching and in-service programmes in the late 1980s. Since then, these original ideas have been refined during the mid and late 1990s to the point that some of the original ideas have been adapted by schools to suit their own needs as later sections in this chapter will demonstrate. In fact, since 1999, the author has been stressing the ideas as much for their potential for school change and for improving school attendance as for the importance of utilising the conceptual base, structure and processes of the schemes. Nowadays, the author recommends utilising the strategic ideas rather than recommending any particular version, as schools' circumstances and needs differ to a greater or lesser extent. For example, the location of schools in rural and inner city regions are so different that this factor needs to be taken into account.

The PSCC scheme emphasises the importance of the transition process between primary and secondary schools and encourages schools to identify potential and actual non-attenders and to take the appropriate action to assist pupils' learning and behavioural needs at as early a stage as possible. The PSCC plan focuses on possible long-term strategic developments which can transform and change attitudes towards non-attendance within schools amongst both staff and pupils. It is particularly geared to changing unfavourable school climates, attitudes and culture, especially in certain schools where public perceptions of a local school are extremely low. Schools in which the PSCC scheme is used often refer to it in their own vernacular. Phrases such as the 'Traffic Lights Scheme', the 'Colour-Coded Concept' and the 'Three Tier Process' are all known to the author as schools have adapted the ideas for their own usage.

Chapter 8 provides some alternative longer-term strategies. One of the key differences between the PSCC scheme in this chapter and the second series of ideas in Chapter 8 is that the former relies upon key information provided by primary school staff as the pupils in the PSCC scheme are initially selected when they are in year 6. Conversely, the schemes discussed in Chapter 8 are dependent upon the secondary school staff choosing the appropriate groups once the transition between the primary and secondary phase has already taken place.

The first part of this chapter focuses on the key concepts behind the PSCC scheme and on the core processes involved in implementing it. In the latter part of the chapter, some novel and alternative approaches towards implementing this long-term strategic scheme to combat pupils' non-attendance based on the original concept are presented and considered. There is also a discussion on the advantages and disadvantages of the PSCC scheme. Finally, there is a consideration of how some of the same concepts used in the PSCC scheme could be built into a school's policy on other related issues such as bullying, behaviour and exclusion. An example of using the ideas for school policies on exclusion is shown in Figure 7.4.

The concept

The PSCC schemes and the SSTG schemes in Chapter 8 have several aspects in common. Each is designed to provide a school with a fresh start approach towards attendance issues. This is the core principle behind the schemes. Ideally, implementing each scheme should involve the willing contribution and participation of *every* member of staff from the head right through the school including form tutors, classroom assistants, learning mentors, attendance support staff and, crucially, the education welfare officer. Each plan is preventative in nature utilising a partial zero-tolerance approach. Each of the concepts is also progressive in nature starting with year 7 and lasts initially for at least a five-year period, culminating with year 11. Thereafter, by the time the scheme reaches the end of year 11, every child in the school will have been through exactly the same process as will every child coming to the school in future years. By following this process rigorously, schools will be able to change their internal culture, ethos and, hopefully, rid themselves of negative pupil (and parental) attitudes towards regular school attendance.

Each of the plans is proactive and provides the pupils and their parents with a single, uniform message – that their attendance matters. In theory, as the importance of making regular attendance is emphasised within a school, so there should be corresponding gains in pupils' behaviour and academic progress; the latter being translated into improved performance in both internal and external 'tests' and examination results.

The plans are flexible. However, they adopt a colour-coding approach in order to facilitate initial pupil and group selection and related 'remedial' activities. The scheme allows for subsequent movement between and into each group or back into the mainstream as individual pupils' circumstances permit.

Plan A: The PSCC scheme in practice

Plan A is called the PSCC scheme for convenience. PS refers to primary secondary to differentiate it from later schemes. CC refers to colour coded.

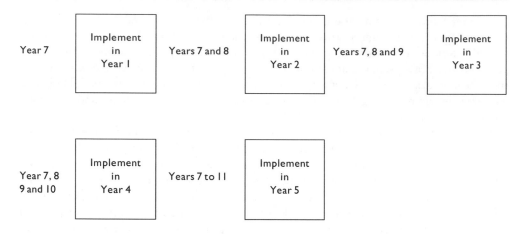

Figure 7.1 The five-year cycle using the PSCC scheme.

The key to understanding the PSCC plan (see Figure 7.1) is that the initial group selections are undertaken in the later stages of year 6 whilst the pupils are still attending their primary/junior school phase. The group selections are also made by the primary headteacher/staff in accordance with criteria given to them from their local secondary school/s in the area. The whole school approach to establishing appropriate policies on attendance and the optimum ways of organising supporting activities in setting up this process have previously been described by Reid (1999) in Chapters 9 and 10 of *Truancy and Schools*.

The scheme utilises four colour codes as follows:

Red group

Pupils who have been identified as occasional or persistent non-attenders or truants whilst at primary school. Research has established that up to 35 per cent of truants or persistent absentees begin their histories of non-attendance whilst at primary school (Reid, 1999).

Blue group

Pupils whom staff deem to be 'at risk' of becoming truants or persistent absentees based on:

(a) evidence collected during their current school profiles;
(b) pupils with a history of non-attendance in the family, e.g. brother or sister or parent with known attendance problems. Reid (1999) has previously reported on families with significant histories of non-attendance sometimes extending into third or fourth generations (see also Chapter 9).

Yellow group

Pupils whom staff consider to be 'at risk' because they are seriously under-achieving at school and whose reading ages, levels of numeracy and literacy are two or more years behind their chronological ages. Research shows that truants tend to come from pupils who have or are under-achieving at school and who have clear literacy and numeracy deficiencies at particular stages (Reid, 1985, 1999). These pupils may or may not be disaffected (Reid, 1986).

Green group

Normally, by far and away the largest group, pupils with no attendance problems are not considered to be 'at risk' for any reason and whose educational progress in school is considered to be satisfactory. Some schools omit the use of the green label on the grounds that it is superfluous.

Progression issues

Pupils from the four pre-selected colour-coded cohorts are included in each form tutor group in year 7. However, periods of time are found within the school week when the pupils in each of the red, blue and yellow groups are brought together within their specialist groups for individual support and/or tuition purposes. One school in South Wales brought the groups together during their designated PSE classes. Another idea is to bring the three risk groups together during, for example, designated modern language teaching time. [NB Few truants are noted for their ability in a second language!] Another possible way of managing this process is through breakfast, lunch-time or after-school clubs, although individual circumstances vary especially in, say, rural schools.

At any point during the process (years 7 to 11), pupils can be transferred between groups. For example, truants who change their behaviour and become good attenders should initially move from the red to the blue group and, then, if their attendance, behaviour and academic progress continue to improve, they could move into the yellow group and, eventually (at least in theory!), into the green cohort. Similarly, pupils from the blue group could be moved to the red group if their attendance worsens or to the yellow group if their circumstances improve. Finally, pupils from the yellow group could progress 'downwards' to the blue or red group if their attendance, behaviour or academic progress deteriorates. Apart from making it clear that a school cares for every one of its pupils, the scheme is ideal used in conjunction with such initiatives as Connexions, Excellence in Cities, mentorship schemes and several others.

Theoretically, the size of the red group should decrease year upon year as remedial approaches begin to bite for the pupils and function well within the school. The same should be true for the blue group. Therefore, the key target is to gradually reduce the pool of pupils who originate in the yellow group or who are likely to be placed in it during their time at secondary school. By working closely with feeder primary schools and by raising academic standards within the school, the potential for pupils to truant, misbehave and under-achieve is gradually reduced. At the same time, by raising pupils' academic profiles, self-concepts and academic self-esteem, and pupils' literacy and numeracy skills (here IT skills are important), the potential for pupils to graduate to either the red or blue group as they get older should be significantly reduced. The PSCC scheme therefore, is about prevention *and* cure.

This is precisely the opposite of current practice as the general trend at present is for the greatest number of absentees in most schools to be located in years 10 and 11. Currently, many secondary schools have at least twice as many absentees or persistent absentees in year 11 as year 7. An OECD Report (2001) recorded that 27 per cent of all pupils in UK secondary schools leave without any qualifications. A high proportion of these pupils have serious literacy and numeracy weaknesses; much the worst in Europe. It is from this cohort that persistent absentees and truants usually originate.

Development issues

Red group

Red pupils require as much individual and/or group time together as possible, ideally on a daily basis. Programmes should include individual and/or group help on all their needs such as reading, writing, oracy (including classroom speaking and/or discussion), numeracy and information technology skills. All of these skills are key to future success in school and later in the world of work. Group time should be spent on such topics as pupils' learning and study skills, e.g. how to write and present an assignment, project or essay or how to use colour in display work. Group tasks could be given on, for instance, preventing truancy from school, how to prepare a CV for potential employers or on how to become a good parent. Specialist preventative sessions on topics like truancy (especially its long-term effects), bullying, preparing for good citizenship are useful subjects to follow as they give non-attenders significant insights into the consequences of their behaviour for themselves and society in much the way as seminars or PSE programmes on drugs, sex education and racial equality currently utilise. Again, the idea is that by empowering the pupils with knowledge on the potential long-term outcomes of their behaviour, pupils will opt to conform. After 2003, with the introduction of vocational GCSEs, existing curriculum-related problems for some categories of less able pupils in some schools should be reduced thereby facilitating this process in a helpful way. As a number of secondary schools may not have the appropriate resources for starting vocational GCSEs (e.g. bricklaying), the number of linked school–FE schemes is expected to increase.

Red group pupils require a staff team to manage the process. These teams will vary between schools according to such factors as availability, need, seriousness of the problems, size of the group, etc. In practical everyday usage, red group management teams have been composed of the following:

(a) One or more governors, a head (and/or deputy head), head of year, school attendance co-ordinator, education welfare officers, learning mentors – or any three from the enclosed list normally encouraging a gender mix.
(b) A member of the senior management team (often with specific responsibility for attendance), head of year and attendance co-ordinator or education welfare officer.

Who sits on each colour-coded management panel is in some ways less important than getting the message across as well as ensuring consistency into the processing of applications and interviews. Some schools prefer a 'heavy' approach; others a 'lighter' touch. Personally, the author believes involving the headteacher and a governor in red group formal processes gives out a strong and appropriate message to pupils, parents and staff alike.

Each school scheme requires a 'champion'. The champion is the overall school co-ordinator of the project. In some ways it does not really matter who it is. The selected person needs to be empathetic with pupils and a very competent organiser. For example, one champion is a former head of year who now works full-time on the project using money provided externally to the school by the National Lottery.

It is exceedingly helpful to involve governors in attendance issues. This is partly due to their position within the community but also because of their experience of human life and current status. Ideally, governors should be drawn from those with an interest in attendance or related issues. It is sensible, because of availability issues, to use one governor per panel meeting who could be drawn from a list of say, three or four governor volunteers. This spreads the workload, keeps the high profile and prevents cancellations or other organisational problems. Every school governing body should have one of their members nominated as being responsible for attendance (and often behaviour, bullying and drugs-related issues). Heads should be asked to provide governors with a detailed report – at least once a year as a standing agenda item – on attendance and related issues. The nominated governor can then comment on the report based on first-hand experience.

Of course, this is a high-risk strategy for some schools with significant attendance problems. It may not be popular with all heads. After all, it is not like providing a report on successful Oxbridge entrants. However, it will help governors understand more readily the realities of school life. Indeed, teacher governors can often support the head in the ensuing discussion of the annual or bi-annual report. Governors will feel that they, and the school, are tackling the issues head-on and doing all they can to prevent and overcome the problems. And there will be some factual evidence to give to Ofsted/ Estyn (in Wales).

Similarly, it is helpful for headteachers to be prepared to make time and provide a lead on the red management task force. In an ideal world, education welfare officers should also always be included in the team. However, given the existing shortage and organisation of education welfare officers, this may not always be possible. This can be problematic and one which the operation of the Connexions Service might seek to rectify.

Arranging the venue and agenda for the meetings is up to the project/school co-ordinator. However, from my own experience, it helps to provide red group pupils with specialist help with their literacy and numeracy skills as often as possible – certainly at least twice a week. Remember that as the red pupils' learning deficits improve, so they become more likely to enjoy and participate in school life.

Similarly, there should be at least one (and preferably two) meetings a term to discuss attendance and progression issues between members of the red group management team and the parent(s) or guardian. At this meeting, evidence is presented on the pupil's progress and attendance and, where necessary, appropriate remedial action taken by all parties (see Chapter 9 on parents and parental-condoned absenteeism). Ideally, these meetings should take place between 2.00 and 6.30 p.m. to give everybody a chance to be present (especially single parents who have to collect younger children from other local schools, or fathers who are on, say, flexible hours or shift work). Some schools prefer to arrange such meetings in blocks during the day and/or at lunch-times as well as in after-school hours. All red group pupils *should* be seen formally at least once a term.

Prior to the point of transfer from the primary to the secondary school, each of the pupils and their parent(s) or guardian(s) should be asked to sign the school's attendance charter and, ideally, a home–school contract before commencing at the comprehensive school. Similarly, the interviews with the Red Group Management Panel should be minuted and, ideally (especially now, with the introduction of the Human Rights Act in the UK) agreed and signed by both parties before departure. The minutes should record an individual pupil's level of attendance, attainment and related and relevant in-school and external difficulties. This is key data in any subsequent short or long-term potential legal action and provides the school with significant legal protection as it is a clear manifestation of a school's attempt to help its under-achieving or difficult pupils.

Pupils should remain in the red group until their attendance (and often related behavioural) problems are no longer causing concern. Procedures for either the blue and/or yellow groups then apply for as long as a pupil requires help and support. Note the potential academic and behavioural differences between traditional, psychological and institutional absentees which are likely to be factors involved in red group pupils (see Reid, 1999, Chapter 2).

Blue group

Pupils in the blue group should follow a similar format to those in the red cohort with the following significant differences:

(a) There is no need for the headteacher or a governor to be included on this team – but, if they are, great – so much the better!
(b) The school attendance co-ordinator, education welfare officer, attendance support officer, a deputy head and/or head of year along with the education welfare officer should be core members of the group.
(c) Ideally, the senior special needs tutor (or deputy) should attend all or most of, at least, the key relevant individual and/or group meetings.

Similar recording processes as for the red group should be used. It is useful to teach each of the colour-coded groups within their designated periods during the week. However, splitting the groups into smaller units for specialist sessions can also be helpful. Again, the formal one-to-professional group session will only take place once a term.

Blue group pupils are in the 'buffer' zone. Theoretically, pupils could go up to the yellow or green groups or down to the red group. The aim of the blue management team is, first, to successfully transfer as many of the initial designated at-risk pupils to the yellow or green groups as soon as practically makes sense. It is, second, to monitor and prevent yellow (and green pupils) from becoming non-attenders or developing further bad habits. Prevention is once more the name of the game.

Yellow group

The role of the yellow management group is also prevention. The purpose of the yellow management group therefore, is on ensuring the learning and special needs of these often less able pupils are met and, ideally, significantly improved. The learning and teaching processes to be followed are identical to those for the red and blue groups although clearly, the specialist curricula will be very much on providing learning support. There is no need to conduct formal interviews with pupils and parents within the yellow group by an appropriate management panel except as necessary or appropriate. However, some schools prefer to do so as part of an overall policy of good practice. Remember, however, yellow group pupils are conformists not deviants; they do have special needs and these can vary greatly.

It will, of course, in some schools (especially in larger schools) be necessary to amend and/or modify individual pupils and group timetables to enable a suitable amount of time to be found for extra learning support. This process has been greatly facilitated since the Secretary of State's decision in 2000 to allow under-achieving and/or disaffected pupils to be allowed time to be given specialist curriculum support as alternative curriculum approaches for disaffected and under-achieving pupils are now permitted for up to 50 per cent of available learning time. Individual schools will have to make their own decisions on how and where this time can be found from the National Curriculum. A consideration of some alternative curriculum schemes currently in use can be found later in Chapter 11.

A number of schools are currently operating the ideas behind the PSCC scheme without establishing and operating the relevant management panels. Partly, this is done to save time. Clearly, to achieve the best results you need to use the whole package. However, the author is assured by staff in these schools that the scheme can function well without using management panels (see later).

Potential outcomes of the PSCC scheme

Primary schools' benefits

Primary school teachers benefit from the focus on attendance and pupils' learning and progression by the secondary school staff in the following ways:

1 early identification;
2 the introduction of earlier remedial strategies;
3 the refocusing of their own experience and practice and gearing it to the needs of their partner secondary school(s);
4 the parents of the poor attenders and under-achieving pupils becoming much more supportive of both their local primary and comprehensive schools;
5 reducing levels of sibling-related absence;
6 making parents realise the importance of attendance and of not, for example, taking pupils away on holidays during school time;
7 increasing confidence between the primary and the secondary school thereby greatly facilitating the transfer process. In particular, it helps to improve the quality of

precision in the recording of data in primary school records and on school transfer documentation;

8 improving the dialogue between primary and secondary schools year upon year especially as knowledge and expertise increase;
9 ensuring that visits by year 6 pupils and their parents to the local secondary for taster classes become the norm;
10 improving attendance within the feeder primary school – especially in the long term.

Ideally, for primary schools with significant attendance problems of their own – and these numbers are on the increase – the PSCC scheme could be introduced into their schools from year 4 onwards. The earlier the preventative activities take place the better, as the younger the pupil the more receptive they are likely to respond to appropriate intervention strategies.

Benefits for the secondary school

Potential benefits for secondary schools could include:

(a) reducing absenteeism significantly over the duration of the project and beyond. The potential to improve a school's rates of attendance are much greater using longer-term than short-term strategies – although both are, of course, mutually supportive;
(b) the secondary school will gradually inherit fewer truants and other forms of non-attenders in year 7;
(c) gradually reducing the number of truants *per se* in the secondary school;
(d) improving the school's levels of literacy, numeracy, external examination passes and, indirectly, improving behaviour and reducing its side effects, e.g. bullying, hostile peer pressure, etc.;
(e) potential gains in academic and behavioural league table positions;
(f) improved home–school and primary–secondary school liaison;
(g) achieving a better understanding of a school's independent variables amongst the governing body (e.g. pupil intake characteristics);
(h) improving team work throughout the school from top to bottom and engineering a managerial success story;
(i) implementing a successful school change strategy;
(j) raising parental confidence in the local or selected secondary school;
(k) similarly, raising the confidence of the local community in the school;
(l) enhancing the school ethos and internal working climate. Projects like the PSCC scheme can help the internal malaise and disaffection of staff to disappear;
(m) a reduction in the pool of potential truants, non-attenders, and other groups of disaffected pupils as academic standards, pupils' performance and behaviour improves;
(n) the school receiving much more positive rather than negative external publicity;
(o) an under-achieving, low-performing school being turned around to the point it becomes regarded as a 'rising' school.

Disadvantages

In truth, very few! However, there are key initial time and organisational issues to be resolved; a re-reading of Reid (1999 Chapters 9 and 10) on whole-school solutions should help re-focus the mind here and answer some of the more obvious questions. Nevertheless, it is worth making a few points.

Yes, managing the project will take time and effort. But, it should be worth it in terms of the school's rising external profile and staff morale. There are a lot of potential avenues of financial support for schools to receive grants or additional funds to help them to undertake this work. For example, the Social Inclusion Pupil Support Standards Fund alone received a total of £174 million a year in 2001 administered through LEAs in England. The Excellence in Cities programme is another potential source of income. So is the £450 million Children's Fund while the Connexions Service offers advice for 13 to 19-year-olds and is intended to improve staying-on rates. In addition, schools which succeed in cutting truancy in challenging circumstances will have the chance to win a 'Truancy Buster' award of up to £10,000. The first 'Truancy Buster' awards were made in early 2001.

In 2001, of the £174 million in the Social Inclusion Pupil Support Standards Fund, £137 million is going directly to schools to help them tackle truancy and poor behaviour; £10 million will support the establishment of new Learning Support Units to ensure that disruptive pupils are taken out of the classroom. The DfES's aim is to have one thousand such units by 2002. Local authorities are receiving a share of £36 million to provide co-ordinated authority-wide support in tackling bad behaviour and providing meaningful education to excluded pupils. A further £1 million will help finance national projects to tackle truancy. Many, if not most, large primary and secondary schools already have learning mentor support and this is gradually increasing to smaller schools and to rural areas which have similar needs.

In this context, it is worth noting that by 2002, all excluded pupils must be offered full-time education. Some LEAs are already making a lot of positive progress in reducing their number of excluded pupils. Compared with 1997, there are now 1,000 more places and 250 more teachers at off-site pupil referral units (PRUs) which cater for excluded pupils. And working in a PRU is really demanding work.

Thus, there is both financial and therefore, potential staffing support to facilitate schools to undertake meaningful projects on improving attendance. So, time and resource constraints should not be irredeemable. Determined schools can succeed and make significant changes when there is a sufficient will. Clearly, however, schools should not undertake a major project on attendance if it is not one of their major problems.

The other big concern of many teachers is that the scheme could utilise negative theory such as labelling. Some teachers feel that by putting a pupil into a 'red' or 'blue' group can adversely affect their pupils' self-image. In theory, badly handled, this is possible. However, the way the project is introduced and managed is key to preventing any stigma from occurring. The whole emphasis should be on: (a) self-improvement, and (b) school improvement.

The project should be 'sold' on the basis of providing *all* pupils with the opportunity to achieve their optimum long-term potential. Similarly, the scheme can be sold to parents. What do all parents want for their children? All caring parents want the best for their children. Ideally, they wish their children to do at least as well as themselves and hopefully, a lot better! This is no less true of the parents of truants and under-achieving pupils as well as anyone else – although you may not always think so given the circumstances in which such parents and teachers often meet!

When a school can assure parents that if their child behaves and attends school regularly, the staff will ensure he or she achieves his or her maximum educational potential – and the parent(s) buy in to this message – there is every chance of parental–school relationships being successful and both parent(s) and the school pulling in the same direction – for the good of the child. Too often, schools are unable to get this positive message across and become defensive with parents. This is precisely why long-term strategic approaches like the PSCC scheme provide real hope for school change and school improvement practice in the future.

PSCC scheme Model 2

A longer term PSCC scheme Model 2 could be introduced within a whole LEA or designated geographical area. This could be achieved by introducing the scheme into local primary schools at year 4 and continuing it through to year 11 in all secondary schools. To date, no experimentation has taken place on this idea although, at the time of writing, it is under consideration by some schools and LEAs.

PSCC scheme Model 3

It has been suggested that the PSCC Model could be introduced into secondary schools from year 8 onwards with selections made at the end of year 7. In the author's view, while this is possible, it is not ideal as it is much too late to do so. But, having a staged scheme is better than not having a scheme at all.

At regional and local one-day courses, a range of alternative schemes based on the author's ideas have been put forward by delegates. A number of these are being tried in individual schools in a practical rather than staged experimental manner. Therefore, it is difficult to be certain what the real benefits of some of these hybrids really are!

PSCC scheme Model 4

Some schools have adapted the PSCC scheme into a different format (see Figure 7.2). At one school, for example, the staff decided to equate the selection processes for red group pupils with those making fewer than 70 per cent attendances. Pupils in the blue group are those making between 70 and 80 per cent attendance. Pupils in the yellow group are those making between 80 and 90 per cent attendance. Finally, pupils in the green group make more than 90 per cent attendance.

In this approach, the emphasis is largely on attendance. Progression issues are secondary. The aim of the scheme is to move pupils upwards to higher attending groups as soon as possible. Thus, the aim is to move all red group pupils into the blue group following appropriate intervention strategies adopted by the school and the education welfare service. Then, ideally, moving pupils from the blue group into the yellow group as attendance improves further.

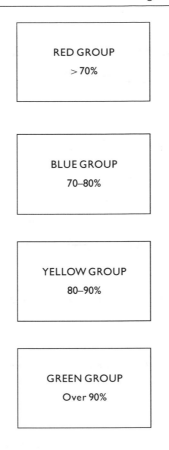

Figure 7.2 Adapting the PSCC scheme in a numerical way.

PSCC scheme Model 5

Some schools have changed the original concept and the colour-coded labels to suit their own convenience, as the example in Figure 7.3 shows.

Case study on East Worthing (project to improve attendance): The RAG scheme

Background

The Pupil Retention Unit introduced a version of the PSCC scheme into local schools using the colour coding for attendance. The project was broadened to include attendance across a family of schools including two first and two middle schools. The idea was to improve relationships between the school, its parents and non-attenders. The timescale for the introduction of the project was as follows:

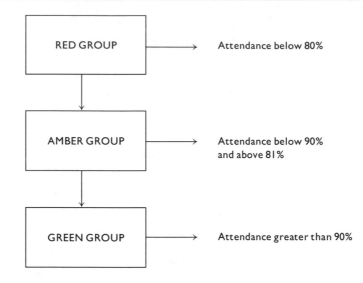

Figure 7.3 The Davison model of the PSCC scheme (the RAG project).

January 2001
Meeting between Davison CE High School for Girls (Technology College) staff and the Education Welfare Service who pledge support for scheme.

February 2001

(a) Family of local schools held a joint meeting. All schools were keen to promote idea and all wished to be involved.

(b) The project was set up under the title the 'RAG' project.
The red group consisted of pupils whose attendance was below 80 per cent. The amber group was for pupils whose attendance was below 90 per cent and above 80 per cent. The green group was for pupils whose attendance was greater than 90 per cent.

(c) The project was then introduced at Davison to the staff. Figure 7.3 shows how year groups 8 and 9 were used to select pupils' group identities.

(d) Colour coding was then introduced by year 9 tutors to parents at a review meeting. The response was highly positive from the parents who appreciated the project's clarity.

(e) The headteacher at Davison met with two parents of truants with behavioural problems. Both agreed to join a 'Parenting Support Group' to be chaired by the principal education welfare officer.

(f) Social services were invited to support the project. Their response was enthusiastic. The project is forming links between all the caring agencies which will include the possibility of work shadowing across all three groups (teaching staff/EWO/social services) in a joined-up professional approach.

(g) The local educational psychologist has become involved with the project. He has agreed to:

(i) meet with parents in schools;

(ii) present intervention strategies to improve parenting skills in relation to attendance.

(h) Early signs from the project are distinctly encouraging. The school has already started to improve its attendance and normal year patterns of attendance.

The Davison scheme is interesting because the school set up its scheme based on the author's work but without his direct input. It suited their needs. It was introduced during a year and not at the start of the year. The colour-coded concept was adapted to suit their individual needs. It is a multi-agency project.

Significantly, the pupils *like* the colour-coding scheme. There is strong competition between them to improve and to move 'up' groups which facilitates and motivates improved attendance and attainment. The school operates the system alongside a positive rewards scheme to encourage its pupils (e.g. prizes for most improved attendance). Contrary to expectations, the colour-coded labels are interpreted positively by pupils and parents alike. The school considers there to be no negative connotations from using the labels, only positive benefits.

Other schools and LEAs are also currently adapting and utilising the PSCC scheme for their own purposes. For example, Blackpool LEA Education Welfare Service began its own scheme in September 2001 under the direction of their Principal Education Welfare Officer. A number of schools and other LEAs are beginning to establish their own PSCC projects managed by themselves, and the number of users of the scheme is growing very quickly.

PSCC scheme Model 6

Chamberlayne Park School

Chamberlayne Park School goes one stage further. It utilises its colour-coding scheme for both attendance and behaviour monitoring and adds in extra coding categories.

The school is a co-educational comprehensive on the south-eastern edge of a large city in the south of England; there are 850 pupils on roll; 23 per cent of these are on free school meals; 51 per cent of the pupils are on the special needs register. The school draws its pupils mainly from two feeder primary schools. Its location is in an area which has considerable social deprivation. The adult unemployment levels for the city are also high. The school's average daily attendance hovers around 90 per cent.

The school has a variety of attendance strategies in place. These include:

(a) weekly letters being sent home for unexplained absence along with half-termly progress reports providing pupils' attendance returns;

(b) 'truancy call' which focuses on first day response for one year at a time facilitated by a computerised register system;

(c) utilising half-termly rewards schemes in a special rewards assembly when the pupils receive certificates and commendations for attendance and credits.

The school has raised its attendance target to 93.5 per cent. To facilitate this rise, pupils have been identified into the following five bands in order to monitor their attendance. These are: Attendance monitoring: Pupil identification bands.

Authorised absence
School target for September 2002 = 93.5 per cent

Gold   =   100 per cent
Green   =   99.9–94 per cent
Yellow =   93.9 per cent–88 per cent
Blue   =   87.9 per cent–80 per cent
Red   =   79.9 per cent and below

Actions
Review each half-term and parent informed of band.

Gold   =   Letters and certificates, pen each term, drinking mug and free visit at end of each year, £50 vouchers and watch at end of year 11.
Green   =   Letters and certificates, free visit at end of each year.
Yellow =   Letter of encouragement and interview with tutor and head of year each half term.
Blue   =   EWO contact, parents invited to meet head of year, EWO and SMT. EWO visit at home and formal caution if did not attend meeting.
Red   =   Parent visited at home by EWO to arrange meeting time in school. Meeting confirmed in formal letter sent by registered mail. Formal Education Planning Review with headteacher, governor and LEA Officer. Parents receive formal warning of prosecution.

Unauthorised absence
School target for September 2002 = 0.7 per cent

Action
Head of year ensures parents are contacted by phone within 24 hours and in writing within 48 hours of not receiving an explanation of any absence. This is done through the Guidance Secretary. Phone calls logged and letters copied. EWO if no response.

Behaviour

Green   =   consistently good behaviour
Yellow =   occasionally breaks code of conduct
Blue   =   frequently or seriously breaks code of conduct
Red   =   at risk of exclusion or returning from an exclusion

Action
Review each half term and parent informed of band.

Gold   =   In June of each year all staff will be asked to nominate pupils from the Green Band to be given a Gold Award. This award is for pupils who demonstrate exceptional behaviour throughout the year. In addition to gaining the awards in the Green Band, Gold Award recipients will receive a special certificate and gift vouchers.

Green = Letters, certificates and credits, free visit at end of each year.

Yellow = Letter of encouragement and interview with tutor each half term.

Blue = Parents invited to meet head of year to plan the way forward. Home–school agreement re-signed. EWO visit at home if parent did not attend meeting. Pupil put on the school's behaviour register and monitored.

Red = A meeting will be arranged with parents, school and appropriate support agencies. Confirmation will be sent to parents by registered mail. The meeting will be to agree a plan of action to improve the pupil's behaviour.

Using the PSCC plan to prevent exclusion

The same colour-coded scheme can be adapted by schools to attempt to reduce their exclusion rates and/or behaviour or bullying problems. The example of exclusion is now used to show how. Since 1998, there has been a fierce national debate about the perceived and actual rising number of school exclusions. After 1997, the New Labour government tried hard to ensure that pupils were not excluded from schools unnecessarily. For example, prior to 1 April 2000, a significant number of pupils were excluded from schools on the grounds of truancy alone; highly counterproductive! This is no longer allowed. The reasons for exclusion and other related issues are considered in *Tackling Truancy in Schools* (Reid, 2000, Unit 20).

Headteachers and professional organisations became concerned that schools were being told to go 'soft' on wilful and destructive conduct including threatening behaviour. After much debate, by mid-2000, it became clear that a compromise position was being reached. Schools were advised that headteachers could always exclude pupils for serious offences and should always do so for serious health and safety issues, e.g. serious assault of a member of staff. However, the DfES asked schools and LEAs to consider a pupil's longer-term interests in their decision-making processes because so many excluded pupils were failing to receive alternative education; in some cases months after being excluded or, in extreme circumstances, never again. Although the DfES agreed that in cases of violent conduct pupils should automatically be excluded, they suggested a re-think on certain less serious, but often persistent categories. It is in this context that utilising the same colour-coded formula as in the PSCC scheme can be particularly meaningful.

The operation of the scheme is shown in Figure 7.4. Red cards are immediately given for offences which lead to automatic exclusion. There are two red card offences. The first is for extreme violent conduct. The second is for persistent serious abuse of school rules on the third occasion; the first two having warranted either a blue or yellow card and both offences having been recorded and the formal warnings being notified to pupil and parent(s).

The introduction of the blue and yellow cards provides a 'buffer' zone between immediate exclusion and a firm warning; a final warning in the case of the blue card. This approach provides schools with some flexibility to give pupils a second chance after a cooling-off period. Some schools may decide – and it is sometimes sensible to do so – to accompany yellow and blue cards not only with a firm warning letter but also a period of time off school to calm down or cool off. Such periods of time can vary from

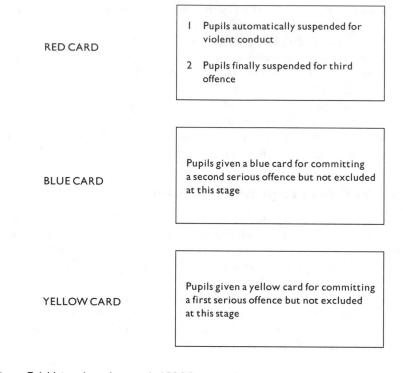

RED CARD

1   Pupils automatically suspended for violent conduct

2   Pupils finally suspended for third offence

BLUE CARD

Pupils given a blue card for committing a second serious offence but not excluded at this stage

YELLOW CARD

Pupils given a yellow card for committing a first serious offence but not excluded at this stage

Figure 7.4 Using the colour-coded PSCC system for exclusion.

the remainder of the day to a full week away from school from the date the offence took place. In extreme cases, a cooling-off period of up to twenty-one days may be appropriate. Cooling-off periods allow all parties to mentally calm down after the initial misdemeanour. If used for exclusion, the scheme should be well publicised to all parents and pupils of the school. Before committing any serious offence, they will both be fully aware of the consequences and of the school's unwillingness to tolerate unacceptable behaviour.

Some schools might prefer to make temporary suspensions last longer (perhaps a full week or more) for blue (second) offences than for yellow cards. It is crucial that this system of agreed penalties should be approved by all teachers in a school at an appropriate staff development event. One school in Watford found that the introduction of this system reduced exclusion rates by approximately two-thirds during the first year of its operation.

Theale Green Community School, an 11 to 18 school in West Berkshire, has by using 'staged' approaches to exclusion not excluded a single pupil for six years. It supports this approach in the following ways:

(a) by establishing a social inclusion unit. Up to six pupils can be in this unit at any time;
(b) by establishing better short-term links with appropriate local off-site units;
(c) by establishing appropriate reintegration strategies for absentee pupils;

(d) making use of videos and drama sessions on exclusion; pupils acting out their frustrations.

The school clears out pupils from its social inclusion unit a month before the end of the summer term in preparation for the new year.

Another school in Merton has a teacher in charge, supported by non-teaching assistants and parents involved in their social inclusion unit. This school believes their unit works effectively because they have appropriately trained staff expertise. Another LEA uses out-of-school panels for primary and secondary pupils with serious attendance and/or behaviour problems. Considerable experimentation is beginning to take place within some schools involving parents sitting-in at the same lessons as their disruptive pupils. This option may provide significant gains for schools to employ and lead to a whole list of related short and long-term benefits. There is a need to experiment and to fully research this concept.

Summary

Establishing the PSCC scheme needs careful thought. It requires a whole-school approach in the fullest meaning of the term. Parents need to be briefed on the scheme as part of the preliminary process before their pupils transfer to the secondary school. So do all the pupils. The 'caring' message given to the parents and the pupils and *how* this is put across are crucial to favourable long-term outcomes.

Ideally, schools will utilise a few short-term approaches alongside this major long-term strategic initiative. Choose three or four of the best short-term strategies outlined in Chapters 3 to 6. Three of the most popular tend to be first day contact, mentoring (however this is done) and appropriate alternative curriculum support. However, whatever works – use it. The causes of non-attendance are so varied and diverse that finding similar solutions which work effectively in every school situation is not easy.

Some schools need to raise the profile of attendance on their agendas. In far too many schools, attendance is too low on their school development plans. Variations in practice abound. One deputy head at a conference held in Bristol in March 2001 stated that she had moved from a school which did everything to encourage attendance to another where the staff never even considered it an issue. Yet her new school had absence rates twice those of her former institution.

The PSCC scheme gives schools a simple and convenient way of raising the profile of attendance in a caring and empathetic manner. The potential gains of the scheme far outweigh the disadvantages as the benefits offer schools and their pupils far more than a simple reduction in non-attendance and truancy. Adopted and set up correctly, it provides a total package. We will now consider variations on the ideas behind the PSCC concept utilised in a different format in the next chapter.

Chapter 8

Long-term strategic approaches II

This chapter focuses on an alternative longer-term strategy for combating truancy and school absenteeism. It is called the SSTG scheme. Theoretically, the three parts to this panel-based scheme can be used independently or treated collectively to form one total integrated scheme. The colour-coded system discussed in the previous chapter can also be adapted into the scheme (see Figure 8.3).

Currently, some schools operating the SSTG only utilise the governors' attendance panel and the attendance support panel (stages one and two). But it works best when all three stages are used as with the PSCC scheme in Chapter 7. Ideally, those schools endeavouring to eradicate absenteeism by using panel-approaches should employ the use of a governors' attendance panel, an attendance support panel and a progress review panel in an integrated manner (see Figure 8.1). As with the PSCC scheme in Chapter 7, the labels used are the author's own terms. However, a number of schools now use different labels based on their own experiences. In fact, it is getting extremely difficult to keep up with all the new terminology being used by schools around the country.

SSTG stands for secondary school three group scheme. It differs from the PSCC scheme in being panel-based rather than using colour-coded categories.

The SSTG scheme

Unlike the PSCC scheme, the SSTG system starts once the pupils have transferred to their secondary school. Some schools however, do select the panel-based groups from data supplied by their feeder primary schools. Others make their own selections after the pupils have been in the secondary school for up to, for example, six weeks or even a term. Again, establishing the groups, advising the parents and pupils on the scheme and its potential long-term benefits are crucial to any outcomes.

The PSCC scheme utilises a three-tier approach. The governors' attendance panel is used for the most serious attendance cases including persistent truants. The attendance support panel is established for less serious cases. The progress review panel is used for pupils whose profiles suggest they have potential to graduate to the other two panels-based groups either because of their specific learning needs or behavioural difficulties and/or needs. We will now consider each of these three stages in turn.

Governors' attendance panel

Some schools currently employ a process whereby a governors' attendance panel is utilised to deal with persistent school absentees and their parent(s). Ideally, the attendance panel will include a governor often selected on a rotational basis from three or more nominated volunteers. The remaining members of the panel will include the headteacher, head of year, education welfare officer and, in some schools, the head of special needs and attendance support teacher co-ordinator.

Some schools manage this process in such a way as to deliberately exclude governors from the panel. In these cases, the panel is sometimes retitled or known as the headteachers' attendance panel or the school attendance panel. The membership is often composed of the headteacher or deputy head in charge of school attendance issues, relevant heads of year, education welfare officer and/or the head of special needs and attendance support teacher/co-ordinator, and possibly, even learning mentors. Whether schools utilise a governors' attendance panel or a headteachers' attendance panel is to some degree a matter of preference. By using governors, a school is bringing local pressure (the community aspect) to bear on non-attenders and their parent(s), thereby reinforcing the school's determination to eradicate persistent absenteeism. The same is true – but to a lesser extent – when utilising a headteacher's attendance panel. It shows that a head is serious about improving attendance in his or her school. It is all a matter of choice. Both can work equally effectively. It all depends upon your individual school's situation and, possibly, location and intake.

However, some schools slightly downgrade the process by utilising attendance panels chaired either by a deputy head or a head of year. Some schools inexplicably appear to exclude education welfare officers from the panel, which is counterproductive – to say the least. Some schools prefer 'hard' approaches; others softer options. The author prefers the former in attendance cases. It is better to give a clear rather than a mixed message.

The process for selecting pupils and their parent(s) to meet the governors' attendance panel (or its equivalent) is as follows. Either the education welfare officer or a senior member of staff with overall responsibility for attendance will sift through the school's registers. Pupils with persistent or erratic attendance will be selected to meet panel members. The panel will normally hold meetings with absentees and their parents up to twice a term. Normally, the panel will hold a preliminary meeting(s) to familiarise themselves with the pupils' profiles. These profiles will usually be drawn up by gathering a combination of evidence from such people as the education welfare officer, form tutor, head of year and head of special needs as appropriate. A list of parents is then drawn up and letters are sent to parent(s) inviting them to attend the meeting. The practice will, of course, have been fully outlined both in a school's policy document on attendance (see Reid 1999, Chapter 9, and 2000, Unit 12) as well as in preliminary information sent to potential year 7 pupils and their parents.

At the panel meeting, the education welfare officer or nominee will provide the parent(s) and pupil with their recent attendance figures and any other relevant information. In cases where the parent(s) do not attend the panel meeting for any reason, the pupil should attend on his or her own. Subsequently, a letter summarising the outcome of the meeting should be sent to the parents' home.

During the meeting, the panel should try to establish the reason(s) for the pupil's poor attendance. An agreed plan should then be devised to support the pupil in school, particularly the pupil's learning support needs. Following the meeting, a letter should be sent to the parental home summarising the outcome of the discussion. In one school in

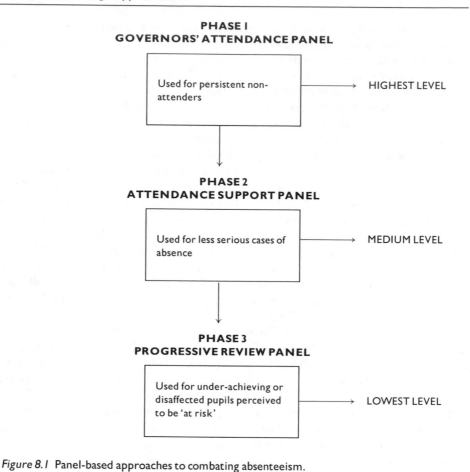

Figure 8.1 Panel-based approaches to combating absenteeism.

South Wales, the aim of the panel is to interview the parents of pupils whose attendance has fallen below 75 per cent without an acceptable reason (Reynolds, 1996).

Governors' attendance panels tend to use the following procedure. A letter is sent to the parent(s) or guardian inviting them to attend the meeting to discuss their child's allowance and academic progress with a pre-stamped addressed envelope and reply slip to be returned to the school. This letter is usually sent approximately three weeks before the panel meeting. If no reply is received within a reasonable timescale, a second letter is sent by recorded delivery approximately one week before the date of the panel meeting. This letter simply confirms the date and time of the meeting. Some schools now prefer to make these arrangements using an attendance support secretary; often the same person who looks after first day responses.

When parents do not attend panel meetings and fail to fulfil their other obligations to their child or school, the panel will normally decide to invoke prosecution procedures. Sometimes schools will issue a final warning first. However, unless there are exceptional circumstances, schools which begin prosecution procedures should see them through to their logical conclusion. Too many schools threaten or start prosecution proceedings only to withdraw them. This final deferment is itself sometimes then undermined to the point that both parent(s) and pupil sometimes feel untouchable.

Attendance support panel

An attendance support panel is covened for use with less serious cases of absence. They are increasingly used to interview pupils with histories of specific lesson absence, post-registration truancy and parental-condoned absenteeism. They can be particularly effect-ive for use with those pupils whose absence is a manifestation of more serious personal, social, psychological or behavioural problems. It is for this reason that a head of year or pastoral co-ordinator and special needs co-ordinator serve on the panel as well as the attendance co-ordinator and/or education welfare officer. Form tutors can also be used for this purpose. The attendance support panel is generally chaired by a deputy head with overall responsibility for school attendance matters. Attendance support panels can be equated with the blue group in Chapter 7.

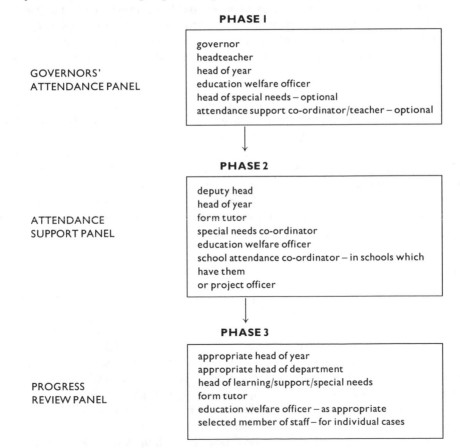

PHASE I

GOVERNORS'
ATTENDANCE PANEL

governor
headteacher
head of year
education welfare officer
head of special needs – optional
attendance support co-ordinator/teacher – optional

PHASE 2

ATTENDANCE
SUPPORT PANEL

deputy head
head of year
form tutor
special needs co-ordinator
education welfare officer
school attendance co-ordinator – in schools which
have them
or project officer

PHASE 3

PROGRESS
REVIEW PANEL

appropriate head of year
appropriate head of department
head of learning/support/special needs
form tutor
education welfare officer – as appropriate
selected member of staff – for individual cases

NB Select a maximum of three or four staff from the above lists. Using too many staff is counterproductive and can 'deter' parent(s) and pupils alike.

Figure 8.2 Key staff who could be involved in the panel processes.

Normally, attendance support panels interview pupils on their own. In cases where attendance either subsequently deteriorates or causes greater concern, the panel can decide to interview parents either with or without their child. Alternatively, the panel can refer the matter upwards to the governors' attendance panel for their action.

The arrangements for these meetings are normally made within schools and within school time. By contrast, governors' attendance panel meetings are usually staggered between early afternoon and evening to enable single parents, parent(s) with younger children or parent(s) who work unsociable hours to attend (see Chapter 7: arrangements for red group pupils).

The duration and frequency of the meetings are up to the individual school, and are dependent upon such issues as time pressures, and the demand and complexity of pupils' cases. Some schools organise these meetings on a twice termly or termly basis. Others prefer to tackle individual cases on a monthly or more frequent basis. The frequency of meetings is less important than their structure and content so long as you get the correct message across.

The meetings are partly aimed at prevention, partly at progression and learning support needs and finally, partly at ensuring the pupil's overall profile for support is being met. From the school's point of view, the pupil should guarantee to attend school regularly. The attendance support panel should inform each pupil that regular attendance is the most essential pre-requisite in making satisfactory academic progress (Scottish Council for Research in Education Study, 1995).

The attendance support panel may often advise that a pupil requires individual or different curriculum support needs from the average regular attender. In this way, there is a clear link with the work of the progress review panel (see Figure 8.1) and ideally, there will be some continuity in membership between the two panels. As individual case pupils' attendance improves, it is likely that they will continue to be monitored by the progress review panel rather than by the attendance support panel.

Careful records of each meeting should be maintained along with agreed action taken. These records should be transferred to pupils' progression files to ensure continuation following any staff or organisational changes within the school.

Progress review panel

Progress review panels can be equated with the yellow groups in Chapter 7. The aim of progress review panels is preventative. The intention should be to endeavour to ensure that potentially at risk and/or under-achieving pupils do not deteriorate into more serious cases of disaffection, absenteeism or under-achievement. The work of the progress review panel is partly diagnostic. It is endeavouring to determine *why* a pupil is not being successful at school, *what* can be done to help the pupil succeed and/or improve and *when* is the best time to provide the support to the pupil that is most appropriate.

The work of the pupil review panel can be utilised to provide re-integrative support to those pupils who have been away from school for a period of time (truants, family holidays, bereavement, illness, etc.) and who need help to catch up with their work in order to prevent them from dropping out again. For schools which use a pupil review panel approach a reading of Chapter 10 on alternative curriculum strategies is essential.

The membership and organisation of the progress review panel can be much more flexible than for the governors' attendance panel and for the attendance support panel which rely on much greater forward planning and structural support. It is suggested that membership of the progress review panel is drawn from appropriate heads of department, the head of learning support and/or special needs, the education welfare officer (as appropriate), and selected members of staff (e.g. form tutors, subject teachers, etc.). In some schools, the form tutor is an automatic member. However, much depends upon *how* schools use their form tutors as practices vary nationwide. In an ideal scenario, the form tutor can be at least as important as the head of year and/or head of a subject department.

Increasingly, some schools are now utilising the yellow group or progress review panel approach with their learning mentorship schemes. For example, one school in outer London ensures that every pupil who is interviewed by a progress review panel is matched with a learning support mentor.

In another example, one pupil received national publicity under the headline, 'Mentor turns tearaway into star pupil'. A classroom rebel had been transformed into a budding newspaper journalist – thanks to a government scheme. Jasmine Stewart, 14, a pupil at Firth Park Community College in Sheffield, was one of the first pupils to have had appointed a 'full-time mentor' to support her needs under the new plan. The teenager admitted her behaviour had previously been 'very bad' and she had been a bit of a rebel. She would shout at teachers and received eleven different formal reprimands in one month for her outbursts. 'My attitude towards the staff and probably the class wasn't very good', she said. 'My work was going downhill.' But when the school appointed three mentors – who work with problem pupils to improve their behaviour – the transformation was amazing.

Jasmine's mentor, Simon Barth, said: 'Jasmine doesn't respond well to negative attention – but does respond to praise.' Simon talked to Jasmine about her interests and found out she loves English. He then signed her up for the Children's Express scheme, which lets pupils write articles for their local paper. Now she is writing for *The Star* newspaper in Sheffield – having researched articles on Christmas shopping and the legalisation of cannabis. Louise Parry, the school's deputy head, said: 'Mentors can do things to boost a pupil's confidence that a teacher just doesn't have time to do'.

The organisation and duration of the progress review meeting *per se* are *ad hoc* dependent upon each individual pupil's needs and set of personal circumstances. Normally, pupils are monitored on their own. However, feedback can be given to parents either at parents' evenings, at specialist meetings for parents of those pupils who are being mentored, by letter, or on such occasions as the school and parent(s) agree and suit one another. Written records should be maintained of all meetings including a note on agreed action(s) taken. These records should be transferred to a pupil's progress file or record of achievement.

As pupils become more successful, they can be taken out of the monitoring processes for the progress review panel. Conversely, if and when pupils' attendance or progress deteriorate, they can be referred to the attendance support panel and/or the governors' attendance panel as appropriate. Some schools adapt the scheme to include specialist group tuition for each panel level during school time in the same way as discussed in Chapter 7 for the PSCC scheme.

Differences and similarities between PSCC and SSTG schemes

There are both similarities and differences between the PSCC system and the three-tier panel approaches, SSTG scheme, considered in this chapter. First, both use three-tier approaches in their ideal mode. However, both can be adapted into single or two-tier approaches dependent upon a school's overall problems, resources, scale of needs, pupils' ability intake and social class distribution levels.

Whereas, however, the red, blue or yellow group pupils are selected in year 6, the selections for the governors' attendance panel, attendance support panel and progress review panel are entirely made within the secondary school. The PSCC colour-coded scheme works best when a secondary school receives a constant intake from local primary schools year upon year. For those schools which do not receive regular intakes from local primaries, the panel approaches described in this chapter are probably more satisfactory. However, some of the same principles apply. For example, the earlier the pupils are selected for the three groups the better. Ideally, the process starts as soon as possible in year 7. Similarly, parents and pupils are notified of the school's strategy to prevent absence and learning difficulties occurring prior to entry and it is constantly reinforced thereafter. Also, as preventative measures begin to bite, pupils can be transferred from the governors' attendance panel down through the attendance support panel to the progress review panel and, hopefully, eventually out of the specialist monitoring exercises altogether.

The colour-coded system used in the PSCC scheme can be adapted for the panel approach described in this chapter. This is a simple process (see Figure 8.3). Indeed, to keep the processes more manageable, the same terms ('red', 'blue', 'yellow') can be used by the staff rather than more cumbersome labels. Therefore, the governors' attendance panel equates with 'red'. The attendance support panel is equivalent to blue. And, the progress review panel group can be labelled yellow. A lot of staff in schools prefer using the colour-coded labels rather than the designated panel terms.

During the author's visits to schools, LEAs, EAZs and during regional staff development events, colleagues have often been asked to undertake an exercise differentiating between the two schemes described in Chapter 7 and here. It is surprising how views vary. Sometimes, respondents strongly prefer the PSCC scheme to the SSTG panel approach. On other occasions, the reverse is true. Sometimes, delegates are evenly split or there is a slight majority in favour of one or the other. It was especially surprising at a one-day conference held in Leeds when delegates generally stated a preference for the PSCC system which caused another teacher to stand up and defend her school's practice. She vigorously defended the panel approach used by her school which they had commenced following a one-day training event organised by the author in 1997. She indicated that attendance levels had been transformed within her school and they would never discontinue it in favour of any other system – however user friendly! So it may be up to you to decide – if you are in a position to choose.

Being objective, my own view is that the PSCC scheme is more easy to manage provided all the key variables are in place. As 35 per cent of non-attendance cases now begin within the primary school phase (Reid, 1999), selecting pupils for the red, blue and yellow groups should be a relatively straightforward issue. Also, all the research evidence is that the earlier the intervention (and prevention techniques), the greater

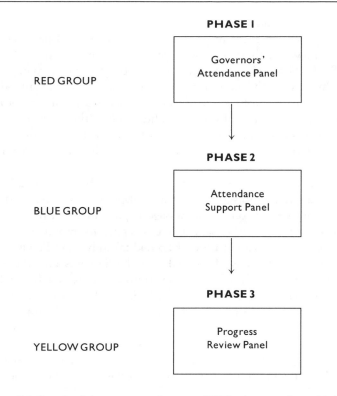

PHASE I

RED GROUP

Governors'
Attendance Panel

PHASE 2

BLUE GROUP

Attendance
Support Panel

PHASE 3

YELLOW GROUP

Progress
Review Panel

Figure 8.3 Standardising processes between PSCC scheme and panel-based SSTG approach.

the chance of success (Reid, 2000). For too many schools, EWOs and LEAs react to persistent absenteeism far too late; often when pupils are in their mid-teens and the families are immune to remedial or court strategies. Intervention works best when pupils are young enough to respect people and processes and wish to improve. Intervention fails when strategies are implemented so late in a pupil's career that chances of significant change (e.g. abrasive conduct) is restricted.

In many LEAs this is not possible perhaps because the structure of schooling within the area is complex and/or multi-layered (e.g. 9–13 schools, 11–14 schools, etc.). In circumstances in which secondary schools do not control their own intake variables, then the SSTG panel approach is easier to set up and control.

Also, the PSCC scheme is dependent upon obtaining accurate input data for year 6 pupils from primary schools. The induction session with parents is also critical. The induction session with parents can be facilitated by using a logical social inclusion agreement (see how to present the case to parents in Chapter 7).

The staff should argue therefore, that provided the pupils attend regularly (supported by their parent(s)), the school will guarantee that their children will receive the best possible education and will be in a position long-term to obtain a career befitting their expertise and knowledge. Most parents will buy into this argument – properly presented – especially (and some of you may be surprised at this point!) those parents who have known genuine hardship as a result of frequent bouts of job changing, unemployment and marital disharmony and conflict often caused by living at poverty levels partly due to their own failure or under-achievement at school. Even truants and persistent absentees will admit that if they had their time again at school, the one thing they would never do is truant (Reid, 1985). This is not only true of truants but of young offenders (Reid, 1986). It is why second chance schools as in the Leeds experiment offer such potential for long-term benefits – irrespective of whether your politics are left or right!

Understandably, the setting up of links with families is often the most sensitive area for discussion with teachers and LEAs in the establishment of new 'truancy' projects. Clearly, this is partially based on the experiences of staff in difficult, often inner-city, multi-racial and high truancy schools.

Nevertheless, it is surprising how some supposedly anti-school, anti-authoritarian parents will change when they visibly perceive their offspring doing well and making good progress. Often, it all depends on *how* a message is presented and the evidence to support that the school meant what it said and is keeping its promises. I can well remember Janine, a mother in her early thirties, who had taken her son Shaun out of his previous two schools because she was dissatisfied with his progress and the teachers' wrong attitude towards him. In the event, after transferring to Olchfa School in Swansea, her attitude changed entirely when her son's SATS showed he had caught up two whole years in his first term. She was delighted. Shaun suddenly started reading novels at home for the first time and his school behaviour and attendance went from strength to strength. Not long afterwards, Janine – herself a school failure – enrolled at the local FE college initially to take some GCSEs. Later, she obtained an A level and a HND and is now working as a classroom support tutor for pupils with behavioural needs within a pupil referral unit.

Nevertheless, in my own professional development exercises with teachers, it is surprising how school–home communication remains the number one issue needing to be resolved according to staff in schools. And, this is consistently true *throughout* the United Kingdom. Even with the SSTG panel scheme, the establishment of appropriate home–school communication is of as much importance as the pupil selection process itself and the general administration of the project within schools. Schools need to have the parents on *their* side; especially parents of under-achieving and disaffected pupils like regular absentees.

In staff development exercises, teachers often perceive the SSTG panel approach to be more 'pupil threatening' than the PSCC scheme. This should not be the case. However, it may be the use of the members of the governing body and headteacher on the panels which conveys this message. If so, it is hardly a wrong one! In both schemes, the school has the option of prosecution open to it in extreme cases.

Some schools have found that emphasising the individual and group support to pupils through the progress review panels (especially in year 7, and between years 7 to 9) can have a significant beneficial effect on reducing longer-term absenteeism. In theory, in both approaches, the more effective the implementation of the scheme, there should be fewer numbers of persistent absentees in the red group or governors' attendance panel, the longer the processes continue. For example, in theory, in year 5 of the scheme there should be fewer persistent truants in the scheme than at its inception. Otherwise the scheme is not working properly. This is precisely the opposite to what currently happens in most schools as absence tends to increase in years 10 and 11 from years 7 and 8.

As with the PSCC scheme, the panel approach can be implemented gradually and progressively within a school (see Figure 8.4) and be cross-referenced with Figure 7.1. In this mode, the three phases would be introduced in year 7 in the first instance. Then, introduced into years 7 and 8. Then, in the third year, reach years 7, 8 and 9. Then, years 7, 8, 9 and 10. Finally, all five years between years 7 to 11. Thus, as with the PSCC scheme, the panel approach can be used to change unfavourable school climates which promote non-attendance, poor behaviour and low academic achievement. Such a progressive introduction is ideal for fresh-start schools, within EAZs, new schools or those which have long-term histories of absenteeism (see case study of Honeywell School in Chapter 2).

It is my own opinion that this longer-term strategic approach is the best way to organise the panel scheme. In fact, in school change projects in which the author has

YEAR 1 OF PROJECT

Introduce Governors' Attendance Panel, Attendance Support Panel and Progress Review Panel with year 7

YEAR 2 OF PROJECT

Organise three panels with years 7 and 8

YEAR 3 OF PROJECT

Organise three panels with years 7, 8 and 9

YEAR 4 OF PROJECT

Organise three panels with years 7, 8, 9 and 10

YEAR 5 OF PROJECT

Organise three panels with years 7–11

Figure 8.4 Longer-term strategic approaches utilising the panel scheme.

acted either as a consultant or change agent, it appears to bring the most effective results. Moreover, as with the PSCC scheme, schools seem to improve their internal and academic results alongside their attendance rates. In fact, the knock-on positive benefits of the scheme are almost too numerous to list. These include:

- improved teacher–pupil relationships and vice versa;
- better home–school contact;
- improved pupils' behaviour;
- less, if any, bullying;
- raising of pupils' academic self-concepts and general levels of self esteem;
- more pride in the school (a feeling generated amongst teachers and pupils alike);
- improved reading and numeracy scores;
- making a contribution towards a managerial success story.

As with the PSCC or this SSTG panel scheme, it is best introduced using whole-school approaches. This is merely good practice. It is especially important that *all* the staff in the school – from the head downwards – are involved in the planning, inception and monitoring work involved in the project (see Reid, 1999, Chapter 9 and Reid, 2000, Units 10 and 11 for guidance on how to implement whole-school policies on attendance successfully).

In the final analysis, schools can adapt, modify and use the best features of the PSCC and SSTG panel schemes to suit themselves and their own needs. What really matters, is having an effective long-term attendance strategy in place, which is consistent, acts both as a deterrent and in a positive, remedial and therapeutic manner. And the schemes are easy to understand and implement. And they work. Moreover, schools get one simple message across to every pupil – your attendance matters and the school intends to keep you involved in your progress and in its learning processes. For schools, it is a win, win, win situation!

Summary

This chapter has considered the second of two long-term strategic approaches to combating truancy and other forms of non-attendance. The scheme considered has been the SSTG panel-based approach. Details on how to apply and set up the scheme including the use of the governors' attendance panel, attendance support panel and the progress review panel have been presented. Finally, the differences between the PSCC and SSTG schemes have been considered.

Chapter 9

Parents and parental-condoned absenteeism

This chapter explores some of the myths and realities of parental-condoned absenteeism. In many studies, parental-condoned absenteeism is the largest single category of non-attendance. However, some recent studies have suggested that specific lesson truancy has now superseded it in scope and importance (O'Keefe *et al.*, 1993). The chapter considers:

- some of the implications for parental-condoned absence and recent developments to prevent it from happening;
- where parents lay the blame for truancy;
- the effects of truancy patrols;
- types of parental-condoned absence.

Under the latter heading, new data is presented suggesting that parental-condoned absence is not a simple continuum. In fact, these data show that there are five categories of parent involved in parental-condoned absenteeism – often coming from entirely different standpoints.

To many people, most notably politicians, blaming truancy and non-attendance on parents has the great merit of deflecting public attention away from schools. It also enables some headteachers and their colleagues to ignore the damaging evidence on schools' differential attendance rates, even those within the same homogeneous location. For them, by blaming parents solely for non-attendance, poor teaching, bullying within schools, irrelevant subject matter and unfavourable school climates can be ignored. Unfortunately, such protagonists fail to explain why it is that if home circumstances and parental attitudes are the sole criteria for non-attendance, most pupils from deprived working class backgrounds attend school regularly. Nor, why some pupils with low social indices and unsupportive home backgrounds in the same classes at school attend regularly when some of their peers do not. Regrettably, there remains a naive body of opinion which prefers to think that schools should have no responsibility and receive no blame for non-attendance issues. Such people argue that pupils should not only be obliged to attend school irrespective of the consequences but to say nothing when events in school go wrong. In reality, of course, this is precisely what does happen as some pupils vote with their feet. The real question is why it is that some pupils will miss school or avoid certain classes, when other pupils in identical personal circumstances do not. And, of the latter, is parental support the only key determinant? The answer is almost certainly 'probably not'.

Parents, however, do play a direct role in helping their children to learn especially at an early age. However, parents often need help if they are to play this role effectively. They need, for example, accurate information and regular feedback about what is happening in their children's schools. Reid (1999, Chapters 2, 4 and 14) has written extensively on parental-condoned absence, the home backgrounds and life styles of persistent absentees, the social indices of truancy and of ways to improve home–school communication.

Surveys on non-attendance from school show that parents tend to under-estimate the amount of unauthorised absence which takes place. So, to a lesser extent, do schools. By contrast, pupil-based surveys often report that absence rates from school are much higher than official studies report. Even high achieving, regular attending pupils will admit to taking time away from school either for specific reasons (to enter a surfing contest, to go and see a pop concert) or simply because they feel in need of a rest or change of scene (Reid, 2000).

Studies into non-attendance also show considerable variations in the reported extent of parental-condoned absenteeism. Between 1999 and 2000, a series of reports produced by a range of LEAs highlight this difference. Whereas, for example, one report conducted in the Midlands found that parental-condoned absence accounted for 93 per cent of total absences, another conducted in the south of England suggested that only 44 per cent of absences could be classified as parental-condoned.

Why should survey results vary so greatly? The answer, of course, lies in the methodology. If, for example, the study took place in a town's shopping centre as in Sandwell (see later in chapter), it will almost invariably contain a higher percentage of parental-condoned absentees than those conducted using other approaches.

Research shows that more parental-condoned absentees tend to be female, tend to stay at home, or in the homes of other relatives or friends, or congregate towards shopping centres. By contrast, traditional truants tend to be loners and so, by definition, avoid company and town centres. Institutional absentees often participate in pre-meditated absence from school (either for the day or when missing specific lessons) and so will stay together in groups often avoiding public places for fear of getting caught. Therefore, a truancy sweep in a town centre will catch a high percentage of absentees but not *all* absentees from a local school or nearby schools. In fact, the pupils with the most genuine reasons for missing school (e.g. illness, visit to a chemist) are the ones most likely to be found in public places like town centres frequently accompanied by parents. Of the remainder of the absentees who make their way to a shopping centre in school time, the strong probability is that they are up to no good (e.g. involved in group shoplifting). Hence, the fact that in London it is estimated that 5 per cent of all offences are committed by children during school hours. Or, the fact that a week-long truancy sweep in Stratford, East London, in 1999 reported that recorded crime dropped by 50 per cent. Car crimes, in particular, fell by 70 per cent. Similarly, research conducted by the Home Office (1995) found that 75 per cent of boys and 50 per cent of girls who play truant once a week or more have committed offences. Clearly, not all these youngsters are parental-condoned absentees.

In ideal circumstances therefore, it is important that studies into school absenteeism utilise appropriate cross-check methodologies which enable them to gather data on all kinds of truancy *per se*, which includes post-registration truancy, illness (when appropriate), psychological absence (as a result of bullying, victimisation or for other psychological or psychiatric reasons) as well as parental-condoned absence. In fact, post-registration truancy and specific lesson absence are often notoriously difficult to detect and are excluded from official statistical returns.

The truth is that nowadays most studies use convenience sampling – often undertaken by staff engaged in truancy patrols. When this is the case, parental-condoned absenteeism will invariably be the highest category. But, whether the highest category or not, parental-condoned absenteeism is highly significant and needs to be properly understood.

This chapter needs to be considered alongside the fact that increasing numbers of parents are beginning to play key roles within some schools. These roles can be quite diverse. For example, parents in schools are now involved as parent governors, through parent–teacher associations, as teacher helpers in classrooms (both paid and unpaid), as learning mentors and in a whole host of other different and often voluntary roles.

An example of good practice involving parents is taking place in the Gloucester Education Achievement Zone. One of the key aims of the Zone is to develop family learning in order to increase the ability of all parents and carers to support their children's learning and especially those experiencing their own difficulties with basic skills (Jeffery, 2000).

As part of the scheme, a team of family learning support workers have been seeking to improve on the capacity of attached family centres to identify and support needy families, whilst, at the same time, building learning capacities in communities without designated family centre facilities. This work is closely co-ordinated with the Sure Start scheme and other community action programmes. Similar schemes exist in many similar EAZs throughout England.

Where parents lay the blame for truancy

Kinder and Wilkin (1998) have reported on their findings of a NFER project on where parents lay the blame for truancy. They found that parents believe children misbehave and play truant because they are bored and the National Curriculum is failing to address their needs. They also blame their own shortcomings as parents, as well as peer pressure and a breakdown in pupil–teacher relationships for truancy and disaffection.

The report found that parents pinpointed the National Curriculum as a culprit in poor classroom behaviour and non-attendance. Parents believed it was not meeting their children's needs and interests, particularly those who have special needs and learning difficulties. The report found that complex factors determined the causes of disaffection, and that children needed a combination of support to overcome their difficulties. Schools which employed a variety of approaches to deal with the problem achieved the best results in improving motivation. Among the most effective were computer registration systems monitoring pupil attendance which enabled teachers to detect patterns of behaviour and absence, and made it more difficult for pupils to truant.

Rewards and sanctions were also effective because they encouraged and reinforced school rules on behaviour and attendance, although some children did not value being seen publicly to receive acclaim. One in eight believed that the giving of prizes and incentives was inappropriate and threw them away.

The authors also found that the prospect of punishment for truancy only worked for those pupils who feared their attendance record could affect their job prospects; others 'beat the system' by intercepting letters home, forging signatures and getting their friends to ring the school. Approaches which provide challenges and offer individual support to pupils were the most effective means of dealing with disaffection. Conversely, those with a strong reprisal element such as withdrawal units, exclusion and suspensions tended not to address the problem.

In another study of persistent school absenteeism (Reid, 1985), 65 per cent of the parents of the non-attenders disapproved of their offspring's absences; 9 per cent 'approved', while 26 per cent of the parents were considered ambivalent. Clearly, there is a great deal of difference between tacit parental approval and outright disapproval, although there was very little overt evidence of parents actively collaborating with the schools in getting their offspring back to school. However, there are undoubtedly major differences between the 'hardened' attitudes of parents of chronic truants with, for example, those of parents of first offenders.

In over half the cases where parental disapproval was acknowledged, the absentees stated that on occasions family quarrels and/or 'rifts' took place within the home because of their non-attendance. These quarrels were especially rife following threats of prosecution, letters from the school and home visits by educational welfare officers. Despite the majority disapproval, only 15 per cent of the parents took any form of 'positive' action against their children in order to discourage their non-attendance. Measures mentioned by the absentees included the stopping of pocket money, returning them to the school gates and detaining them at home in the evenings 'being grounded'. Many of the absentees specifically mentioned that they disliked being punished by their parents far more than their schools and, according to the absentees, it seems that a large proportion of the parents simply took the easy way out by 'just telling me to return to school and then doing nothing about it', or 'telling me off and then sending the school a false note'.

There is also evidence that more girls than boys are parental-condoned absentees. Research suggests that mothers often keep their daughters at home as company, to help them to undertake specific chores, or, in extreme cases, for protection from violence and/or child abuse. It is also clear that there are occasions when the reasons given by the schools for the absence contradict, or are different from the evidence collected either by the social services or health agencies or both. Illustratively, cases where teenage girls are pregnant and have abortions are often classified as either illness or truancy by schools because they are unaware of the truth. A high proportion of parental condoned absence is reported on studies which include pupils from ethnic minority backgrounds especially amongst some Asian-background pupils.

Truancy patrols

There is little doubt that far too many parents fail to take seriously their responsibilities for ensuring their children attend school regularly. The failure of some parents to fulfil their legal obligations under the 1944 Education Act has been highlighted in a number of ways. First, a spate of recent surveys have reported that most truants from school have their behaviour condoned by their parent(s). For example, Sandwell (2000) Borough Council reported on a four-month study conducted in the main shopping centre in which truancy patrols stopped and questioned school-age pupils when out of school during term time. The findings show that 627 of the 715 were in the town centre accompanied either by a parent(s) or a carer(s). Only 88 pupils were found to be on their own, and 28 per cent of those who were not in school were found to have medical reasons for their absence. The report concluded however, that there was a degree of difficulty in ascertaining the truth from those interviewed as some parents naturally stick up for their children when questioned. The researchers also found it difficult to be certain as to when parents were giving them true or false information. In the Sandwell study, only 6 per cent of those missing school were considered to be truants *per se* rather than parental-condoned absentees.

A similar set of statistics was reported from a truancy patrol set up in the Bonymaen part of Swansea. In April 2001, a twenty strong anti-truancy patrol blitzed the area around Cefn Hengoed Comprehensive School over a three-hour period during the morning. The patrol was sub-divided to form five 'hit squads' to round up school-age pupils not attending school. The squads collected up no fewer than fifty-nine pupils who were returned to Cefn Hengoed School to have their details taken and to be 'signed' for. Although few of the truants were accompanied by their parent(s) at the time, most of them subsequently had their absence condoned by their parents during follow-up visits from the police. Even more worrying is the fact that in repeat exercises many of the same pupils were rounded up again. In fact, in one part of Swansea, some pupils rounded up by a truancy patrol in the morning and returned to their schools were picked up by the same patrols in the afternoon, often in exactly the same places. This amounted to exactly half of those picked up in the afternoon by the patrol. The local paper reported on the exasperation felt by members of the truancy patrols who felt their best efforts were being undermined by the lack of support they received from parents and local schools alike. Clearly, a lot of schools do not have any re-integration strategies.

Truancy patrols came into effect in February 1999 as part of new powers introduced under section 16 of the 1988 Crime and Disorder Act. Under section 16, the police may remove truants from the streets if they believe they have 'reasonable cause' that the pupils are absent from schools without good reason.

The introduction of truancy patrols has had four major consequences. First, they highlight the failure of many schools to have appropriate early warning systems to prevent and detect truancy and post-registration absence. Second, they illustrate how easy it is for some pupils to enter and leave schools at will. Third, they have reinforced the failure of certain parents to support their children's schooling and their willingness to condone their non-attendance. Finally, and perhaps most importantly, they have reinforced the seriousness of many of the cases reported on by truancy patrols. For example, truancy patrols in London have found numerous cases of:

(a) pupils excluded from school with no alternative provision being made sometimes months after the initial exclusion order has taken effect;
(b) pupils engaged in criminal activity when out of school (e.g. shoplifting);
(c) girls who were away due to pregnancy without the knowledge or consent of the school;
(d) under-age pupils living rough in London having run away from other parts of the United Kingdom;
(e) pupils engaged in drug-related activities;
(f) children of illegal immigrants who did not go to school and who were not on the registers of any local school, and whose whereabouts would not otherwise have been known;

(g) pupils missing school because they were afraid to attend due to either bullying or other forms of victimisation;

(h) children who were accompanying their mother at her request because the parent was afraid of their partner or former partner;

(i) cases which when investigated uncovered child abuse;

(j) under-age work conducted either during the daytime and/or the evenings. One recent Report (TUC/MORI, 2001) found that nearly half a million pupils are working illegally in England alone; the worst record in Europe. Of those, over 100,000 are 'truanting' from school to do so.

A significant number of children apprehended by truancy patrols have subsequently had their cases and/or those of their parents referred to the social services as well as being returned to their schools and/or local education departments (dependent upon local policies).

The ease with which some pupils enter and leave schools at will is currently a source of concern to the DfES. Some schools have now started to act to prevent this freedom of access. None of the 1,700 pupils at New College, Leicester, are able to leave its grounds during the day without being issued with a pass. As a consequence, non-attendance has been reduced by nearly 10 per cent. The New College scheme is backed by police, parents and shopkeepers. Local shopkeepers in Leicester from high street chains like Boots to local bakers refuse to serve pupils during school hours unless they can produce the pass. The police find it helps their truancy patrols. Only pass-less pupils are taken back to school. The scheme helps to deter parental-condoned absenteeism as all out-of-school pupils with legitimate reasons have the pass; the remainder are considered to be truants and are treated as such.

It is thought that this scheme will help local magistrates who often have difficulty in distinguishing between parental-condoned absence and genuine truancy. Since March 2001, magistrates have been able to impose a higher maximum fine (initially of £2,500 per parent) and/or imprisonment for up to three months for cases of truancy. They can also impose alternative sentences such as parenting orders under which parents must accompany their child to school or attend parenting classes. If a child is truanting, schools and education welfare officers normally agree an action plan with the parents and this is subsequently monitored closely. Usually, only when parents refuse to co-operate and fail to impose their child's attendance will legal proceedings be taken.

By 2001, New Labour was becoming increasingly concerned about the role of parents in condoning absenteeism from school. Therefore, between 2001 and 2004, they have allocated £450 million via the Children's Fund towards supporting families, including help to prevent children from becoming truants. Similarly, the Connexions Service (see Chapter 11) is also putting resources into increasing the numbers of pupils who stay on at school. As part of the Connexions Scheme, youngsters are given a personal adviser to help them to find solutions with their learning difficulties and encourage them into supportive learning or training situations. Local Connexions services often include members drawn from the youth service, careers, education welfare and schools.

Unfortunately, and indeed often unwittingly, some schools and parents inadvertently collude over non-attendance rates. For example, it is the policy in some schools not to record unauthorised absence immediately. Upon returning to school, pupils who have not brought a supportive note from their parent(s) are instructed to bring one the following day. Therefore, some unauthorised absence subsequently becomes classified as authorised, thereby helping to reduce the school's official rates of unauthorised absence. Similarly, a study of twenty-six schools by the University of Leicester (2001) found that: (a) some difficult pupils were encouraged to drop out of school; (b) some headteachers were recording excluded pupils as authorised absences; (c) truancy was being condoned by some of the schools.

The recording of attendance – particularly of unauthorised absence – is so variable from school to school that it is almost impossible to be certain how many pupils miss school daily, how many pupils really play truant, as well as the full extent of parental-condoned absence. In fact, on one training day organised by the author, the staff present stated that: (a) in some schools holidays are never marked as unauthorised absence; (b) the school policy was to mark all illness and illness-related absence as if the pupils were present provided a note was received by the school.

One headteacher from Manchester told the author that her school was in special measures partly because her staff were instructed to mark the registers accurately. By contrast, she asserted that several of her neighbouring schools fudged their figures by 'authorising unauthorised absence' in order to protect their league table position. Most people agree that the extent of parents providing supportive and often false notes to justify their children's unauthorised absence is now so widespread that it makes inter-preting differences between unauthorised and authorised absence extremely difficult, and in some cases, impossible.

In both Swansea and in parts of London, truancy patrol have reported that up to two-thirds of pupils found missing school have been carrying false notes in their pockets. Some of these have been written by the pupils themselves. Others by friends. Some by parents anxious not to be prosecuted. Either way, the pupils are really truanting. Too many people falsely equate parental-condoned absence with authorised absence. It is not. It is truancy. The situation is now so ludicrous that some schools are even authoris-ing pupils who are returned to schools by truancy patrols provided there is evidence of a note. And the pupils are aware of this practice!

Types of parental-condoned absence

In most studies and reports into school absenteeism, parental-condoned absence is considered to be a single generic category. This is both wrong and misleading as it is most certainly not. My own evidence – based on over thirty years of work in the field – suggests that there are five different, if sometimes complementary, categories. The categories are presented in Figures 9.1 to 9.6. Each of them will now be described in more detail. The five categories are: anti-education (belligerent) parents; *laissez-faire* (weak) parents; frustrated (failed) parents; desperate (anxious) parents; and, adjusting (vulnerable) parents.

There is considerable utility in these categories because an understanding of them dispels the myth that all parental-condoned absentees are the same. Some politicians and teachers who like to blame all school non-attendance upon parents tend to make this assumption. If you are of this persuasion, ask any experienced education welfare officer, and they will soon tell you that you are wrong! In fact, variations in parental attitudes abound and, in some ways, restricting these differences to only five categories is not easy.

Category	Type
1	Anti-Education (Belligerent)
2	*Laissez-Faire*
3	Frustrated
4	Desperate
5	Adjusting

Figure 9.1 Categories of parental-condoned absence.

Category 1: Anti-education parents

The first category, anti-education parents, is composed of parents who are anti-schooling and tend to be belligerent in nature (see Figure 9.2). Typically, these are parents who are hostile and aggressive towards teachers and schooling. They tend not to be avid readers or even to read well, to have extremely low educational standards themselves and to be people who were brought up in households where gaining academic qualifications was not regarded highly.

Some of them were truants and non-attenders themselves when of school age. We know, for example, that male truants tend to marry female truants and to experience a whole host of personal, social, economic and employment woes in adult life (Reid, 1985). They also tended to leave school at the first opportunity.

Many anti-education parents are beset, if not overwhelmed, with a multitude of social, economic and other personal problems. A high proportion are on the lowest incomes or on income support. Many are in need of regular support from the social services. A large percentage are currently living in single parent families, in poor quality housing, and on council estates. Even in families which have remained together over time, marital discord can be the norm with arguments, shouting and tempter tantrums occurring regularly.

Many absentees brought up in these homes enjoy no kind of social or educational support whatsoever. Their daily lives are miserable, compounded by poor quality food and other low order forms of material support. The deprivation known by some of these pupils is almost beyond the competence and understanding of teachers, the vast majority of whom emanate from middle-class backgrounds (Reid *et al.*, 1985).

The tendency of many of these anti-education parents is to shout and be aggressive when they are put onto the defensive. Unfortunately, it is these very kind of parents who cause some teachers to be afraid of all kind of home–school initiatives; often with good reason.

For example, Jez is a persistent truant at 14. When his education welfare officer visited his mother, she was shocked by the verbal abuse which she received. After three visits within a five-week period, the level of abuse was so severe that she asked her principal education welfare officer whether she could avoid going to the home again.

Profile

- Tend to dislike visiting schools
- Hostile towards teachers and schooling
- Tendency to have low educational standards themselves
- Possibly former truants
- Unlikely to be regular readers
- Low tolerance thresholds
- Attempting to cope with effects of a variety of social, personal and economic difficulties
- Often early school leavers themselves
- Tending to be on low incomes
- Many in regular support of social services
- A high percentage on income support
- Often coping with life as single parent
- Children receive little, if any, homework support
- Tendency towards defensive aggression
- Can be quite brazen when provoked
- Will be prone to change interview situation into an argument when interviewed by headteachers or teachers

---

Figure 9.2 Profiles of categories of parental-condoned absence: Category 1; Type: Anti-education (belligerent).

Subsequently, she spoke to Jez's form tutor and headteacher. Both had similar experiences as well as abusive letters sent to the school in response to first day absence telephone calls.

A few days later, the principal education welfare officer phoned to say that he had been advised that the family was well known to the local social services department. Apparently, the father, mother, Jez and his younger brother had all been brought to the attention of the social services for a variety of different reasons. Social services had advised against prosecution because the family was already in debt and at risk of losing their council home. The mother's social worker had similarly informed her line manager that she was tired of being verbally abused despite trying to help her.

Category 1 – anti-education parents – are precisely those who tend to give all parents a bad name in the eyes of authority. It is usually these kind of parents that teachers and politicians have in mind when attributing all absence to the home and the family background. In one sense, they are most certainly right!

Category 2: Laissez-faire parents

There are more *laissez-faire* (weak) parents around than many people appreciate (see Figure 9.3). Unlike their anti-education peers, they differ in three key respects. First, they are conformist and certainly not aggressive. Second, they tend to be weak parents. Third, they will almost certainly support and condone any action taken by their offspring – almost as a mark of family loyalty. With teachers, they will tend to be meek

Profile

- Tend to be conformist
- Wish to avoid trouble or being in the limelight
- Often 'weak' parent(s)
- Will usually support and condone their children's actions even when they are unaware of them; a belief that this is a hallmark of family loyalty
- Often meek and apologetic in visits to school when interviewed by teachers and headteachers
- Tendency to have low educational expectations of their children
- Were low achievers themselves at school
- Tendency to give in to own children rather than making moral stand or remaining firm on a point of principle
- Believe children's long-term happiness is key goal
- Cannot be relied upon to support schools or other forms of authority during times of crisis; will often take the weak option
- In some homes, the parent(s) will deliberately shield themselves from the truth even when it is obvious

Figure 9.3 Parental-condoned absence: Category 2; Type: *Laissez-faire* (weak).

and apologetic. Many *laissez-faire* families have comparatively low educational expectations. They tended to be low achievers themselves at school and probably expect their offspring to follow suit.

Jackie is a persistent truant. She is now 15 but became a regular absentee from school at the age of 13. She spends a lot of time when away from school with her boyfriend who is 19. Although the parents are unhappy about the relationship, they feel there is little they can do and are reluctant to interfere in case it forces their daughter to leave home.

Jackie's father is a mechanic who works extremely long hours at the local garage; a job which he believes gives him a lot of street-cred and local prestige. He has worked in the same garage since he left school at 16 with three GCEs to his credit. Her mother is a part-time cleaner in a local nursing home and works three evenings a week and at weekends in the local supermarket. They make ends meet financially but life is hard. They have not taken a family holiday since Jackie – the last child of three – was born.

All they want for Jackie is for her to be happy. They are saddened that she misses so much school and know it will be to her long-term disadvantage. Yet, whenever telephone calls or letters come from the school they always support their daughter claiming she is suffering from the after-effects of glandular fever. Whilst they are afraid of being taken to court, they are also afraid that Jackie's boyfriend's influence might grow if they take any more severe measures. They just hope that Jackie and they will get away with her persistent absences.

When questioned, Jackie's mother admits to being unsure when her daughter is in school and when she is not. Jackie leaves home dressed to go to school every morning.

Sometimes she arrives; more often she does not. Sometimes she goes straight to her boy-friend's home. On other occasions, she visits one or two of her girlfriends who are similarly away from school.

Jackie herself is completely aware of her parents' dilemma. She has little against school claiming it is boring and irrelevant as her main aim in life is to become a hair-dresser. She says she hopes to get married soon after leaving school and to go and live with her boyfriend who is already looking for a better job so they can settle down together.

Category 3: Frustrated parents

Category 3 – frustrated (failed) parents – are the precise opposite of those who condone their children's absences from school (see Figure 9.4). In fact, frustrated parents are to some extent let down by the system. Their home lives are often ruined by their children's poor behaviour and erratic attendance at school. In some cases, they have and are doing everything possible to ensure their children go to school and fail in the attempt.

Frustrated parents are often misunderstood. They will have tried everything to get help and support for their child. Their child's non-attendance is a constant source of acrimony and worry. Rows frequently occur within the home because the parent(s) are at their wit's end and do not know what else they can do. Whereas some politicians and teachers blame parents for failing to send their children to school, these type of families tend to blame politicians and teachers for doing too little to help them to get their children to school and to make sure they remain there throughout the day.

Profile
- Feel let down by the 'system'
- Do not tolerate their child's absences from school
- Pressure of attempting to ensure their child attends school can lead to serious family arguments, to a breakdown of relationships within the home and the secondary problems
- Often have poor parent(s)–child relationships
- Little respect between parent(s) and child
- Child perceived as a 'rebel'
- Worry a great deal about their children's behaviour and attitude
- Willingness to support headteacher and staff in school but lacking the necessary skills to know how to do so
- In extreme cases, parent(s) feel at their 'wit's end'
- In some families there is a history of strife between mother and father over child-rearing practices
- Tendency to blame others for their domestic difficulties and for the failure of their child(children) to attend school regularly
- Feel failures as parents

Figure 9.4 Parental-condoned absence: Category 3; Type: Frustrated (failed).

Mr J believes his daughter's behaviour and truancy have ruined his life. Partly disabled, Mr J was shocked when at the age of 12 his daughter first started 'mitching' school. By the age of 13, she was on soft and hard drugs. At 14, she had become a daytime prostitute in order to finance her daily routine of drug and alcohol abuse. At 14½, Marie was taken into care.

Mr J believes he took every possible measure to help support his daughter. He also thinks that all his best efforts were in vain and feels he was let down by the caring professionals. The steps he took included:

(a) reporting his daughter for truancy to the headteacher of her secondary school;
(b) calling in the social services and the police to seek help with Marie's drug problems;
(c) asking Mrs Thomas, the school's education welfare officer, to call in daily at his home to check Marie was in school;
(d) paying for a taxi daily to take Marie to school.

Everything he tried failed and the situation has gone from bad to worse. Marie is currently allowed to visit home at weekends. Whenever she does, the situation soon degenerates into verbal abuse, shouting and swearing. Marie normally leaves early for town and, on occasions, does not come home again. He often has to phone the police or social services for help.

Mr J represents a larger proportion of parents than some people currently comprehend. There is little doubt that amongst the high proportion of daily absentees that exist in Britain, there are many parent(s) who dearly would like their children to attend regularly and make suitable academic progress. Currently, there is no way of telling precisely how large this category really is. Whereas anti-education and *laissez-faire* parents tend to be grouped together to form a single category in the minds of many politicians, teachers and writers, there has been no single study into the lives of those frustrated parents who do everything to get their children to go to school – and who, despite their best efforts, regularly fail.

Such a study is urgently needed. At present, apart from individual case study reports, there is no way, for example, in which magistrates can differentiate in sentencing practices between the various categories of parenting.

The worst case of this kind the author came across happened a few years ago on the Gower. Here, a middle-aged father, only five foot six inches tall, tried to 'make' his six foot, much heavier son go to school after receiving a final warning letter from his EWO. After the ensuing argument, which took place in front of pupils on the school bus, the father required 122 micro stitches, hospitalisation and treatment for several broken bones. His son was subsequently taken away from home and placed in care.

Category 4: Desperate parents

There is a subtle difference between frustrated and desperate parents. Frustrated parents are upset by their own inability to get their child to attend school. Desperate (anxious) parents are the precise opposite (see Figure 9.5). They are *afraid* to let their children go to school. They need their child(ren) to stay home to look after them, possibly for medical reasons or, much more likely, because they are unable to cope with life's

Profile

- A significant but minority group
- Tend to be single parent(s)
- Often afraid to let their child(children) go to school regularly
- Child often provides parent with emotional support on a daily basis
- Parent often 'afraid' of consequences of daily pressures
- Possibly need child's help for medical reasons
- Possibly afraid of physical abuse or retribution
- Often require specialist counselling
- Social backgrounds can be very similar to category one parents
- Will make up excuses for their child(children)

Figure 9.5 Parental-condoned absence: Category 4; Type: Desperate (anxious).

pressures. In extreme circumstances, they are afraid of a partner, former partner or another threatening adult.

Desperate parent(s) need counselling and support. Their personal problems are frequently exacerbated by a host of other social, home and economic deficiencies, often not dissimilar to Category 1 parent(s). These parent(s) *cause* their child(ren) not to go to school. Sometimes, they are so desperate, they will make up excuses or situations to ensure their child does not leave the family home.

Zoe is 12 and wanted to go to school to be with her friends. She enjoyed learning and being in school. She hated having to stay home but she was afraid to leave her mother and her mother's last partner threatened to beat her up when she asked him for money to pay an electricity bill. Since then her progress at school has gone downhill. Zoe does all the shopping with her mother and makes sure she is hardly ever on her own. Both Zoe and her mother realise the situation cannot go on for much longer. The education welfare officer has visited them three times and called in the police and social services. To date, the situation has not improved and Zoe is beginning to wonder how she will cope when she does eventually return to school.

As with Category 3 parents, there has been no major study undertaken on the plight of desperate families and its relationship with school attendance. In case study reports and in the literature on attendance, there are occasional references to the plight of this category of parent. There is a clear link between one-parent families and the need to keep a child off school for emotional and therapeutic support (Reid, 1989a, volume 1, Chapter 6, and 1999, Chapter 14).

Category 5: Adjusting parents

There is a clear link between Categories 4 and 5. There are however, some subtle differences. Parents in Category 5 tend not to be afraid to let their children attend school or

Profile
- Two major types:
  (a) parents who come from ethnic minority backgrounds – often first or second generation British families
  (b) young parents or young single mothers
- Strong family bonds fuelled by deep religious, culture, social, economic and mutual inter-dependency needs
- Can be a lot of 'hidden' pressures exerted upon children
- Sometimes boys and girls can be treated very differently
- Can be genuinely confused about the skills required to be successful and competent parents
- Problems often accrue from a lack of experience or knowledge
- Can be diffident with teachers and/or other professionals
- Often confused about legal requirements
- Sometimes need children to fill in forms or to help them with maternal responsibilities
- Often poor readers
- English may or may not be 'mother tongue' or first or second language
- Young mothers can feel 'ashamed' and many have very low levels of self-esteem; some do not even like going out in their community without company.

Figure 9.6 Parental-condoned absence: Category 5; Type: Adjusting parents (vulnerable).

to feel in need of protection or medical help or other forms of emotional support. The parent(s) do feel a similar need for the company of their child(ren) during the day but often for pragmatic reasons. Many adjusting vulnerable parents emanate from ethnic minority backgrounds (see Figure 9.6). Some are of Asian origins; others can be Afro-Caribbean. Typically, they will either not have been resident in Britain for very long or are still adjusting as second generation families. There will be a strong bond within the family often fuelled by deep religious, culture, social, economic and mutual inter-dependency needs. These dependency needs will often be manifest in the form of a close bond, often perceived to be much closer than in a lot of other kinds of households. In certain adjusting families, there will be a lot of hidden pressures upon both boys and girls, sometimes for entirely different reasons.

Asha is 15. She really enjoys school and gets on with all the other pupils in her class. She is studious in nature and would eventually like to go to university. Unfortunately, she feels very confused within herself. She enjoys the 'freedom' which her friends at school receive from their parents and would like to join in more by going out with them in the evenings to discos and parties. Her parents will not allow her to do so and impose a 'curfew' on all her evening activities. She is aware that her parents wish her to leave school early and have already discussed with her the prospect of an 'arranged' marriage. She is desperate not to participate in an arranged marriage and deeply envies her brother who she feels is treated entirely differently from herself and seems to be 'favoured'. Asha perceives both parents operating double standards – emphasising compliance and the need to take a secondary role in life with her whilst, at the same time, urging her elder brother to make a success of himself in later life as a businessman and encouraging his study at Nottingham University.

Asha's attendance at school was normal until the age of 13. Since then, her mother has regularly requested her to go shopping with her, to visit relatives and to participate in other social and recreational activities. Although Asha would rather go to school, she does not wish to cause major offence to her parents, especially her father, who she knows would take any form of rebellion very badly. Privately, she admits to being at a crossroads in her life. She knows she either has to stand up for herself very firmly – with all the distress this will cause, or alternatively, she has to continue to be compliant and face the same long-term expectations from life as her mother. She is currently 'too confused' to know which way to turn.

Another group contained within this category are young parents. These can frequently be parent(s) who have either married young or had their first and/or subsequent child whilst a teenager or in their early twenties. Sometimes the parents or the single mother can be genuinely confused about the skills required to be successful and competent parents and to lack experience or knowledge of how to relate to professionals and meet their social and legal requirements. Many of these young parents, especially young mothers, have very low self-esteem and lack confidence. The confidence of some can be so low they do not like leaving their own homes without company.

Implications

A lot more research is needed into the detailed effects of the five categories upon attendance issues and upon parental-condoned absence in particular. An understanding of these issues could lead professionals towards better treatment and/or remedial strategies for working with parents of absentee pupils. A knowledge and understanding of the five categories should be fundamental in the training of education welfare officers and education social workers. It would also be extremely helpful for form tutors, heads of year, deputy heads and headteachers to appreciate the subtle differences between groups. Too many teachers hold single isomorphisms of parents and parental groups in their mind sets.

Similarly, these five parental categories need to be understood in terms of their relationship with traditional, psychological and institutional absentees/truants (Reid, 1999, 2000). An understanding of the inter-relationships between these two forms of categorisation for absentee pupils (traditional, psychological or institutional absentees) and their parental backgrounds – provides an opportunity for professionals (especially psychologists) to begin to develop appropriate treatment strategies for dealing with non-attendance scientifically. These approaches could take several forms. One way might be to develop compensatory remedial packs for use with particular types of absentees/truants and/or with their parent(s) or with the whole family grouping together. Another could be to help parents to develop appropriate parental skills including overcoming their rational or irrational fears or prejudices. A third possibility might be to use existing personality inventories (e.g. repertory grids) or, more likely, use specially developed new personality inventories to help identify and/or treat absentee/truant and/or their parent(s) appropriately. If this could be done, it would be a major step forward.

Summary

This chapter considers what is known about the relationship between parents and persistent school absenteeism. It discusses some of the reasons for parental-condoned absenteeism and the implications for this action. It presents evidence of where parents lay the blame for truancy. It outlines the issues involved in truancy patrols returning pupils to school. It then goes on to consider the variations between five categories of parents who condoned their children's absence from a variety of different perspectives. Finally, the chapter highlights the subtle issues involved in any discussion of parental-condoned absenteeism especially as more and more politicians are tending to blame parents for all forms of truancy and non-attendance irrespective of their personal circumstances or views. Blaming parents *en masse* minimises a complex and delicate phenomenon. It also does nothing to help reduce prejudice amongst some teachers and professionals in some of the other caring services prejudices. Nor does it help promote better school–parental relationships especially when there is a great deal of evidence to show that communication between parents and some schools is in need of considerable improvement (and even a total overhaul) especially in some of today's weakest, under-achieving and, sometimes, failing institutions (Reid, 2000). There are for example, a lot of staff in some schools who would benefit from short courses on how to improve their interpersonal skills when communicating with parents.

Chapter 10

Alternative curriculum schemes

The move towards greater flexibility

Prior to the introduction of the National Curriculum alternative curriculum schemes abounded in British secondary schools. Once the National Curriculum was introduced, most innovative alternative curriculum schemes ceased overnight. During 1999, the DfES began to reconsider its position with regard to alternative curriculum strategies through Circular 10/99. This Circular was the first to allow schools to begin to disapply parts of the National Curriculum whether for reasons of pupils' special needs, disaffection or ethnicity. For example, section 4.24 states that:

> If staff consider that it would help a pupil to concentrate for several weeks on areas of particular weakness, this can happen without formal disapplication although staff will need to comply with the programmes of study.

On work-related learning and work experience for 14 to 16–year-olds the Circular states:

> Work-related learning allows greater curriculum flexibility that may widen the horizons of 14 to 16–year-olds at risk of disaffection. The law allows such pupils to spend some of the week on work-related learning programmes either in school, further education colleges or with an employer. The extra time for work-related learning is freed by dropping two of science, design and technology or a modern foreign language.

Section 4.26 enables some FE colleges to offer tailor-made programmes for secondary-aged pupils at key stage 4, either on a part-time or full-time basis. Some voluntary bodies also offer a range of activities for this age group, often in conjunction with the FE sector. The majority of alternative curriculum schemes focus upon providing pupils with opportunities to catch up on the basics supplemented by acquiring skills in information technology and, often, opportunities to undertake vocational subjects. In the remaining part of this chapter we will consider a few of these different practices.

For example, Dwr-y-Felin School in Neath organises an innovative link with Neath Tertiary College. Disaffected key stage 4 pupils from the school spend up to two and a half days taking vocational subjects such as bricklaying, hairdressing and ICT at the college. An evaluation of the project by Morgan (1999) found that the vast majority of

1 The use of corrective schemes to overcome literacy and numeracy
2 The use of independent learning systems such as Plato, Pearson Technology Developments, Success Maker and the Pacific Institute Programme
3 Utilising classroom assistants to facilitate slow learners and reintegration strategies
4 Mentoring schemes (see Chapter 13)
5 Second chance opportunities
6 Use of homework clubs and ICT
7 Summer school initiatives
8 Establishing learning support centres
9 Breakfast and after-school clubs
10 Vocational-orientated curriculum strategies
11 Individual or group key skills lessons
12 Flexible tuition times
13 Utilising individual student progress planners
14 Buddy systems
15 Providing school FE links with disaffected pupils
16 Managing individual learning programmes for pupils
17 Utilising specialists in-school projects
18 Using special needs assistants
19 Providing a range of compensatory programmes
20 Establishing a school-based social inclusion unit
21 Alternative year 10 and 11 projects
22 All-the-year round learning schemes
23 The specialist role of Education Action Zones, Excellence in Cities Projects and Connexions
24 Voluntary schemes, e.g. Millennium Volunteers; The Duke of Edinburgh's Awards Scheme; The Prince's Trust.
25 Individual school-based schemes, e.g. the Mountain Ash Map Project
26 Gateway Learners Project

Figure 10.1 Some existing alternative curriculum strategies.

the disaffected pupils, which included a significant number of non-attenders and truants, made 100 per cent attendance at the college even though they had been poor attenders at school. Clearly, for some disaffected pupils, relevance is a key factor.

Figure 10.1 provides a list of some existing alternative curriculum strategies at key stage 4. It cannot really do more because the range and extent of alternative curriculum strategies throughout and across the UK are so vast, different, and often unique. Therefore, those presented in Figure 10.1 represent some examples which have already been discussed in some of the short-term strategies between Chapters 3 to 6. However, some different and/or new schemes are now considered in this chapter. Similar lists to Figure 10.1 could be devised for key stages 1 to 3.

In a series of comparative and controversial articles for *The Guardian*, Davies (2000) suggested that most pupils who drop out of school or truant do so because of their disaffection with the National Curriculum. He went on first to outline some alternative curriculum schemes which are operating effectively in London and the South East and then to compare UK strategies unfavourably with more enlightened approaches in Holland. Subsequently, the DfES has been taking a much greater interest in alternative curriculum schemes.

Kinder and Wilkin (1998) have also produced a report based on work undertaken by the NFER which shows that parents blame the inadequacies of the National Curriculum for pupils' truancy and disaffection from school. They suggest that some pupils are bored with their prescribed learning in school. Parents believed the National Curriculum is not meeting children's needs and interests, particularly those who have special needs and learning difficulties. They also blamed the National Curriculum for the rise in poor classroom behaviour as well as for non-attendance. Schools which provided variety in their approaches to the curriculum appeared to be achieving the best results with their potentially disaffected pupils.

Disaffection in Scotland

The growing interest in alternative curriculum approaches has already led to a number of new developments. A major initiative has been launched on the delivery of the curriculum to disengaged young people in Scotland. This study will identify the range of initiatives across Scotland that are aimed at addressing young people's disaffection and disengagement from learning. It will assess and evaluate the effectiveness of the major approaches identified, in terms of the curriculum content delivered successfully; the impact on young people's motivation to engage or re-engage in learning; and the impact on their attendance, attainment, aspirations and attitudes. Methods will include surveys and in-depth case-study work with secondary schools, FE colleges and a range of other provider agencies and services, including careers services, training providers and involved employers.

Recent research carried out in England and Wales by the NFER has shown that alternative provision, involving an adaptation of the traditional content and/or contexts of learning, has proved to be a successful way to re-engage disaffected young people with educational opportunity. The contribution of other agencies, e.g. community education services, youth work, social services and FE colleges, has been highly evident in a wide range of strategies and interventions aimed at re-engaging disaffected young people. By working with schools in a range of ways, these agencies can provide a learning experience that previously disengaged young people value. This can then form a bridge enabling them to follow positive progression routes back into mainstream education, training or employment.

The study will seek to apply NFER research experience in the area of pupil disengagement to the Scottish context. Furthermore, given the specific characteristics of Scotland's school population and education system, it is anticipated that new issues and factors will be identified. These may include, for example, insights into strategies to counter disaffection in rural communities and insights into the impact of education for work and enterprise on the delivery of the curriculum to disengaged young people.

This study by Kinder *et al.* (2001) will:

- identify the range of strategies and provision across Scotland that are aimed at addressing young people's disaffection and disengagement from learning;
- assess and evaluate the effectiveness of the major approaches identified, in terms of:
  - the curriculum content delivered successfully;
  - the impact on young people's motivation to re-engage/engage in learning; and
  - the impact on their attendance, attainment, aspiration and attitude to learning/training.

The first aim will include the identification of successful interventions across the lower secondary, upper secondary and relevant post-18 sectors However, the main focus will be on the 14–18 age range. The study is sub-divided into two phases: the audit stage followed by the use of in-depth case studies.

During the audit stage, questionnaires will be sent to all secondary schools and FE colleges in Scotland, as well as to a wide range of other provider agencies. A target sample of 700 institutions is anticipated. The questionnaire will request information on the existence and nature of strategies and provision for disaffected young people according to age. It will also note any specialist client focus, the agencies involved, the perceived effects and benefits, the main aims and objectives of the provision and sources of funding. Subsequent analysis will highlight any trends or differences in the availability and emphasis of such provision. In addition to this analysis, telephone interviews will be undertaken with respondents representing the main types of provision and providing agencies.

For the case studies, up to sixteen initiatives will be selected for in-depth analysis. These will reflect a range of variables including: geographical locale, age range and type of client group, agencies involved, focus of provision and learning context. This case study phase will include observations of the strategies/provision in action, interviews with providers, young people and key senior personnel, as well as the collection of relevant documentation and hard data (e.g. relating to attendance and attainment).

Disaffection amongst minority groups

More research is to take place on disaffection amongst Muslim pupils within state secondary schools. Recent research has highlighted the over-representation of pupils from minority ethnic groupings excluded (school-based, fixed-term and permanent) from compulsory schooling. Previously, the main focus for much of this research has been on the experiences of African-Caribbean pupils. It is becoming increasingly clear however, that other minority ethnic groups are experiencing a similar situation. Gillburn and Gipps (1996) and Pathak (2000) have reported that there is evidence both of under-achievement and higher rates of exclusion in relation to pupils from all minority groups. There are suggestions that the causes of truancy and non-attendance are often different amongst ethnic minority pupils, with the nature of the curriculum being one of the main reasons.

The DfES is also conducting a review being undertaken by Kinder et al. (2001) on the role of the LEA in reducing truancy. Part of this review is focusing upon 'curriculum disengagement' as well as upon the role of the education welfare service. Finally, there are a whole range of innovative schemes being organised by a variety of education action zones across England which will now be considered.

The role of Education Action Zones

Why Education Action Zones? The government's agenda is to raise standards in all areas of the country. If this is to be achieved in areas with particular problems, there is a need to explore imaginative ways of working using sustainable local partnerships which build on the roles of schools, local communities and LEAs. They will operate in the context of the national policies to improve levels of achievement in literacy and numeracy.

What are Education Action Zones? They are local clusters of schools – usually a mix of not more than twenty primary, secondary and special schools – working in a new partnership with the LEA, local parents, businesses, TECs and others. This partnership encourages innovative approaches to tackling disadvantage and raising standards.

In some cases these partnerships build on local networks already in place; in others, new ones are created. The partnership certainly involves a central role for business. It also draws upon local and national agencies and charities involved in, for example, health care, social care and crime prevention. In some areas Education Action Zones are linked to health or employment zones and with projects funded by the Single Regeneration Budget. All of this will enhance the work of the LEA.

How do the zones work? The initiative challenges schools, working with other partners, to meet demanding targets for improvement and put in place plans for achieving them. In return, zones will have priority access to many of the department's other initiatives, such as:

- specialist schools – the DfES wishes to establish one in each zone (provided that good applications are put forward). This will be a resource for local people and other schools in the zone to draw on, helping to revitalise education in the area. Schools in zones will work in partnership to decide which specialism will best meet local needs and where it should be based. In doing this, they will have particularly close support from the Technology Colleges Trust (for technology, language and arts applications), and the Youth Sports Trust (for sport colleges);
- early excellence centres – these will bring together education, childcare and integrated services and help to identify emerging special needs, and provide training and a focus for dissemination of good practice;
- Advanced Skills Teachers – this will be a new teaching grade to reward the best classroom teachers. The DfES expects that a number will work in action zones;
- literacy summer schools – these are a key part of the government's literacy strategy and help pupils who have fallen behind at primary school to make a better transition to secondary education. Following evaluation of a pilot of fifty summer schools in 1997, the total was raised to 500 in 1998. The DfES now expects that there will be a place within each zone for a summer school;
- family literacy schemes – the DfES sees a need to link efforts to improve literacy among adults to their proposals for improving reading standards in primary schools. Following the success of the pilot schemes run by the Basic Skills Agency, the DfES wishes to see family literacy schemes being set up within zones as a central part of raising reading standards;
- out-of-school hours learning activities – these can bolster confidence and motivation, boost achievement in school and help to develop skills for life. They can benefit both secondary and primary pupils as well as offering childcare facilities to allow

parents to work. The DfES is enabling priority to be given to schools in zones through lottery funding from the New Opportunities Fund;

- work-related learning – this can help to raise pupils' levels of achievement and broaden their experience by allowing them to learn in a different environment such as a further education college, with a local employer or at a community organisation. The DfES extended the GNVQ initiative to zones and encourages bridging courses to employment or training;
- information and communications technology – this will be invaluable, both for working within the zone, and for sharing ideas beyond it on the new National Grid for Learning.

As well as having priority for the departmental programmes above, zones receive an annual grant to help with running costs, including hiring a project manager, and for specific locally planned initiatives. The DfES has explicitly encouraged innovation and flexibility within EAZs. These proposals have ensured that the needs of each child are met so that they will reach the highest possible standards. They also build on national initiatives such as the literacy and numeracy hours. Proposals have included:

- adapting the National Curriculum – or even radically redesigning parts of it – to meet local needs. For example, by providing additional opportunities for work-related learning and community work or an extra focus on literacy and numeracy;
- attracting outstanding educational leaders as heads of schools in zones through the use of flexible contracts which recognise the importance of experience and high performance in school leadership;
- employing extra teachers to work across several schools, perhaps acting as subject specialists to improve performance for pupils in the last two years of primary school;
- using accommodation across the zone more flexibly. For example, allowing space in a school to be used as a centre for the community – including as a homework centre in out-of-school hours; or allowing spare space in a school in the daytime to be used as a crèche by other schools, which could help to attract additional staff;
- providing new incentives to attract outstanding teachers to zones, perhaps by:
  - finding ways to relieve teachers of their administrative burdens, including providing more support staff;
  - offering contracts which reward teachers for working a more flexible school day or year;
  - finding ways to bring other adults – including youth workers – into the classroom in support of teachers;
  - rewarding outstanding performance by individuals or teams.

The grant comes in part from the government and in part from other partners such as business. The DfES provides up to £500,000 a year to be available to each zone depending on its size. Some partners will also provide valuable support in kind. For example, businesses might encourage their employees to mentor pupils.

Who organises action zones? The local partners run action zones through an action forum. Members are selected locally and include participating schools, the LEA, local and national businesses, the TEC, religious bodies, voluntary and community organisations and other local government agencies. The Secretary of State may also wish to appoint a representative.

Different zones are run in different ways, with various types of organisation taking the lead; but there will always be a range of partners. In many cases, the LEA is the driving force behind a proposal and will take a lead part in running the zone. In such cases there is still a central role for business and for community and voluntary organisations.

In others, a proposal to create a zone might come from a business, the community or a voluntary organisation, in conjunction with a group of schools. This allows for new and exciting groups to become involved in running an action forum, bringing with them fresh ideas on school improvement. In such cases, the LEA is consulted in the development of the proposal. The DfES expects LEAs to work closely with any successful bids which come through this route.

The day-to-day running of a zone is usually carried out by a project director, who is employed directly by the action forum. The director works closely with the headteachers in the zone to deliver the forum's action plan. In some cases, directors have come from an LEA or have been seconded from a school. In others, they are senior staff from local or national businesses. Within zones, there is an additional flexibility in the way that schools are governed. Governing bodies can choose to contract with a forum to provide specific services relating, for example, to staffing or the curriculum. A more radical option allows governing bodies formally to cede the majority of their powers to the forum. Action zones are located in areas of educational underperformance whether urban or rural, where schools need additional targeted support. In these areas, it is even more vital than elsewhere that levels of educational achievement are raised, especially to improve the life chances of pupils living in them.

In some education action zone areas there are schools which have been found to be failing to provide adequate education for their children. Action zones provide a framework for pursuing the government's strategy to turn round failing schools in difficult areas. This includes ensuring that the schools are given the support and leadership they need, helping them to recruit skilled and experienced headteachers, helping them to develop strategies to improve performance and, if necessary, offering a 'Fresh Start'.

- Zones are, therefore, to be found in areas of educational under-performance where schools will benefit from this kind of focused and targeted support;
- The programme is only open to partnerships between schools, businesses and others. It is not available to LEAs acting on their own, nor to individual schools, nor to a group of schools operating without other partners.

For example, Barnsley Education Partnership serves North and East Barnsley. It is innovative because it utilises:

- smart card and ICT to keep records of pupils' learning progress;
- an extension of the literacy and numeracy centre on their Internet to all schools in the zone;
- advanced skills teachers across the zone;
- and provides an interactive homework service;
- education, health, social services and voluntary sector professionals working together.

It aims to achieve the following:

- a 10–15 per cent improvement in levels of attainment at all key stages and at GCSE-level above targets included in the LEA's Education Development Plan;
- ensuring the percentage of pupils not achieving any grades at GCSE level will be reduced by 50 per cent, i.e. from 20 to 10 per cent;
- achieving a minimum 93 per cent attendance in secondary schools and 96 per cent in primary schools;
- ensuring that every child in the zone will have an e-mail address and links to the National Grid for Learning.

The key partners in this scheme are: Barnsley College; Barnsley and Doncaster TEC; Barnsley LEA; British Telecom; Bretton Hall College; Bull Information Systems; Nord Anglia. The zone includes eighteen primary schools, three secondaries and one special school.

The Learning Gateway Project

Another area of growing concern revolves around the number of pupils who are leaving school without any formal qualifications. Many of these youngsters 'job drift' and end up eventually on income support and other forms of state benefit. In an earlier section of the book, we reported on the Leeds experiment with the first 'second chance' school in Britain. There are, however, a number of other projects aimed at facilitating the lost generation of disaffected youth by providing them with a 'second chance'. One of these is the Learning Gateway Project.

This project operates in the following way. Youngsters aged between 16 and 18 who have been failed by the conventional school system are being coaxed back to education by the prospect of improving their own skills and earning money. Trainees currently receive a £40 a week training allowance plus a £50 incentive bonus for starting the course and another bonus for going on to further study or training.

The Learning Gatework Project attempts to improve pupils' learning while, at the same time, helping them to change their often initially hostile attitudes and raise their low self-concepts. Trainees include those who are 'disaffected by attitude'. For instance, those not in school or work, or those who are moving between dead-end jobs; or those who are disadvantaged by circumstances or characteristics such as homelessness, health problems, care history, family difficulties or offending behaviour. One of the key options in the Learning Gateway Project is a life skills programme of at least sixteen hours a week over a three to four-month period to help equip youngsters with the basics needed to do further educational courses or training. The skills included are: reading, spelling, mathematics, communication, using numbers, information technology, working with people and problem solving. The programme also helps students to pinpoint job areas of interest and helps them to prepare for job interviews.

The Learning Gateway Project is part of the local Connexions Service which started on 1 April 2001 (see Chapter 11). As such, every participant has a personal adviser to listen and identify the support needed, to discuss their most suitable short and long-term job opportunities and options, and to encourage a positive attitude and boost confidence and self-esteem. The personal adviser will help youngsters with their claims for benefits, completion of applications to employers and colleges as well as with learning interview skills. The student can then move onto another education course or to work-based training such as a Modern Apprenticeship or National Traineeship. Alternatively, the student can progress by returning to mainstream education with their learning skills enhanced. The personal adviser continues to support the client for as long as necessary in order to ensure that he or she does not drop out. Therefore, the Learning Gateway Project is a mixture of utilising individual learning requirements, alternative curriculum approaches and mentoring techniques. Similar schemes are also available for excluded pupils around the United Kingdom.

Alternative schemes for excluded pupils

Once again, there are so many different alternative education and curriculum schemes for excluded pupils that it is only possible to highlight a few examples. A number of these schemes are managed by either religious groups or voluntary organisations or both. These include: the YMCA, Home Initiative; Youth for Christ; Waltham Forest; 'Fresh Start', Southwark, London; The 'Bridgeworks' Project, Gosport; The Matson Youth and Community Project, Gloucester; The Luton Educational Trust Project; Club 2000 (throughout England and Scotland); The Zacchaeus Centre, Birmingham; Level 3, Toxteth, Liverpool; The Cornerstone Gap Project, Swansea; and, finally, the Surrey Skillway Project. Like the Learning Gateway Project, these schemes also combine a mixture of raising personal self-esteem, alternative curriculum strategies as well as a variety of approaches towards mentoring (SVN, 2001).

Exemplar: Scheme I

For example, in Birmingham the Zacchaeus Centre is the product of co-operation between the local authority's ten Roman Catholic secondary schools. An intervention programme of four weeks operates in a special unit jointly sponsored by the ten schools, the diocese and the LEA. After two years of pilot project status, it is now fully accepted and receives a substantial annual grant from central government. The unit is able to vary the National Curriculum (though still teaching many of the normal schools subjects), and can concentrate on the life skills programme. The Centre is located in an adapted church cellar with ample space for the unit at its present size. The space is also used for club activities after school. Parents are involved as much as they want to be, and can visit the Centre at any time.

The ten schools identify pupils from year 9 who are seen as heading for permanent exclusion and after a positive interview send them to the Centre for four weeks. The process of re-integration into their school is carefully planned, and, in the rare case of a pupil not responding well to the course, there is the possibility of a further four weeks' placement. The programme uses a developed approach known as 'Positive Discipline'. There is no contract but there is a clearly stated code of conduct. Each child is given five points at the beginning of a lesson and points can be lost by wilfully breaking this code. At the end of each day, the grades are recorded with comments on a progress record which is sent home for the parents to see and sign. This is aggregated. An overall score of 80 per cent is needed to maintain progress. At the end of the four weeks, award certificates are given out and a Centre 'Record of Achievement' report goes back to the school with the pupil.

Attendances at the Centre are counted as normal school attendance on a student's record and the normal procedures of schooling are followed. There are three full-time staff members (all of whom are experienced qualified teachers), several part-time and volunteer helpers and a chaplain. Students on initial teacher training programmes also make a valuable input. The weekly timetable includes emphasis on numeracy and literacy, group work on behaviour management, and for a small amount of the time, students are placed on individual study programmes. The emphasis is on coming to terms with living and working with others. A high proportion of its students are able successfully to rejoin their school programme.

Exemplar: Scheme 2

The level 3 scheme in Toxteth, Liverpool, operates in a different way. This project serves a slightly older group of pupils who would otherwise be permanently out of school. 'Level 3' is an initiative taken originally by members of a local church (Toxteth Baptist Tabernacle) and uses the adapted basement of the original church building. It aims to cater for 14–16-year-olds excluded or disaffected from mainstream schooling who have been referred to it by local EWOs. The pupils come initially on a one-month trial and follow a full-time structured programme that can continue until they reach normal school-leaving age of 16. It is an alternative to normal school education with a strong emphasis on marketable skills. The subjects taught include technology (offering IT, pottery, textiles, woodwork and electronics), personal and social education, religious and moral education, environmental studies, social studies and humanities, French, in addition to maths and language. The Unit is well staffed by qualified teachers, instructors and volunteers and individual tutorials monitor progress, difficulties and behaviour. In addition to these regular timetabled activities, students are involved with community projects, work experience, youth award schemes and careers guidance.

Level 3 now enjoys the full endorsement and support of the LEA and has the practical backing of the EWOs. Its finance comes in part from donations. The original setting-up costs were all gifts from Christians and others who wished to see it succeed. Now it is recognised as an alternative school, the LEA provides funding on a per capita basis for each of the enrolled students.

Exemplar: Scheme 3

The Cornerstone Gap Project in Swansea has taken up the challenge of serving its local community by working with disaffected young people. The area is one of extreme deprivation with high crime, unemployment and drug abuse. The church established a centre that has now received approval as an Accredited Training Centre with the Open Colleges Network and offers courses that command the full approval of the LEA, HMI, Community Education and local schools. The premises were purchased from local collections and a loan as the church has few high earners. However, day-to-day funding comes from tithes and covenants. It enjoys high levels of success with the local young people.

The project cares for fifteen students, currently all girls aged 14–16 from one local school. It runs for thirty-nine weeks, in parallel with the school year. The Gap programme is unusual in that students register at school but after one hour are collected and taken to the Centre and are returned shortly before the end of the school day. These students already have strong negative reactions to school and work better in a non-school environment. For part of each week, they follow a programme at the Centre, including activities that take them out of the Centre into the community for work experience and Outward Bound activities. The days spent in the Centre are largely concerned with a life skills programme, counselling and continuing education.

The MAP Project: A school-based project

Despite the profileration of church-inspired schemes, most alternative curriculum projects are currently taking place and organised within mainstream secondary schools. Thus, we will now consider one such project in some detail; the MAP scheme. MAP stands for the Mountain Ash Partnership: Out of School Learning Project (Reynolds, 2000). It is funded by the New Opportunities Fund for out of school hours learning.

The aim of the MAP Project is to identify pupils who are disadvantaged and/or showing signs of disaffection in Mountain Ash Comprehensive School and its feeder primary schools. Each of these pupils is given personal and curricula support both inside school and within the community. They are guided into a series of community projects, chosen for their impact on the development of self-esteem and confidence. Reid (1982b), for example, found that persistent school absentees had significantly lower academic levels of self-esteem and general levels of self-concepts than regular attenders from the same forms and academic bands when matched by age, gender and home background. These findings clearly provide a major clue as to why some pupils decide to miss school when their peers from a similar cycle of disadvantage do not.

In school, the pupils work with the MAP Project Out-of-School-Hours-Learning-Link and Development Officer (OSHL – SLD) to identify the causes of their disaffection and to establish the type of out-of-school learning which they would most like to do, from a range of exciting programmes on offer. The MAP Project officer then develops an appropriate package of support and variety of activities for every pupil referred to her. She subsequently works in liaison with parents and with programme providers. Within the community, the selected pupils are supported by volunteer mentors and youth workers. The MAP Project is a good example of joined-up inter-agency professional practice.

The MAP Project operates with up to 250 pupils a year and in total nearly 700. This represents 32 per cent of the 8–16–year-old age range in the region which suffers significant deprivation. For example, 50 per cent of the pupils in the catchment area have free school meals. The project is managed by a multi-disciplinary group comprising representatives from schools, a young person, a parent, staff from voluntary organisations and the local education authority. Preliminary research prior to the start of the project showed that:

> There is a cycle of social disadvantage leading to educational disadvantage leading to further social disadvantage. This project has been developed to attempt to break that cycle by addressing what are recognised as some of the core symptoms of disadvantage which lead to young people failing to thrive in the school environment.

Activities	Year 7	Year 8	Year 9	Year 10	Year 11
Homework Club	10%	5%	15%	0%	0%
Revision Club	10%	11%	25%	8%	8%
Art	56%	45%	53%	25%	33%
Drama	28%	32%	50%	12%	25%
Healthy Living	11%	8%	23%	8%	8%
Computer skills	51%	50%	55%	45%	28%
Reading	10%	8%	13%	0%	6%
Film	34%	42%	38%	16%	19%
Language	7%	21%	8%	6%	6%
Music	31%	26%	28%	12%	19%
Chess	13%	8%	8%	6%	0%
Scrabble	15%	3%	0%	0%	0%
Sport	72%	53%	50%	73%	44%
Science & Technology	31%	24%	25%	10%	11%
Residential events	20%	3%	60%	2%	14%

Figure 10.2 Pupils' preferred out-of-school activities by year.

These symptoms included:

- low aspirations;
- low self-esteem;
- unrealistic expectations;
- aggressive behaviour;
- lack of respect for others;
- difficulties with relationships with parent(s), friends and/or teachers.

The key objective of the MAP Project is to help people develop the personal skills they need to do well at school. Young people doing least well in school are also the ones least likely to be involved in organised leisure or community activities. Some are even excluded from youth club provision because of their behaviour. With these issues in mind, the partnership decided to undertake a survey of years 7 to 11 within Mountain Ash Comprehensive School. The survey asked pupils what they would like to do after school. Their responses are presented in Figure 10.2.

The partnership then contacted a number of providers who could work with the project to develop and deliver tailored programmes for out-of-school learning. These included:

- the Arts Development Team of Rhondda Cynon Taff County Borough Council;
- the University of Glamorgan Extra Mural Department;
- the Wildfire Project, a voluntary initiative which works with girls aged between 12 and 18 years of age to enable them to gain skills which increase their choices.

The key elements of the project are:

- Personal support – each participant is identified through their school, and given personal support throughout their involvement in the project. Their involvement is monitored and developed by the OSHL-SLD Officer who may assign them to a mentor as appropriate.
- Exciting and effective projects focusing on creative arts, cultural activities, multimedia, personal development, outdoor activities and sport.
- Community development – the project fosters links between young people and organisations working within their community. It encourages participation in community initiatives.
- School links – the project is linked into the partner schools through the OSHL-SLD Officer. The post is carried out through a secondment from Mountain Ash School, by an experienced and respected teacher who has long-term experience of working on truancy reduction programmes. She already had existing links into all the partner schools and knows many of the pupils that the project aims to target and their families.

The key principles in designing the project programme are:

- pupils should wish to participate in what is offered and the experiences available should be new and exciting for them;
- there should be a good geographical spread of activities so that pupils can become involved in their own community;
- there should be personal support available in as much depth as the individual needs.

Therefore, the Out-of-School Hours Learning School Link and Development Officer works closely with staff in the partner schools to identify pupils who are showing signs of disaffection or withdrawal from school. These signs include truancy, absenteeism, frequent misbehaviour, poor attitude in class, refusal to take part in school activities and failure to achieve academic potential.

The pupils are then monitored both in and out of school. Some of the activities are organised after school; some are run at weekends or during school holidays, not dissimilar to related activities in French schools.

The OSHL-SLD Officer closely monitors each pupil's involvement. Special steps are taken to ensure that each pupil can participate in every activity. Thus, dependent upon need, arrangements may be taken to include:

- taking the pupil to the first few sessions until they have settled in;
- setting up a mentor within the activity who can support the pupil on a one-to-one basis;
- establishing appropriate teaching and learning arrangements with the school.

The MAP Project is characterised by a uniform approach to each issue. Sessions are deliberately informal, inviting and inclusive. Additional personal and group support is provided as required. The MAP Project gives pupils a choice and mix of activities, enabling them to choose those in which they most wish to participate. The range of available choices is shown in Figure 10.3. There are a number of mentors participating in each activity. The full extent of the MAP Project is shown in Figure 10.4.

Name	Activity
Arts programme	Performing arts courses in areas like rock music, creative writing Visual arts courses in crafts, murals, etc.
Information technology	Presentation of course work using computers
Sports programme	Taster sessions with qualified coach/expert; use of computers and library materials to learn about sport; practical coaching sessions
Homework Club	Library-based homework clubs that use computers and library materials
Mesus	Multi-media project with the University of Glamorgan
Cybercycle	Build your own computer and take it home
Lads and Dads	Monthly club for fathers and sons with leisure and issue-based work
Wildfire programme	Groupwork course for girls only including discussion sessions, visits and special arts sessions
Outdoor Pursuits	An annual camp for all MAP Project participants with a range of outdoor activities An annual camp for girls through the Wildfire Project

Figure 10.3 Activities available through the MAP programme.

The programme outcomes are six-fold. These are:

1 Improved school performance amongst the young people and their school. These performance outcomes are measured through examination results and the results of course/class work assessed in school.
2 Improved attendance.
3 Attitudinal changes, as identified by the young people themselves, their parents and their teachers.
4 Increased involvement in organised leisure/community activities.
5 A reduction in the number of pupils excluded or not attending full-time schooling.
6 Improved support for needy pupils within their schools at all levels including the curriculum.

Re-integration strategies

Most schools are currently weak on re-integrating their long-term or returning absentees back into the fold. This includes any kind of absentee whether for reasons of illness, travel, holidays, familial disharmony or indeed, for any form of non-attendance. In fact, many schools have no re-integration strategies whatsoever. All too often pupils are left to their own devices to endeavour to catch up with work they have missed as best they can. For less able and disaffected pupils this is neither ideal nor easy. It can be extremely difficult even for the most able pupil.

A number of re-integration strategies have already been considered between Chapters 2 and 8, so these will not be reconsidered in detail now. Re-integration strategies

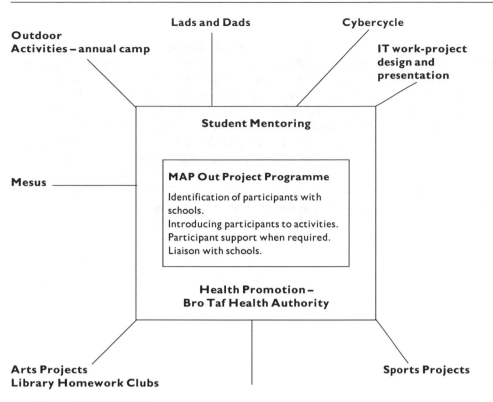

Figure 10.4 The MAP Project.

previously discussed include: corrective schemes to overcome literacy and numeracy deficiencies, the use of independent learning systems on the web such as Plato and Success Maker, various mentoring schemes (e.g. Buddy systems, able with less able pupils), 'catch up' units or clubs, having appropriate return to school policies and/or re-integration strategies, second chance opportunities, homework clubs, summer school initiatives, breakfast and after school clubs, the use of key skills lessons, student lesson planners, limiting school exit points, monitoring school transitions, one-to-one case reviews, providing compensatory programmes within school hours, tackling social exclusion, establishing inclusive school policies through the setting up of a social inclusion unit, providing specialist in-school projects especially at key stage 4, utilising an arrivals and departure lounge, providing parental convoys, parental sit-ins, and, finally, ensuring all-the-year-round learning.

It is not suggested that schools should adopt any or all of these ideas. Rather, that each school should have its own appropriate written policy on social inclusion and on re-integrating pupils back into their learning fold. These schemes should be user friendly and conducive to good practice. Schools might decide to select four or five of the above ideas and adapt them to fit into their own circumstances. Details of each scheme can be found in Figure 3.1 and at appropriate points in the text between Chapters 3 to 6.

Ideally, re-integration strategies are best facilitated when a returning pupil is provided with an individual learning mentor. It is for this reason that the next chapter focuses upon the emergent theme of mentorship.

Summary

This chapter has provided some specific details of alternative curriculum schemes and the reasons why these pupil-friendly projects are gaining in momentum. Alternative curriculum schemes are often largely focused on disaffected pupils like persistent non-attenders. There is no one ideally agreed alternative curriculum scheme. Variations in alternative curriculum schemes abound throughout the UK. Some of the best alternative curriculum schemes can be found in the innovative work being undertaken by the education action zones in England. The Learning Gateway Project and the MAP scheme are two good local examples of existing alternative curriculum provision which have close links with mentoring. Finally, there are a range of current alternative curriculum schemes specifically focused upon excluded pupils of which this chapter has provided a few examples from schemes based in Birmingham, Liverpool and Swansea.

Chapter 11

Mentoring

Mentoring schemes are growing rapidly. The art of mentoring in schools is practised in many different forms, shapes and sizes. Mentors come from a range of different backgrounds and expertise. Some are highly qualified, well trained and skilled. Others are untrained support staff with minimal qualifications and limited expertise other than a desire and willingness to work with young people. Many mentorship schemes are aimed at needy and vulnerable pupils. These can include pupils from ethnic minority backgrounds, those who are less able, disaffected, truant and who may even be bullied. These pupils may or may not have other forms of special needs including learning deficiencies as well as, very often, low levels of self-esteem. Figure 11.1 provides an outline of popular mentoring schemes.

Mentors in their role as learning tutors, require both process and academic skills. Tasks need to be clearly defined and realistic. Goals should be attainable. Mentors require appropriate and relevant knowledge and experience of both life and learning. When both pupils and mentor alike enjoy the companionship provided by a tutoring relationship, the potential for learning is usually greater (Dearden, 1998; Batty *et al.*, 2000).

Approaches to mentoring

The majority of mentoring schemes are based on a simple premise. Most young people will 'look up to' and admire someone who is empathetic, non-judgemental and who understands and listens to you. Studies have shown that young people who have a significant adult or 'mentor' in their life, other than family members, are more likely to achieve in a variety of ways, including socially and academically. Some mentoring schemes spring up completely by chance and are often informal. Others are pre-planned and focus upon aspects of schooling, employment, self-esteem and behaviour.

Most mentorship schemes involve an older adult working with an individual or group of young people. However, other forms of mentorship abound. These include older pupils working with younger pupils and a range of peer support schemes (see Figure 11.1). Mentorship schemes require a clear set of achievable aims and significant resources including a major time commitment. The recruitment, selection and induction processes involved in the appointment of suitable mentors are a vital part of establishing successful schemes. Matching the right young person with the right mentor is also crucial. This stage determines whether or not the relationship will be a success.

Adults with pupils	– Pupils can be disadvantaged, slow learners, recent immigrants, handicapped, disabled or have particular learning difficulties or unfavourable attitudes towards schooling (e.g. truants, disruptive pupils, bullies or bullied).
Connexions	– The DfES-supported scheme.
Excellence in Cities	– Learning mentors are school-based employees, who together with teaching a pastoral staff, assess, identify and work with those pupils who need extra help to overcome barriers to learning.
Older pupils with younger pupils	– Year 12 and 13 pupils with younger pupils; able pupil with less able; good attenders with poor attenders; young carers scheme; use of former pupils.
Peer support	– Able pupils from same tutor groups as less able; good attenders from same tutor group as bad/poor attenders; teenage sports leaders scheme (soccer, hockey, cross country); role models scheme (e.g. art, drama, performing arts, etc.).
Parents with pupils	– Parent(s) with own child; parents with other people's children; parental support groups within school or in out-of-school locations (e.g. local homes or social club).
Business links	– Mentors and/or mentorship schemes supported by local business; business link mentors.
Voluntary sector	– Mobilising the voluntary sector and/or 'grey army' of retired locals to help in schools in a variety of individual and/or group mentoring schemes.
Undergraduates	– Using undergraduates to help part-time in mentoring schemes in schools (e.g. Birmingham).

Figure 11.1 Popular mentoring schemes.

Mentors require appropriate supervision and training which makes them feel valued and part of a team. They will need to be supported in the often daunting task of mentoring a young person or young people. Mentoring schemes need to be properly monitored and evaluated bearing in mind that the safety of young people, including pupils, is of paramount importance.

There are many positive benefits of a mentoring relationship. It can be a very rewarding and fulfiling experience for mentor and the young person alike. It can, for example, provide a young person with emotional and behavioural problems, like a persistent truant, the opportunity to be listened to and valued as an individual in his or her own right. It can allow a young person the time and space to examine the situation they are in, reflect on it, and develop goals and targets for the future. The relationship can also create opportunities and broaden the horizons of a young person's experience. The mentoring process can give them the opportunity to succeed in a number of ways in both their social and developmental stages in life. It can provide an appropriate adult–young person role model as too many children these days have inappropriate and psychologically unrewarding relationships with the key adults in their lives.

Within the schools situation, mentors can be used in a variety of ways. They can encourage a single pupil or a group of pupils working together. They can be used to help pupils with specific learning or behavioural difficulties or both. They can help and support vulnerable pupils like those who are being bullied. They can be used to raise self-esteem or to help pupils who are falling behind with schoolwork to catch up or to help those who are under-achieving or disaffected to achieve and become happier.

Mentoring is a key part of New Labour's policies on education and is essential to their social inclusion policies. Within these policies, three initiatives are critical; the role of small education action zones, the Connexions Service and Excellence in Cities. We will now consider each of these three as major EAZs have been discussed in the previous chapter.

The Connexions Service

The Connexions Service began in April 2001. It is a new multi-agency support service for all 13–19-year-olds which is to be fully operational by 2004. Connexions brings together a range of partners currently working with young people in a 'joined-up' approach. These partners include schools, colleges, career services, the youth service, education welfare or education social work, health agencies, youth offending teams and, where appropriate, social services. The Connexions Service aims to provide a coherent, holistic package of support that enables every young person to remain engaged in learning and make a successful transition to adulthood, the world of work and/or higher education.

In many parts of England, the introduction of Connexions is leading to inter-departmental mergers with, for example, youth, career services and educational welfare beginning to function together.

For schools, the Connexions Service will mean:

- a new integrated support service for all young people, with personal advisers at its heart, some of whom will be based in schools. Headteachers will have a key role in planning and delivery of the service in their area;
- a range of personal advisers, appointed and managed by headteachers, to help raise pupils' aspirations, support progression and remove barriers to learning.

It is hoped, for example, that the implementation of a successful Connexions Service will lead to a reduction in truancy and other forms of non-attendance, poor behaviour in schools, disaffection and bullying.

The personal adviser

The personal adviser (or mentor) is at the heart of the Connexions Service.

- The personal adviser will provide a wide range of support and play a central role in helping young people to deal with the problems they experience, raising their aspirations and removing barriers to effective engagement in learning. This might include barriers associated with the young person's academic under-achievement, health, ethnicity, and social, cultural or home life.

- Extra support will be given to young people from neighbourhoods with concentrations of barriers to participation in learning, and to young people who often face particular difficulties such as those from black and minority ethnic communities; those in and leaving public care; young people with learning difficulties and disabilities; teenage mothers and young carers; offenders; and those who misuse drugs or alcohol.
- Working with schools and others, personal advisers will over time also call on networks of voluntary and community mentors which are being developed to provide extra support and role models for young people. Advisers will also broker specialist support for the young person where needed, for example, in Child and Adolescent Mental Health Services.
- There is a phased introduction of the new service taking place between 2001 and 2003, with a clear focus on developing best practice, testing out what works through pilots and building on that experience.

Local organisation of Connexions

The structure for delivery of the new service includes an inter-departmental Connexions Service National Unit, forty-seven Connexions Partnerships at the level of local learning and in Skills Council areas responsible for funding and strategic planning, and with local management committees responsible for the operational delivery of the service. These are usually based on local authority boundaries. Each committee has appointed a local manager who is responsible to it for day-to-day management of the service, working closely with headteachers and others. Schools have an important role to play in planning and delivering the service, and headteachers will be represented on local management committees.

The role of Connexions

(a) The Connexions Service is providing valuable help to schools in meeting the needs of their pupils, particularly the disaffected and those facing disadvantage. Their work will contribute both to Connexions targets (including relevant local education authority targets) and the institution's own targets for raising achievement and reducing truancy and exclusion rates.

(b) Although personal advisers working in schools and in pupil referral units will be appointed and managed by the headteacher or teachers in charge, they are also operating as part of the integrated Connexions Service. Managers from the service are working closely with headteachers to ensure that Connexions staff complement the pastoral and other support systems and objectives of the school.

(c) School-based Connexions advisers undertake a range of activities, depending on the needs of each school and the level of adviser resource available. Working alongside teaching and other staff, they conduct assessments and reviews, provide one-to-one support for those not fully engaged in learning, and make referrals to specialist support services, such as study support, the Community Drugs Team or specialist guidance, where needed. This role is similar to that of the learning mentors, introduced through the government's Excellence in Cities (EiC) initiative (see later in chapter). In EiC areas, Connexions advisers work alongside EiC Learning Mentors.

(d) Connexions advisers will assume responsibilities from the Careers Service for the provision of impartial information and guidance on learning opportunities and careers, encouraging young people to aim high in their choices. Advisers will also offer first line support to schools in relation to their careers' education programmes and their obligation to make available careers information to pupils.

(e) Personal advisers work closely to support children with SEN. Where personal advisers identify previously unrecognised SEN, they will need to ask SENCOS whether extra support from the school is needed, or a formal assessment for a statement. Where a child already has a statement, the Connexions adviser must attend the year 9 transition review and contribute to drawing up and monitoring the transition plan. In addition, for those with statements in their last year of schooling who are moving from school to further education or training, the Connexions Service is responsible for arranging assessments of their needs and the provision to meet those needs in these settings. Advisers are also able to identify others with SEN but without statements, who would benefit from an assessment covering post-16 learning.

(f) Personal advisers will also work with school-age children who have been excluded from school or who are truanting, to encourage them back into mainstream education and onto a school roll as quickly as possible.

(g) Part of the personal adviser's role within the Connexions Service is to monitor and act upon the information provided on each student's individual Connexions card. The main functions of the Connexions card are:

- to accurately record the attendance of each student. Thus, deterioration in the attendance patterns are quickly picked up at the local level enabling early intervention schemes to operate. The automation of attendance monitoring will also provide fast accurate information for learning providers.
- to provide appropriate rewards and loyalty models and bonuses to students making good progress at a variety of levels. These include rewards for attendance, punctuality, completion of homework, achievement of agreed milestones, making good progress generally, participating in community-based activities and sports, recreational, cultural and artistic events. Experience shows that rewards are motivational if they offer 'prizes' which young people regard as valuable. Rewards can include educational items such as books or stationery. Young people like 'sensible' rewards and/or discounts. Other popular rewards include vouchers for entertainment events (e.g. pop concerts), sport, driving lessons, clothes or opportunities for travel and/or holidays.

Excellence in Cities

Excellence in Cities is part of a major new DfES initiative which has a massive budget and is a key part of New Labour's strategy for raising standards in schools. Excellence in Cities provides secondary schools with additional support for gifted pupils, learning mentors, disaffected pupils and new learning support units to remove disaffected pupils from the classroom. State of the art city learning centres as well as beacon and specialist schools along with mini education action zones are also a key feature of the programme.

Alongside this support, schools set challenging targets to improve their exam results at the end of key stage 3 and GCSE.

Another important part of Excellence in Cities is the desire to transform failing schools. Failing inner-city schools will be replaced by new city academics. Other failing schools and low performing schools will be rebuilt out of a large capital budget which is part of the programme. Extra money is also provided to primary schools for catch-up classes for weaker pupils – alongside extra help or training in secondary schools for key stage 3 support.

Following successful pilots in six major conurbations, Excellence in Cities was extended from September 2001 to a large number of major towns and cities throughout England. These include: Leicester; Stoke-on-Trent; the Wirral, St Helens and Halton (all part of Merseyside); Greater Manchester (Rochdale); Tyne and Wear (Gateshead, Newcastle-upon-Tyne, North Tyneside, South Tyneside and Sunderland); Teesside (Middlesbrough, Hartlepool, Redcar and Cleveland, and Stockton); Bristol; Nottingham; Hull; and, in London, the boroughs of Brent, Barking, Dagenham and Ealing. Other cities in England will soon follow suit.

As part of the Excellence in Cities programme, learning mentors are school-based employees who, together with teaching and pastoral staff, assess, identify and work with those pupils who need extra help to overcome barriers to learning inside and outside school. In this way, they support teachers and help take some of their burden off them. Teachers can therefore, focus upon their teaching *per se*. They can be safe in the knowledge that the learning mentors are helping their pupils to overcome problems inside and outside school.

The Excellence in Cities scheme is proving to be a very exciting and popular initiative with teachers. One of the key complaints however, is the fact that it is restricted to only certain high density parts of England. Teachers in Wales, for example, feel increasingly disappointed to be outside the initiative. So popular is Excellence in Cities proving, that a large number of schools outside the designated geographical areas have taken it upon themselves to use their own or alternative funds to recruit their own learning mentors.

Another part of the Excellence in Cities initiative is the extra funding to provide Education Maintenance Allowances to encourage young people to remain in education. Primary schools in Excellence in Cities areas are now also allowed to employ learning mentors as well as to provide extra programmes for their able pupils. By the end of 2001, there were already 1,500 learning mentors in post in Excellence in Cities secondary schools. There were 900 in primary schools in the same areas. By 2004, there will be an estimated total of 3,200 learning mentors in primary and secondary schools within the Excellence in Cities scheme itself along with the developing new Excellence clusters. In addition, there will be a countless number of learning mentors operating in areas outside the scheme such as in Hereford and Worcester, Devon, Dorset and Wales. The provision of learning mentors within schools is as popular with parents and the pupils themselves as well as with teachers. Examples of specific initiatives operating in Excellence in Cities areas include:

- clustering schools into groups of families in order to raise achievement;
- raising the number of pupils applying for Oxbridge places from inner city regions;
- widening access, participation and entry to higher education;

- improving links between primary and secondary schools by, for example, delivering extension classes in maths for the gifted;
- sharing schemes of good practice around the LEA and amongst regional customers;
- developing e-mentoring schemes by:
  - connecting hundreds of high school students with adult mentors;
  - involving e-mail correspondence between students and mentors;
  - providing students with access to information and on-line resources that support their learning.

The key emphasis is that ICT is to be used to develop independent learning, to widen access to learning opportunities and to enhance the quality of learning, all with the underlying aim of raising achievement. Evidence from evaluations of Excellence in Cities initiatives reveal some outstanding transformations of individual pupils based on detailed case studies.

Small Education Action Zones

Several Excellence in Cities initiatives are benefiting from working alongside large Education Action Zones as previously considered in Chapter 10. However, in some smaller density urban areas there is not always a natural cluster of secondary schools on which to base a large zone. So, typically, small EAZs often focus on the needs of a single secondary school and its associated primary schools.

Like large EAZs, small zones aim to tackle deep-rooted social and educational problems through innovative approaches to school improvement, in partnership with parents, other schools, businesses and local authorities. Initially, each zone receives a cash grant of £250,000 a year for three years. They then have the chance to extend that period to five years. These small zones are also encouraged to work closely with local businesses. Any additional sponsorship is matched pound for pound by the DfES up to the value of £50,000. By April 2001, there were already 86 small EAZs operating across inner city areas involving 10 per cent of all schools in England.

Small EAZs in inner cities are combating a whole range of social and educational problems including low educational achievement across the community, truancy, a high number of exclusions, and youth crime. The emphasis in every zone is on raising standards. There are, however, a whole host of individual and different ways in which small EAZs tackle the particular challenges faced by their schools. Many zones, for example, specifically focus upon literacy and numeracy, science or ICT. They try to ensure continuity across the curriculum in, for example, the partnership between secondary and primary schools by smoothing the transitions between the key stages.

Small EAZs are at the forefront of innovation. Therefore, a lot of experimentation is taking place. Some specialise in providing for the needs of gifted and talented pupils or those with special educational needs. Some are at the forefront of performing arts, sporting or musical endeavours.

Many of the small EAZs have set themselves targets to reduce exclusions and improve attendance. Schools are utilising a range of schemes to improve attendance and to make existing services work better. Support for families is another of their main target areas. These activities range from schemes to encourage parents to become more involved with the school to community-based initiatives such as family literacy schemes. All the small

EAZs are based on a strong local partnership. A wide range of mentoring schemes are in operation within these EAZs. Some, for example, use students from higher education institutions or businesses. Therefore, we will now consider one of these schemes based in Birmingham.

The Birmingham Mentoring Consortium

The Birmingham Mentoring Consortium (BMC) organises a scheme which enables degree-level students to apply for Millennium Awards worth £2,000 each to spend a day a week mentoring less able and difficult pupils to reach their full potential. At the same time, participation in the scheme enables the students to enhance their own personal development and makes them more attractive to prospective employers. The students act as mentors for young people at secondary school who are under-achieving or at risk of exclusion. They also design and carry out a related project in a local West Midlands community. Each mentor supports two or three young people and, together with four hours a week on the community project, this works out at about a day a week. The scheme is mainly aimed at second year university students because for them year one can be stressful, while third years usually face their final examinations.

The Birmingham Mentoring Consortium is part of the National Mentoring Pilot Project which was established by the DfES in 1999. Under the scheme, sixteen universities and one higher education college have been linked with schools in education action zones. Each HE institution involved in the project has between forty and a hundred students working as mentors.

The first twenty-nine Millennium Award volunteers started a range of community-based projects in Birmingham. These included schemes to help refugees into employment, to support young mothers and to teach computer skills to African-Caribbean elders.

The Birmingham Mentoring Consortium is an inter-cultural mentoring organisation which embraces the Hindu, African-Caribbean, Bangladeshi and Sikh communities, as well as people from white and ethnically mixed backgrounds. Most mentees are supported by mentors from the same ethnic background as themselves. The Birmingham Mentoring Consortia scheme focuses upon raising the self-concepts of mentees by providing them with someone to whom they can relate, talk to, seek advice and gain a bit of leadership. Both troublesome and less able boys as well as girls have benefited from the mentoring.

Early evaluations of the scheme suggest that some of the mentees are capable of achieving good passes at GCSE level. Unfortunately, their innate intellectual abilities are often diminished by unstable home backgrounds, anti-social behaviour at school and a breakdown in normal teacher–pupil relationships. For ethnic minority pupils, these difficulties can be compounded by language problems at home and in their local community by cultural, social, economic and, in some cases, 'adjustment' problems.

Other forms of mentoring

Apart from government-sponsored initiatives, a wide range of other forms of mentoring currently exist (see Figure 11.1). These include schemes in which adults mentor pupils who can be disadvantaged, slow learners, recent immigrants, handicapped, disabled or have particular learning difficulties (e.g. speech impediment) or have hostile or unfavourable attitudes towards schooling. They include projects with truants, disruptive pupils, excluded pupils, bullies and/or bullied.

Another variant is for year 12 and 13 pupils to mentor younger pupils. Or, for able pupils to work with the less able. Or, for good attenders to help poor attenders. The Young Carers scheme is popular in some parts of the country. An interesting idea used by some schools is to match former pupils who have stayed locally to work or enter higher education with existing pupils attending their old school.

Peer support schemes are beginning to gain an increased recognition in the literature. These include able pupils working with their less able peers in the same form tutor group. Similarly, matching good attenders with bad or poor attenders from the same tutor group is becoming more popular. The teenage sports leaders scheme encourages able pupils to support novice or less natural sporting pupils at, for example, soccer, hockey, netball, cross country, tennis, swimming and many others. This model is, of course, part of the culture of schools throughout many of the states in North America. Similarly, the role models scheme applies the same principle to aesthetic and cultural studies such as art, drama, music and the whole range of performing arts.

Morrison *et al.* (2000), in an interesting variant of the above, describe a cross-age tutoring scheme in two very different settings. The first was a rural primary school and the second an urban secondary school. In each setting the aims were social as well as academic. The academic focus was on language work, including reading. In the primary school, year 4 pupils (aged 8–9 years) worked with reception pupils (aged 4–5 years) to produce storybooks with illustrations and a text which incorporated individualised key words. In the secondary school, year 9 pupils (aged 13–14 years) worked with year 7 pupils (aged 11–12 years) whose reading age made it difficult for them to access the curriculum.

In the primary school, both boys and girls were involved. In the secondary school, only boys. There was no clear pattern of improvement in the language skills of either group of tutees. However, both groups felt more positively about reading. There were some indications that relations between younger and older pupils were developing in positive ways. In both projects the tasks were clearly defined. Even the 8-year-old pupil tutors had a sound grasp of what the tutoring process entailed.

Such projects have potential. Pupils, especially in secondary schools, often say they wish to be given more responsibility and to be treated more like adults. For them, and for the younger primary-age pupils, peer tutoring can provide opportunities for early leadership. They can also establish a way of learning – learning from one another – which may well be the main informal learning mode in life after school. Peer mentoring has the potential for embedding it in the curriculum (Dearden, 1998).

Another potentially rich area for further research is the possible mentor role between parents with pupils (their own or other people's) in the school setting. This idea certainly has the potential to reduce alienation, truancy, bullying and other forms of anti-social behaviour. Currently, some EAZs are experimenting with parental school-based schemes and/or community-based projects. One such example of good practice is the Gloucester EAZ.

More common mentoring schemes involving parents include parental support groups within school or in out-of-school locations such as youth clubs, after hours clubs, holiday clubs or in a whole range of sporting and cultural activities (e.g. drama clubs).

Business links in mentoring schemes have grown especially in work with, for example, EAZs, the National Strategy for Neighbourhood Renewal (NSNR) and through the development of the Children's Fund.

The National Strategy for Neighbourhood Renewal is about turning round the most deprived neighbourhoods by tackling the underlying causes of moral and urban poverty. It is a key plank in New Labour's social exclusion policy. The severely deprived estate of Townhill in Swansea, for example, was considerably boosted by the opening of new all-weather sport facilities, a large indoor leisure complex and a range of other recreational and community-based initiatives supplemented by a series of traffic calming measures in order to combat joyriding and car theft.

The Children's Fund (see Chapter 1) was established to tackle child poverty and social exclusion. It is part of a range of measures to ensure that vulnerable children get the best start in life, remain on track in their early years, flourish in secondary school and choose to stay on in education and training at 16.

Finally, the voluntary sector is probably more active than ever before. Voluntary groups include a whole range of organisations, from CARE (Christian Action Research and Education), the SVN (The Senior Volunteer Network) and the YMCA to Age Concern. For example, Age Concern organise first day response in some schools in some parts of the country. Mobilising the voluntary sector and/or a 'grey army' of retired or non-working people in local communities does require initiative. But, it can pay rich dividends. Young people, including disaffected pupils, will often relate to the elderly in an entirely different and better way than to peers of their own age. Often elderly people are more naturally empathetic and can replace the missing extended family which is so sadly lacking these days.

Residual issues

Not every aspect of mentoring schemes is rosy. The recruitment and retention of suitable mentors are proving difficult in some parts of the country. Some people are beginning to change or re-enter employment by starting as mentors only to leave as soon as other opportunities arise. Some mentors have been considered to be too young, inexperienced or unsuitable for their role. Some mentors have been unable to cope with their mentees, especially in cases where pupils have serious special needs or behavioural difficulties or disorders. A number of mentors have subsequently decided to retrain as teachers.

Some professionals have suggested that a few mentors being used in government-run schemes have been making things worse for the young people they are trying to help. For example, some mentors have reinforced classroom-based problems due to their lack of training or professional competence and they soon become critical of their mentees. Similarly, some mentors have forged inappropriate relationships with their youngsters, leading to a breakdown in communication and long-term development. These early warning signs need to be heeded.

Summary

This chapter has considered some of the emergent and best known mentoring schemes. First, a variety of approaches to mentoring were discussed. Second, this was followed by a consideration of the Connexions Service, Excellence in Cities, small education action zones, the Birmingham Mentoring Consortium, and some other forms of mentoring. There is little doubt that a whole range of mentoring schemes are making a major impact upon our schools. It is still too early to be certain about the long-term outcomes. But, mentoring schemes are providing hope and help to a whole new generation of learners. Their outcomes need urgent evaluation. Their long-term potential includes significantly raising standards in schools and pupils' individual and collective levels of achievement. They also have the potential to reduce bullying, disruptive behaviour, exclusion rates, underachievement, disaffection, truancy and other forms of non-attendance. There is also considerable potential for using parents more actively in mentoring and other support roles within schools. Whether the various mentoring schemes will prove as effective as current optimism suggests, only time will tell.

Chapter 12

The way forward

The purpose of this short but significant final chapter is to pull together a number of the key issues previously discussed throughout the book. This will be achieved by making a series of recommendations which, hopefully, will lead to further good and better practice and help to move the prevention and combating of truancy and other forms of non-attendance onto a new level. No one should think that either achieving or managing this process will be easy. However, nothing ventured, nothing gained. Certainly, there currently seems more will in high places to try initiatives to combat truancy, school absenteeism and other forms of disaffected behaviour than ever before.

Key recommendations

1 There should be a National Inquiry into truancy and non-attendance from school. This inquiry should take the form of a Dearing-style (HMSO, 1997) investigation and produce the first major report of its kind into the subject. The report should not simply analyse the retrospective history of truancy but look forward to finding solutions in an increasingly technologically based society. The aim of the inquiry should be to find some nationally agreed ways of moving forward in as much of a concerted and joined-up approach as possible. Truancy has for far too long thrived on inadequate, piecemeal and haphazard local solutions. As local solutions have not proved effective, there is a clear need for sound national initiatives, national co-ordination and a national plan to combat truancy and other forms of non-attendance from school.

2 There should be a related National Inquiry into the role of the education welfare/education social work service. This service has long suffered from a crisis of confidence for a number of inter-related reasons. There need to be agreed national aims and objectives for the service. Professional staff working in education welfare/education social work should do so operating from the same base line. There should also be nationally agreed rates of pay and conditions of service. The service should be given full professional status.

3 The widespread disparity between the differential pupil/school ratios to numbers of education welfare/education social work employers needs resolving. Truancy thrives when pupils know there is little risk of being caught or, when they are caught, knowing that court action is often ineffective and takes much too long to implement. Truancy also thrives when the decisions taken in court run counter to the seriousness of the offence, which is all too frequently the case.

4 Apart from education welfare officers/education social workers, there are a whole array of semi-professionals becoming involved in attendance and attendance-related issues. These include attendance officers and attendance support staff and local variations abound. There is a need to ensure that all attendance issues are placed directly under the control of headteachers and the education welfare service. Currently, too many individual cases of attendance-related issues are being over complicated because of the number of professionals and semi-professionals involved in them. Serious consideration needs to be given to the wisdom of allowing education welfare/education social workers and attendance officers to operate separately and from entirely different professional perspectives with different reporting procedures. Consideration also needs to be given formally to determining the professional status of attendance support teacher/officers/staff. Further consideration needs to be given to whether these staff should be amalgamated into the education welfare service.

5 The role of education welfare/education social work within the Connexions Service needs reviewing. Research evidence clearly shows that the prevention and combating of truancy are continually hampered because of the lack of early intervention. Thirty-five per cent of truancy and other forms of non-attendance begin whilst pupils are at the primary stage. Therefore, consideration needs to be given to the full effects of linking education welfare to the Connexions Service for post-13-year-old pupils as well as its implications upon younger pupils.

6 In March 2001, the DfES announced plans to establish multi-disciplinary and inter-disciplinary regional local panels to work together in a joined-up approach to combat truancy and crime within their areas. This initiative should be encouraged and supported by the provision of sufficient resources to undertake the task. Appropriate training to bond these local teams based on their inter-disciplinary and multi-disciplinary needs should be provided.

7 A national web-site, along with supporting regional web-sites on good practice in truancy cases, should be established to enable professionals to learn from one another's experience. The national web-sites should be overseen by the DfES, Welsh Assembly, Northern Ireland Assembly and Scottish Parliament. The regional web-site could be managed by the local panels.

8 There should be a full-blown audit into the current processes used by schools to register and monitor pupils' attendance. The audit should be conducted randomly and regionally on a sampling basis. The purpose of the audit should be to:

(a) ascertain variations in registration practice used by different schools;
(b) discover the rationale as to why some schools are currently 'authorising' unauthorised absence;
(c) assess the effects of league tables and inspections upon registration practices;
(d) examine the role of headteachers in defining individual school practice in registration processes;
(e) reconsider the position of recording pupils absent on family holidays in registration processes;
(f) report on variations in practice even within clearly defined local boundaries.

The aim of the audit should be to stabilise existing practice into a uniform state as well as to advise on how to improve existing procedures.

9   There should be a related reconsideration about the difficulties between recording the categories 'authorised' and 'unauthorised' absence. It is widely felt throughout the teaching profession that authorising absence and determining which box to tick for authorising pupils' absence place teachers and headteachers in an invidious position which, on occasions, can be professionally demeaning. There is a strong belief that marking the register should be made a simplified task. If, for example, registers were simply marked 'present' or 'absent', appropriate and more accurate follow-up of information could be provided using such processes as recording finite responses to first day absence enquiries.

10 Better ways need to be found for accurately recording post-registration truancy and specific lesson absence. Currently, both these categories are often omitted from official returns on attendance. In a legal sense, this can be extremely serious.

11 There needs to be more research into parental-condoned absenteeism, taking account of the categories outlined in Chapter 9. The role and responsibilities of parents in truancy and non-attendance cases need to be both re-examined and reinforced. A national advertising campaign on this issue could help to reinforce the key points. The wider usage of parenting orders in attendance cases should be carefully examined by magistrates.

12 All magistrates and magistrates' clerks involved in hearing attendance cases should be provided with appropriate training.

13 Whenever possible, attendance cases should be heard on the same day in each local court. There should be a consistency in approach at both local and national level on agreed outcomes in non-attendance cases brought to court. Pre-hearing meetings should be arranged locally to resolve issues before they are finally brought to court. The process of bringing attendance cases to court should be speeded up. The role of the social service department in attendance cases should be re-examined as should the issue of 'confidentiality'. Currently, the issue of 'confidentiality' is proving counterproductive to effective joined-up professional activity.

14 Legislation should be introduced to make one member of each governing body responsible for overseeing attendance issues within a school. Headteachers should be required to provide governors with a full report on attendance and attendance-related issues at least once a year.

15 Each school should be required to update its school policy document on attendance on an annual basis.

16 Each school should be required to inform pupils and parents of their appropriate reintegration strategies when pupils return to school after a period of significant absence whether because of illness, family-related reasons or for non-attendance.

17 There should be an appropriately funded research study into the relationship between staff absence from schools and pupil absence.

18 Each school should include at least half a dozen short-term measures as part of its school policies on attendance. Ideally, every school should, whenever possible, implement appropriate first day response schemes. Other practical short-term solutions can be selected from the lists provided between Chapters 3 and 6 dependent upon local circumstances and need. All pupils need to be made aware that their attendance matters.

19 Truancy should be included as a topic in personal and social education programmes. The topic should be covered from a preventative standpoint in much the same ways

as 'drugs', 'alcohol abuse', and existing sex education programmes. Ideally, the topic of truancy should be introduced no later than in year 7 so that pupils fully understand the long-term consequences of such behaviour.

20 Schools with serious attendance problems should investigate the appropriateness of introducing some long-term and more strategic approaches to combating their difficulties. Too often, truancy thrives in schools with an unfavourable school ethos in which the issue of non-attendance has become accepted as the norm by pupils, parents and staff alike.

21 The DfES, Welsh and Northern Ireland Assembly and Scottish Parliament should consider examining the role of alternative curriculum strategies as a palliative to truancy from schools. Schools involved in linked FE-school projects with disaffected pupils should not be financially penalised. The funding methodology for this process needs rethinking. Currently, schools lose half funding per pupil for those schemes with FE colleges which are half and half. Equally, FE colleges only receive half funding. Given the potential to prevent long-term adult disaffection and reliance on state support, it would seem appropriate to give both schools and FE colleges full funding for all pupils engaged in collaborative alternative curriculum initiatives.

22 Although the causes of truancy and non-attendance have been well researched, there is a need to re-examine the genesis of truancy and other forms of non-attendance amongst ethnic minority pupils. There is also a need to re-examine the similarities and differences between boys and girls in cases of parental condoned absence.

23 The short and long-term effects of mentoring on disaffected pupils like truants and absentees need a proper evaluation. Some funded research into this topic would be beneficial.

24 The potential for extending the range and activities conducted by small local education action zones should be considered especially in schools with serious attendance problems. The potential for extending these small local education action zones should not only be re-examined throughout England but in Wales, Scotland and Northern Ireland as well.

25 Evidence from research, as well as the positive benefits and knowledge acquired from Excellence in Cities, Connexions, the work of education action zones and other recent initiatives, should be appropriately disseminated across schools throughout the UK.

26 It is unsatisfactory that new teachers are starting work in schools without any formal training on attendance and truancy and, often, without any experience of registration or form tutor responsibilities. It should be mandatory that all new teachers receive appropriate training on these issues. Furthermore, the induction of new staff in school (whether new to the profession or a school) should always cover attendance matters including an understanding of the school policy document on attendance. Whenever possible, education welfare staff should be involved in this process.

27 Holiday periods involving all local educational establishments including FE colleges should be standardised. Too many children miss days and/or weeks from school because of differential practices between local schools and/or colleges.

28 All schools should only be allowed to take one-week for half-term breaks (and not two as is traditional in some local schools, often those with a minority foundation basis).

29 There needs to be a review of:

(a) the effects of schools' occasional and/or staff development ('Baker') days on pupils' regular attendance;

(b) the consequences of teacher absence upon pupils' absence. In particular, the effects upon pupils' learning and attendance of those staff who frequently resort to taking time off work on a fairly regular basis.

30 Attendance issues should become a core item in the training of staff for potential leadership positions within schools; most notably headteachers, deputy headteachers and heads of year/house. This applies to senior staff in primary, middle and all other types of secondary schools. Attendance issues should also feature in training events held for members of school governing bodies.

Bibliography

Audit Commission (1996) *Misspent Youth*, London: The Audit Commission.

Batty, J., Rudduck, J. and Wilson, E. (2000) 'What makes a good mentor? Who makes a good mentor?', *Education Action Research*, 7(3), 369–78.

Cabinet Office (1998) *Truancy and School Exclusion Report*, Social Exclusion Unit, London: Cabinet Office.

Cullen, M.A., Fletcher-Campbell, F., Bowen, E., Osgood, J. and Kelleher, S. (2000) *Alternative Education Provision at Key Stage 4* (LGA Research Report 11), Slough: NFER.

Davies, N. (2000) *Schools in Crisis*. Series of Articles in *The Guardian*, 10, 11, 12 July 2000.

Dearden, J. (1998) 'Cross-age peer mentoring in action', *Education Psychology in Practice*, 13, 4, 250–7.

Dearing Report (1997) *Higher Education in the Learning Society*, London: HMSO.

Department of Education and Science (1975) *Survey of Absence from Secondary and Middle Schools in England and Wales on Thursday, 17 January 1974*, London: HMSO.

DfEE (1997) Command paper 3681, 'Excellence in Schools', London: The Stationery Office.

DfES (1998) *Recommended Daily Home Learning-Based Activities Extracted from Homework Guidelines*, London: DfES.

DfES (2000) *Schools: Building on Success*, London: DfES.

Gann, N. (1999) *Targets for Tomorrow's Schools*, London: Falmer Press.

Gillburn, D. and Gipps, C. (1996) *Recent Research on the Achievements of Ethnic Minority Pupils*, London: Ofsted.

Home Office (1995) *Young People and Crime; Home Office Study 145*, London: Home Office.

Hoyle, D. (1998) 'Constructions of pupil absence in the British Education Service', *Child and Family Social Work*, 3, 1–13.

Jeffery, K. (2000) *The Action Plan for the Gloucester Education Achievement Zone*, Gloucester: GEAZ.

Kinder, K. and Wilkin, A. (1998) *Where Parents Lay the Blame for Truancy*, Windsor: NFER.

Kinder, K., Atkinson, M., Wilkin, A. and Kendall, S. (2000) *The Role of the LEA in Reducing Truancy*, York: NFER.

Kinder, K., Cullen, M.A., Kendall, S. and Bruce, D. (2001) *The Delivery of the Curriculum to Disengaged Young People in Scotland*, York: NFER.

Lee, B., Pye, D. and Bhabra, S. (2000) *Research on Disaffection amongst Muslim Pupils within State Secondary Schools: Exclusion and Truancy*, London: IQRA Trust.

Lewis, E.J. (1995) *Truancy – The Partnership Approach*, London: Home Office Police Research Project.

Morgan, M. (1999) 'An evaluation of an alternative curriculum project at key stage 4', unpublished DBA dissertation, Swansea Institute of Higher Education.

Morrison, I., Everton, T., Rudduck, J., Cannie, J. and Strommen, L. (2000) 'Pupils helping other pupils with their learning: Cross-age tutoring in a primary and secondary school', *Mentoring and Tutoring*, 8, 3, 190–7.

O'Keefe, D. *et al.* (1993) *Truancy in English Secondary Schools*, London: DfES.

Pack (1977) *Truancy and Indiscipline in Schools in Scotland (The Pack Report)*, Scottish Education Department, London: HMSO.

Pathak, S. (2000) *Race Research for the Future: Ethnicity in Education, Training and the Labour Market*, Research Topic Paper, London: DfES.

Reid, K. (1980) *Whose Children?*, Cardiff: Gibbs.

Reid, K. (1982a) 'The self-concept and persistent school absenteeism', *British Journal of Educational Psychology*, 52, 2, 179–7.

Reid, K. (1982b) 'School organisation and persistent school absenteeism: An introduction to a complex problem', *School Organisation*, 2, 1, 45–52.

Reid, K. (1985) *Truancy and School Absenteeism*, London: Hodder & Stoughton.

Reid, K. (1986) *Disaffection from School*, London: Methuen.

Reid, K. (1987) *Combating School Absenteeism*, London: Hodder & Stoughton.

Reid, K. (1988a) *Staff Development in Primary Schools*, Oxford: Blackwell.

Reid, K. (1988b) *An Introduction to Primary School Organisation*, London: Hodder & Stoughton.

Reid, K. (1989a) *Helping Troubled Pupils in Secondary Schools*, 2 vols, Oxford: Blackwell.

Reid, K. (1989b) *Staff Development in Secondary Schools*, London: Hodder & Stoughton.

Reid, K. (1999) *Truancy and Schools*, London: Routledge.

Reid, K. (2000) *Tackling Truancy in Schools*, London: Routledge.

Reid, K. and Hopkins, D. (1985) *Rethinking Teacher Education*, London: Croom Helm.

Reid, K., Hopkins, D. and Holly, P. (1987) *Towards the Effective School*, Oxford: Blackwell.

Reynolds, E. (1996) 'An in-depth analysis of an initiative to improve attendance in a South Wales comprehensive school', 2 vols, unpublished MPhil thesis, Swansea Institute of Higher Education.

Reynolds, E. (2000) *The MAP Project*, RCT: Mountain Ash Comprehensive School.

Sandwell (2000) *Report of a Project on School Attendance*, Sandwell LEA.

Scottish Council for Research in Education Study (1995) *Understanding Truancy: Links between Attendance, Truancy and Performance*, Edinburgh: SCRE.

Scottish Office (2000) *Focus No. 5 on Truancy*, Edinburgh: Scottish Office.

Sharp, S. and Smith, P.K. (1999) *Tackling Bullying in Your School*, London: Routledge.

Smith, M., Goodban, L. and Ford, R. (1994) *Attendance Matters: A Guide for Schools*, Herts: Herts LEA.

Social Exclusion Report (1998) *Truancy and School Exclusion Report*, London: Cabinet Office.

SVN (2001) *Excluded but not Rejected*, Nottingham: The Society for Voluntary Network.

TUC/MORI Poll (2001) *Half a Million Kids Working Illegally*, TUC, 21 March 2001.

Waterhouse, R. (2000) 'Rescued after dropping out: learning gateway', *TES*, 21 January 2000, FE Focus IV.

Weston, M. (2001) *The RAG Project: An East Worthing Project to Improve Attendance*, Worthing, Davison CE High School.

Woodward, W. (2000) 'Mentoring may not help children', *The Guardian*, 7 September 2000.

Wragg, E.C., Wragg, C.M., Hayes, G.S. and Chamberlain, R.P. (1998) *Improving Literacy in the Primary School*, London: Routledge.

Youth Cohort Study (1998) 'Truancy and youth transitions reporting No. 34', quoted in Social Exclusion Report op. cit.

Index

adjusting parents 153–5
advice to schools 28–30
Afro-Caribbean officer 65
after hours support 62; tutors or clubs 62
after-school clubs 58
all-the-year round learning 110
alternative curriculum schemes 157–72
alternative schemes for excluded pupils
    165–7
anti-education parents 148–9
anti-truancy teams 79
appointing a home-school co-ordinator
    60–1
appointment of specialist attendance staff
    84–5
approaches to mentoring 173–5
arrival and departure lounge 103
Asian liaison officer 65
asthma clinics 105
at-risk registers 40
attendance: certificates 63; cups 97; hot line
    71; league tables 97; literacy, attainment and
    target setting 51–3; notice boards 96–7;
    panels 97, 130–40; support panel 133–4;
    support secretary 86; support teachers 84–6;
    targets 50–2; tribunals 100

basic skills 25
Birmingham Mentoring Consortium 180–2
blue group 118
breakfast clubs 57
buddy system 66
bullying 24–5
bus passes 74
business sponsorship 99

case reviews 80
case studies 14–18, 20–30
catch up units 101
challenge of truancy and school absenteeism
    1–19

Chamberlayne Park School 125–7
Children's fund 7
closer FE-school links 67
combating lateness 78–9
community police 102
compensatory programmes 87
Connexions Service 7, 175–7
consistency of staff policies 101–2
corrective schemes to overcome literacy and
    numeracy 36
costs: of non-attendance 18; of truancy and
    exclusion 81–3
counsellors 86
court action 5–6
crime 81–3

desperate parents 152–3
detentions 98–9
developing strategies for punctuality and
    lateness 78–9
development issues 116–18
differences between PSCC and SSTG schemes
    136–40
disadvantages of PSCC scheme 121–2
disaffection amongst minority groups 160–1
disaffection in Scotland 159–60

East Worthing scheme 123–5
education action zones 8, 161–4, 179–80
effective monitoring 26–7
effective targets 46–53
e-mails 61
end-of-day registrations 99
e-registration schemes 105
EWO's interviewing pupils and parents 70
Excellence in Cities 8, 177–9
exclusion 127–9
extension of primary school practice 87
extent of effort 1–2
extent of truancy 2–4
external: consultants 102; volunteers 68

familial breakdown 9–10
first day response 31–4
flexibility within curriculum 157–9
flexible tuition times 61–2
format for a school attendance order 75–7
formation of anti-truancy teams 79
free bus passes 74
foundation programmes 65
frustrated parents 151–2

good and poor attenders' 'runs' 104
good attenders' attitudes towards persistent
    school absentees 15
governing body review on attendance 95–6
governors' attendance panel 130–3

half-day rewards 63
headteachers' attitudes towards truancy 14
home–school contracts 78
home–school co-ordinator 60–1
home–school relations 25–6
homework clubs 53
homework clubs and ICT 53–5
homework guidelines 53–4

illegal under-age work 105–9
improved health checks 84
improving the quality of registration time 68
improving special needs facilities 45
incentive initiatives 38–40
inclusive school policies 93
initial school-based review 88
in-school projects 83
inter-agency co-operation 80–1, 82–7
Internet 96
involving community police in school 102

joined-up professionalism 80–7

key recommendations in book 184–8
key skills lessons 60

laissez-faire parents 149–51
law 74–7
Learning Gateway Project 164–5
learning support centres 56
legal powers 74–7
letters to parents 103
limiting school exit points 77
local organisation of Connexions 176
long-term strategic approaches 112–40
lottery-type schemes 40

management of learning programmes scheme
    67–8
managing school transfers 42–4

managing subject choices for GCSEs/GNVQs
    44–5
MAP Project 167–72
mentoring 8, 173–88; programmes 37–8; wider
    issues 181–3
missing from lessons slips 100
monitoring school transitions 77

national advertising schemes 79
National Curriculum 9, 21, 157–72
National Strategy for Neighbourhood Renewal
    (NSNR) 7
New Labour's key policies on truancy 69

Objective 3 scheme funding 68
one-to-one experiences 80
on-line registers 105
on track 8

Pacific Institute Programme 110
paging systems 79
parental: -condoned absence 3, 141–56;
    convoys 103–4; days 98; fines 69; sit-ins 105
parenting orders 76–7
parent–pupil contracts 78
parents 141–56; and parental-condoned
    absenteeism 141–56; and truancy 143–4
parents' evening 98
pastoral training 73–74
Pearson technology developments 109
personal advisers 175–6
personal and social education programmes 35
personal congratulation schemes 96
Phonemaster 105
planning stages: school based review 89
Plato concept 36–7
policies for habitual truants 101
positive reinforcement 38–40
premiership 103
presenting attendance certificates 63
pressure of truancy 10–11
preventing exclusion 127–9
primary school practice 87
primary schools' benefits 119–20
primary–secondary links 42–4, 112–29
prizes 38–40
professional issues 4–5
progression issues 115–16
progress review panel 133–5
projecting achievement targets 46–53
prosecution for irregular attendance 76
PRUs 110–11
PSCC scheme 112–40
pupil panels 93–4
pupil referral units 110–11
pupil-school contracts 78

pupils': common rooms 56; perspectives 17–18; photographs 98; school council 72–3; traits 11–13
punctuality 78–9

questionnaires 90–1
quiet room 104–5

RAG scheme 123–5
reasons for not going to school 15–16
red group 116–18
red lists 61
reducing illegal under-age work 105–9
registration processes 2–6
registration time 68
reintegration strategies 41–2, 170–2
return to school policies 41
rewarding good attendance 27–8
role of Connexions 176–7
role of education action zones 161–4

school attendance orders 75–7
school-based project 167–72
school-based review 87–91
school: council 72–3; newsletters 98; transfers 42–4; trips 96
Scottish Shilling 109–10
secondary school benefits 120–1
second chance opportunities 45–6
short-term solutions 31–111
similarities between PSCC and SSTG schemes 136–40
small education action zones 179–80
social exclusion 91–2
social inclusion – pupil support (SIPS) grant 7
social inclusion units 93
social workers in schools 83
specialist counsellors 86
specialist pastoral training 73–4
special needs 45; assistants 86–7
sports clubs 62–3
spot checks 72
SSTG scheme 130–40
staff absenteeism 102
staff development 88
staggered start times 101
strategic approaches 112–40

student progress planners 66
Success Maker 110
suggestion box schemes 63–5
summer school initiatives 55–6
Sure Start 8
swipe card systems 105

tackling social exclusion 91–2
target setting 46–53
targets: for nursery and infant schools 47–8; for primary schools 48–50; for secondary schools 50–1
teachers' attitudes 13–17
text message support 61
truancy: buster scheme 66–7; call 104; and crime 4–6; and exclusion 127–9; patrols 144–7; sweep schemes 70; in the UK 11; watch schemes 103
types of parental-condoned absence 147–56
types of targets 46–53

under-age work 105–109
unemployment and homelessness 81
use of: at-risk registers 40; classroom assistants 37; external consultants 102; foundation programmes 65; pupil referral units 110–11; role play 38; school-based questionnaires 90–1; security firms 77; stickers and badges 96; the web 36–7
using legal powers decisively 74–7
using local sports clubs 62–3
utilisation of colour-coded groups 35–6
utilising: external volunteers 68; paging systems 79; pupils' common rooms and learning support centres 56; specialist in-school projects 83; social workers in schools 83; the Internet 96

viewmaster scheme 66

way forward 184–8
where parents lay the blame for truancy 143–4
work-related curriculum strategies 58–9

years 10 and 11 projects 99–100
yellow group 119

Index 204